—

OUR JOURNEY
IN THE
VALLEY OF
TEARS

—

To
Tom Roberts
with our compliments

Anny Joy   *Karoline Jus*

12 July 1991

Andrzej and Karolina JUS

OUR JOURNEY IN THE VALLEY OF TEARS

TORONTO

1991

TO THE MEMORY
of Karolina's parents, and her only sister, who perished in the Holocaust. To the memory of all the Jewish people who were exterminated by the Nazis,
becoming victims of a mass crime unique in history.

TO THE MEMORY
of Andrzej's parents and to that of many other Poles,
among them many Catholic priests and nuns, who,
risking their own lives, enabled Karolina, and others
like her, to survive the times of contempt.

This book is also dedicated to all people who are
devoted to peaceful and respectful relations between
human beings, independently of their race, nationality, and religion, and are fighting against any kind
of fanaticism and segregation.

Authors

And the LORD said to Moses . . . You shall not take vengeance or bear any grudge against the sons of your own people, but you shall love your neighbour as yourself; I am the LORD.

Leviticus
19:18

And one of the scribes came up and heard them disputing with one another, and seeing that he answered them well, asked him, 'Which commandment is the first of all?' Jesus answered 'The first is, "Hear, O Israel: The Lord our God, the Lord is one; and you shall love the Lord, your God with all your heart, and with all your soul, and with all your mind, and with all your strength". The second is this, "You shall love your neighbour as yourself". There is no other commandment greater than these.'

The Gospel of Mark
12:28–31

ACKNOWLEDGEMENTS

We would like to take this opportunity to thank the staff of the University of Toronto Press and, in particular, Jim Paterson, for his congenial and continuous assistance in organizing this book. Jim gently guided us through various aspects of book production and expertly advised us on such matters as word processing, copy editing, cover and text design. He immediately understood our wish to keep manuscript editing to a minimum in order to preserve the original emotional flavour of this true story.

We are grateful for the dedicated and thoughtful work of the design team, headed by Laurie Lewis, who translated onto the cover, in a symbolic interplay of colour and design, the tense atmosphere of a book in which all the incidents are true and the people real, whether named or unnamed.

We appreciate the emotional involvement of the word processing specialist, Nellie Paterson, who, while performing this apparently mechanical task, treated the content with respect and sympathy. Nellie told us, during consultations on word processing, that 'I was always your companion in this journey and I was suffering with you.'

Although some people towards the end of their journey in this valley might think that they are left with 'no flower of their kindred,' our experience with the people at the University of Toronto Press has given us the feeling that around us there are people able to 'reflect back one's blushes' and to 'give a sigh for a sigh.'

CONTENTS

PART ONE

—

BEFORE THE LAST SUNSET

The wind blows where it wills,
and you hear the sound of it,
but you do not know
whence it comes
or whither it goes;
so it is with everyone who is born
from the Spirit.

The Gospel of John
3:8

I

THE GERMAN PLANES DROPPED THEIR FIRST BOMBS ON THE city of Lwów in the morning, at ten o'clock. It was 1 September 1939. Only a few hours after Hitler's armed invasion of Poland began, a city 400 kilometres from the Polish-German frontier was attacked by air. The first victims were registered – some dead, some dying, some wounded.

For many hours, Polish radio repeated that, before dawn on 1 September 1939, German military aggression against Poland had begun. In Poland the idea of what war is like was, in most cases, based on the memories of the First World War. The 'colonels' ruling Poland after the death of Marshall Piłsudski were convinced that the cavalry was the pride of the Polish army and that the horse was, and always would be, an important element in contemporary warfare. Poland also had an excellently trained but very modest number of pilots. There were not enough Polish planes to fight against the staggering numbers in the Luftwaffe.

In the first hour of war, Poles looked anxiously to the sky. They saw very few Polish planes; the air above was dominated by planes bearing the hated swastika. Already in the first hours of war, everyone knew that not only the Polish army, but all the population of Poland was exposed to mortal danger, that the merciless enemy was bombing the open cities, shooting from low-flying planes at people in the outskirts of cities, at peasants working in the fields, at civilian evacuation trains, at civilians in flight by road towards the east.

A few days after the outbreak of the war, the Polish population understood the meaning of 'Blitzkrieg.' People of Lwów had seen the first Polish refugees from the western parts of Poland, which were occupied by the German army. Soon afterwards, one could see elegant limousines, carrying officials of the Polish government fleeing to Romania. The Polish-Romanian frontier had been open since the beginning of the war, and the frontier bridge in Zaleszczyki was the main escape route from the dying country.

Poland approached total defeat, although many divisions of the Polish army defended their homeland with heroism and extraordinary courage. History has noted the attack of the Polish cavalry on

German tanks, and of peasants, armed only with scythes, on heavily armed German infantry.

Lwów was not a good place to live in September 1939. The city was under frequent bombardment by the German air force. The population had to spend many hours, day and night, in shelters in cellars. The hospitals were overcrowded. The city was full of refugees from the western areas. The miserable, disorganized remains of the Polish army were crossing the city, aiming to reach the bridge of Zaleszczyki.

On 12 September 1939, the German army entered the western suburbs of Lwów – and stopped there. No one understood why the Germans were not attacking the defenceless city. This situation lasted for about one week, and afterwards all was clear. On 17 September 1939, the Soviet army crossed the eastern frontier of Poland in the north (the region of Mołodeczno), and a few days later entered the eastern suburbs of Lwów.

It was calm in the city between the two armies – no bombardments, no new fires. It was known then that, according to a treaty signed between Stalin and Hitler in August 1939, the Soviets were occupying the eastern part of Poland, populated predominantly by Ukrainians and Belorussians. The people knew also that the Soviets were entering Poland, not to fight with German invaders, but perhaps to delay their own involvement in the developing world tragedy. The nation that had felt relieved when, on the third day of the hostilities, France and England declared war on Hitler, now felt abandoned.

After the Red Army entered Lwów, the German army withdrew about 100 kilometres to the west. The new frontier in the south of pre-war Poland between Germany and the Soviet Union, was now on the river San. The first act of the tragedy of the Second World War came to an end, although the heroic defence of Warsaw, under President Starzyński, lasted until the end of September 1939. Westerplatte was taken after a most heroic battle.

The Red Army that entered Lwów was not very impressive: old cars, shabby uniforms, mostly horse-driven artillery. The new rulers of Lwów were very suspicious and treated the majority of the population as capitalists and enemies of the working class. Lwów was now the capital of Western Ukraine, and the Ukrainian population was favoured. What was previously the south-eastern part of Poland became Western Ukraine, a part of the Ukrainian Soviet

Socialist Republic, which itself was a part of the Soviet Union. The official language of the republic was Ukrainian.

The history of Lwów was complicated, and so was the life of its population. Before the end of the eighteenth century, Lwów belonged to the Kingdom of Poland. After the third partition of Poland in 1795, it belonged to the Austro-Hungarian Empire and was the capital of Austrian Galicia for 120 years. After the First World War, it belonged again to Poland. Before the end of the war, there was great bloodshed in Lwów between the young local Polish population and the Ukrainians who wanted an independent, free Ukraine, and Lwów. From the end of September 1939 to June 1941, Lwów belonged to Ukraine, but it did not provide the type of free Ukraine for which, in 1918, the Ukrainians were fighting with the Poles. After the German invasion in 1941, Lwów belonged to the occupied territories of the at that time victorious Germany. The population of this part of the world experienced living in a new country, obtaining new citizenship, and changing their official language without the trouble of moving or the expense of travel. The cost of all these changes was always the same: blood paid by the soldiers of various armies, invading and invaded, and by the citizens of this unfortunate region.

The Soviet population that began arriving in 1939 and continued to do so until June 1941 had mixed attitudes towards the pre-war inhabitants. Some of them were friendly, helpful, and understanding the tragic situation of the Poles after the defeat of Poland. However, many Soviet citizens who came to Lwów to occupy high administrative positions in offices, schools, and universities appeared to the Polish population to be brainwashed, puppets of Marxism-Leninism. To them, the Polish population was a defeated capitalist nation.

Especially difficult was the situation of Poles who, after the German invasion of the west of Poland in 1939, fled in September 1939 to Lwów and other cities in the eastern part of Poland. For some obscure reason, this migration was viewed by the Soviet authorities as very suspicious. They could not and would not understand that the people were fleeing to the eastern parts of Poland because they were afraid of Nazi atrocities. The Soviet authorities were convinced that Poles from the western part of the country were dangerous capitalists, coming to spy on Western Ukraine and to sabotage the Soviet regime. Whereas the indigenous population of the part of Poland occupied by the Soviets were given

Soviet passports without special annotation, the refugee population's passports included the famous paragraph 11. The great majority of those with such passports were forcibly deported at night later in 1939 and 1940 to various distant regions, in the Soviet Union, mostly to Siberia. The conditions of deportation were very hard, and the life of those deported to Siberia was extremely difficult.

Even worse was the situation of Polish officers of the defeated Polish army. As a rule, they were arrested and sent to prisons in various parts of the Soviet Union. In the official opinion of the Soviet authorities, Polish officers were the worst class of capitalist Poland. The fact that they fought with great heroism against the German invader did not change this opinion. The Soviet Union, after all, had a non-aggression pact with Hitler's Germany.

Very soon after their arrival, the Soviets opened schools, universities, offices, and shops, and tried hard to normalize life in the occupied region. The Ukrainians were favoured by the Soviets. The Poles who lived in the region that now was Western Ukraine were not, as a rule, especially persecuted; neither was the population of Polish Jews. However, they were issued passports by the Soviets that listed their nationality as Jewish, not Polish.

The majority of the population in this part of pre-war Poland, regardless of their nationality or religion, was shocked by the rigid, bureaucratic, and inhuman attempts by the Soviets to enforce Marxist theories. Was it a childish illness of a new social regime, a flaw in the system? Or was it simply impossible to make such a regime workable before necessary changes appeared in human nature after a long evolutionary process? Maybe Marxist theory was simply the wrong theory, inadequate to the task of giving a better life to humanity. Nobody knew the answer at that time, but, from the beginning of Soviet rule in Lwów, everybody knew that it would be very difficult, if not impossible, to make Marxist theory work in life. In 1939, it was not yet known what the cruel years of Stalin's dictatorship would do to the people of the Soviet Union, nor was it known how long this system would survive after the revolution of 1917.

II

WHEN THE GERMAN BOMBS FELL ON LWÓW, ANDRZEJ was passing his last exam for the medical diploma at the University of Lwów. He was twenty-four years old and had finished his medical studies at the University of Jan Kazimierz in Lwów. Two days after his last exam, a small ceremony took place at the university during which the Dean delivered to Andrzej and his colleagues their medical diplomas. It was at the beginning of September 1939, and all of western Poland was already occupied by the Nazis. Lwów was still an open Polish city, and although the academic year usually began in October, the university was, in light of the special circumstances, open for exams in the Medical Faculty and conferring Polish medical diplomas on students who had passed all exams.

Even with Lwów still alive as a Polish city, nobody could deny that Poland was dying and that in only a few days Lwów might surrender. The work in hospitals continued, and some of them were crowded with the victims of bombardments.

In these circumstances Andrzej went immediately to work in the teaching hospital of the Faculty of Medicine. During the last years of his studies, he worked as a volunteer in the Psychiatric Department of this hospital, and returned to it in September 1939 as a physician.

Andrzej was born in Lwów, in the teaching hospital, at the beginning of the First World War, on 16 October 1914. His father, Ludwik Jus, was a professor of Latin and Greek languages, teaching before the First World War in the gymnasium (an academic high school in various Central European countries). Andrzej's mother was also a gymnasium teacher, specializing in the French language.

Andrzej's father had a very difficult life. He was born as one of the five sons of poor peasants in a small village in the sub-Carpathian region of Austrian Galicia. He had also one sister. He went to the elementary school in his village until the age of ten. The family was so poor that he had to work as a cowherd before and after school hours. He was such a brilliant student that he was admitted without any difficulty to the gymnasium in the nearest town, Sanok. There he had an uncle who was a shoemaker. This uncle was so proud to have a nephew admitted to a gymnasium that he offered him lodging in his house. However, he was too poor to feed Ludwik. Therefore, at the weekends, on Saturday afternoons in summer's heat and the cold and snow of winter, Ludwik had to walk the 20 kilometres from Sanok to Końskie, his native village, to pick up bread, butter, cheese, and eggs with which to feed himself during the six-day schoolweek. The journey took about four hours, and was quite harsh in winter. Sunday afternoon, he would be back in Sanok. During the week, after school hours, he gave lessons to some of less able and less impoverished students to earn money for his clothes and shoes.

After graduating with honours from the gymnasium, he enrolled in the Faculty of Philosophy at the University of Lwów to study classical philology, especially Greek and Latin. His knowledge of Latin and Greek was already substantial, because of his gymnasium studies, and he was fascinated by the beauty of languages and the ancient history of Greece and Rome. He dreamed of becoming a teacher of those two languages – a dream that was realized before the First World War when he became a teacher of Latin and Greek in a gymnasium in Lwów and began to prepare his doctoral thesis to start a university career.

At that time he met, fell in love with, and very soon married Estelle Kober the future mother of Andrzej. He met her while he was giving private Latin lessons to the same students she was teaching French privately. Her lessons were very much in demand because she had an incomparable Parisian accent. In addition to private tutoring, she was also teaching in a gymnasium, as was Ludwik. She was a girl of great beauty and charm, very open minded and helpful to people, and had many friends who adored her. She was born in Paris in 1885. Her mother, Caroline, was French, and her father, Paul, was Polish. He came to Paris, abandoning his relatively wealthy home because he was bored with the life-style of the son of a well-to-do landlord. He wanted very much to become independent and self-supporting, and to know the world better. When by chance he met Caroline, he fell in love with her. 'C'était un coup de foudre,' he used to say. They married and had some difficulties with working in Paris. Seduced by the stories of a better life in North America, they went to New York.

This move was a complete disaster. After life in Paris in the 1880s, New York seemed so terrible to them that, after five years, they returned to Paris, where they started a family. They had two daughters and one son. Soon Paul's family asked them to come to Poland and to bring all three children with them: 'Everything is forgotten and forgiven. Paul, return home with your wife and children. We have prepared a nice place for you to work.'

They packed their modest belongings and went to a part of Poland that, at that time, belonged to the Austrian Empire. Very soon after they arrived in Lwów, they discovered that life there would not be very easy for them. Caroline had special difficulty adapting to Lwów after Paris. However, all the three children – Clémentine, Lucien, and Estelle (the youngest, who was then seven years old) – adapted to life in the new place. All of the children finished elementary school and gymnasium easily in the Polish language, in Lwów. Estelle became a teacher of French in the gymnasium and also gave private French lessons, which led her to meet Ludwik.

Before the First World War, Lwów was a capital of Galicia, a part of the Austro-Hungarian Empire. At that time, although the schools and universities were still Polish, the Poles had Austrian citizenship. With the outbreak of the First World War, Ludwik, although he was of Polish origin, was inducted into the Austrian army to fight for the Austro-Hungarian Empire. This event was a great disaster for Estelle, because she was already seven months pregnant. It was a still greater disaster when she was informed that Ludwik had been taken as a prisoner of war by the Russians.

In October 1914, fighting was going on in Lwów, and at that time she gave birth to Andrzej. Her husband was not with her to assist in the birth of their first child, and she was, as was her sister-in-law Madeleine (Madzia), wife of her brother, Lucien, without any male help. She returned to her modest home with the new-born baby, realizing that she was left on her own to fight during wartime for her and her baby's life.

One evening hour, when the baby was already two months old, she heard a knock at her door – and there was Ludwik, standing on the porch with a Russian soldier. They were on the way to the POW camps in Siberia. The soldier, touched by Ludwik's story that he left his pregnant wife in Lwów, promised him that, if the POW echelon passed Lwów, he would be permitted, under guard, to see his wife and the new-born baby. Ludwik saw Andrzej at two months of age, and would not see him again for the nearly 7 years of his captivity in Siberia. All through the First World War and for several years afterward, Estelle fought alone to save herself and her child.

The emotional ties within this family that was reunited after seven long years were strong and tight. After his return from Irkutsk,

Ludwik took up working in the newly born Poland. Lwów was now a booming city in free Poland, with an excellent university, a great cultural life, and one of the best theatres in the country.

There was always an excellent atmosphere at Andrzej's home. Ludwik was very open-minded. The years of captivity before, during, and after the Russian Revolution taught him a lot about human nature and the disasters of war and revolution. His political opinions were liberal; he was never a member of a party, but sympathized with the Polish Socialist Party (PPS). He was a man of great integrity, respected by those who shared his opinions and equally by those who did not. This integrity and his philosophy of anti-discrimination he taught Andrzej from early childhood.

Ludwik was fighting against many racial and national discriminations, the anti-Ukrainian feelings in Lwów, and the anti-Semitism, which was increasing in Poland in the years before the Second World War. Raised in the tradition of fervent Catholicism held by Polish peasants, he arrived, in adulthood, to a *sui generis* atheism – *sui generis*, because, at the same time, he treated people of various religions with respect. Andrzej was brought up in a home where he felt no pressure to attend church. Although Estelle's mother was Lutheran and her father Catholic, Estelle herself was brought up in the Lutheran faith. As Ludwik's parents, especially his mother, were fervent Catholics, she accepted the conversion to Catholicism, and they were married in a Catholic church.

Since childhood, Andrzej lived through various phases of faith and atheism. From both of his parents he learned to respect any faith and any kind of atheism, any race, any nation, and any class. What was important to him was honesty and a non-discriminative attitude in any human being. As soon as he perceived discrimination of any kind, he fought against it, especially when he was a medical student and encountered the attitudes of nationalist students from the far right, who were propagating anti-Semitism. Ludwik disliked deeply the way Poland was administered by the clique of colonels who came to power after the death of Marshall Piłsudski.

The new, free Poland after the First World War period, the same Poland that had suffered, for over 120 years, partition among Russia, Prussia, and Austria, was not a good mother for minorities. The Poles, who for many years were a national minority in the Austro-Hungarian Empire, in Russia, and in Prussia, knew how painful it was to be treated as second-class citizens. Nevertheless, they themselves persecuted national and religious minorities – Ukrainians, Belorussians, and Jews. Andrzej's father held that persecution by the once persecuted makes the government 'the persecuted persecutor.' Ludwik taught Andrzej how to avoid a *false* patriotism, where instead of pride taken in belonging to a nation, the predominant emotion was a contempt for other nations. Understanding that all other nations have the same reasons to be proud, and to respect everyone, was patriotism with a *human* face.

Estelle had instilled in Andrzej, since his early childhood, a practical understanding of how to face hard times, how to work with very modest means during and after the war, how to help other people, and how – even under great hardship – not to lose confidence. She endured the last two years of Ludwik's captivity without any information on his fate in Russia during the revolution, and she never lost hope that he would return. It was a great day when she first learned that he had survived the hunger and diseases and revolution and was on his way home from the far regions of Russia.

In addition to the theoretical moral code taught at school, Andrzej had practical lessons of moral integrity from both of his parents. He described his father as a non-believer and his mother as a moderate believer, one who does not take up too much of God's time with too many prayers. In difficult situations in her life, Estelle asked God for help, and she was certain that God is present in the souls of all honest people. Andrzej had from his parents the best, from the intellectual, moral, and emotional point of view.

After the Soviet authorities entered Lwów in 1939, the school system was reorganized. In the framework of this reorganization, lessons in Latin and Greek were deleted from the high schools and colleges, and Ludwik lost his position as a teacher in the gymnasium. He had now to teach geography and mathematics in an elementary school. Fortunately enough, his political activity in the inter-war period was minimal, and therefore he was not suspected of any anti-Soviet action and was allowed to stay with his family in the home they occupied before the war. Some others were not so fortunate: those considered to be enemies of the Soviets were expelled from their homes.

At the same time the Soviet authorities reorganized the universities. The University of Jan Kazimierz was renamed as it could no longer bear the name of a Polish king from the seventeenth century. The Faculty of Theology was liquidated, and the Faculty of Medicine was transferred from the university and the jurisdiction of the Ministry of Education to form an autonomous medical institute under the Ministry of Health. Andrzej was appointed assistant professor of the Psychiatric Department of the Governmental Medical Institute of Lwów in the same teaching hospital in which he worked as a student volunteer and later as a physician.

The chairman of the department was a former associate professor of psychiatry at the Lwów university. One of the newly nominated associate professors in the same department had previously been his teacher and chief of the department under whose guidance Andrzej was working. This associate professor was a brilliant psychiatrist with great theoretical and clinical experience, very respected by all the staff. Two other associate professors were from the Soviet Union, one from Kiev, the other from Moscow. Both were well educated and cultivated, and exhibited friendly attitudes towards the Polish staff, never trying to indoctrinate them with political theories. The associate professor from Moscow was very helpful in dealing with the Soviet administration of the hospital. Among the younger medical staff was only one young physician from the Soviet Union. She was working on her doctoral thesis and had a friendly relationship with the Polish staff. The general atmosphere in the department was very good, and Andrzej felt satisfied that, in the difficult times of war, he could still work and specialize in psychiatry.

The department was relocated to one of the pavilions of a big psychiatric hospital in the outskirts of Lwów. The administration of this big hospital was totally in the hands of the Soviet officials, mostly party members. They were suspicious of Polish physicians, assuming that since they had been brought up and educated in capitalistic Poland they might automatically be enemies of the Communist system. The best method to counter that, in the opinion of the Soviets, was to teach all the physicians the principles of Marxism-Leninism. Therefore, all the Polish doctors had to participate in special political seminars and discuss the contents of books written by Marks, Engels, Lenin, and Stalin. Above all, they had to know perfectly the history of the Communist party, how and why it came to power and how this power was protected by the genius of Stalin. The Soviet administrators believed that such an indoctrination could easily change a human being and make him or her believe in Marxist dogma. They also insisted the doctors adopt a critical attitude towards the past and all the errors of capitalist Poland.

Auto-criticism was believed to be one of the best methods for converting capitalist thinking patterns into those favouring Communism.

The doctors decided to bring to the attention of the associate professor from Moscow these primitive and unbearable methods. This very intelligent and honest man was a party member. With extreme patience he tried to explain to the worried Polish doctors that you might sometimes meet in the Soviet system some overly zealous and rigid people, and that all the phraseology and rhetoric should not be taken too seriously and certainly would not be enforced because they did not take into account human psychology. An enforcement of such attitudes would mean disaster. As history proved, his opinion was right, although at that time the cruel past and future of Stalinist activity was not yet known.

There were some positive signs in the administrative work of the Soviet people. It was amazing to see how the same people who seemed to be completely brainwashed politically could very well understand that the ultimate goal of the hospital administration was to furnish the best possible services and treatment to sick people. Their task was facilitated because, at the time of their arrival, there were more doctors working in the hospital than ever before. Many eminent psychiatrists from the western part of Poland fled to the east, and stopped in Lwów. Hearing what was going on in the part of Poland under Nazi occupation, they decided not to return. They had no difficulties obtaining work in the big hospital, which, until the war, was always understaffed. Thus, although distrusting the Polish intelligentsia, the Soviet administration positively evaluated the knowledge of the psychiatrists who fled from the west, and the patients in the big hospital found themselves under excellent care.

A very intelligent Soviet teacher working with Ludwik at school explained to him that the distrust towards the Polish intelligentsia was implanted in the Soviet population, starting with their early elementary-school education. Seeing how unjustified this was, the teacher and some of his colleagues were trying to change such attitudes. However, he added with a special smile: 'Please don't mention to anybody our conversation.'

III

THREE DAYS AFTER THE BEGINNING OF THE WAR, IT WAS clear, that soon Cracow would be occupied by the Nazis.

On the third day of the war, Juliusz left Cracow with his wife, Dorota and his elder daughter, Karolina. They were fortunate enough to catch the last evacuation train leaving Cracow. The journey by train was very dangerous, because the German planes were, day and night, patrolling the railway tracks, and the German pilots were engaging in low-flying bombardment of the trains they spotted. The train journey from Cracow to Lwów lasted three days because it had to avoid the bombardment of the main track. Frequently the passengers had to get out and hide in the deep ravines beside the track. The train eventually reached Lwów with nobody killed or injured. Waiting for them in great anxiety was Juliusz's younger daughter Zofia ('Zosia').

Hearing the rumours of impending war, Juliusz sent Zosia with some of their belongings – bedding, etc. – to Lwów, which he considered to be a safe place. He had some relatives in Lwów who offered him and his family their hospitality for the duration of the war. The prevailing opinion in the Polish population was that the war might last a couple of weeks, or perhaps months, and that the German army would be defeated very soon because the Polish army was very courageous and because France and England had joined in the fight against Hitler. Surely, it was felt, the German army could not survive for long, caught between the Polish army on one side and the Allied Forces of France and England on the other. Everybody on the train felt optimistic about a victorious end of the war.

Juliusz Frist and Dorota Bannet were born in Cracow, the ancient Polish capital with the Royal castle Wawel on a hill above Vistula. Wawel was a reminder to all the population that Cracow was *the* capital of Poland, although one of the kings in the seventeenth century moved the capital to Warsaw.

When Juliusz and Dorota were born, towards the end of the nineteenth century, Poland was not a free country. It was divided into three parts, each under control of a neighbouring country: Austria, Prussia, and Russia. The Polish nation was persecuted during this occupation, which lasted nearly 130 years.

The Polish language was banned from the schools in Prussia and Russia; it was not banned under the Austrian occupation which was the most tolerant of all the three. The part annexed to the Austro-Hungarian Empire had the name of Galicia and Lodomeria. It had its own Parliament in Lwów and was represented in the Austrian Parliament by Polish politicians. Life under the reign of the Emperor Franz Joseph was, for the minorities, like the Poles, rather smooth compared to that of Poles under Russian and Prussian, and then German occupation. However, always there was a strong desire to regain independence and have a free Poland. This feeling never subsided.

Juliusz enrolled in a Polish gymnasium and, after graduation, in the Law Faculty of the Polish University in Cracow. This very old university was founded in 1365 by the King Casimir the Great as Cracow Academia and, in 1400, fully reorganized by Władysław Jagiełło, the first King of the Jagiellonian dynasty. Therefore, it had the name of the Jagiellonian University. The law taught at this university was Austrian because the jurisdiction of this part of Poland was Austrian after the partition of Poland. However, the lectures and exams were conducted in the Polish language. The law students had to know also the German version of the laws observed in Galicia. In case of doubt, the German version of the law always took precedence. The lawyers educated in this university had the right to practise law in any part of the Austro-Hungarian Empire.

Juliusz chose to start practising law in Bolzano. At that time Bolzano (Bozen then) was also a part of the Austro-Hungarian Empire, although the population was mostly Italian. He had selected Bolzano for its great beauty and because it reminded him of Cracow. Also, it was nested in the mountains of Tirol, close to another city of his dreams, Verona in Italy.

Dorota, after graduating with her Matura from a Polish gymnasium, enrolled in chemistry at the Jagiellonian University. Cracow was famous for its chemists, who had a world reputation. After she married Juliusz, she left her studies and never returned to them, because of her children and the outbreak of the First World War.

The families of Juliusz and Dorota had been living in Cracow for many years. They considered Cracow to be one of the most beautiful and cultivated cities in Europe. They were deeply attached to Polish culture and Polish literature, especially poetry, and were proud of the heroic history of the Poles; understandably they were very unhappy that Poland was divided and not a free country, and they dreamed of a united, free Poland. Their religion was Judaic; however, their national feelings were exactly the same as those of Poles whose religion was Catholic. They considered themselves Poles with a Judaic religion. Both families were open-minded, and they accepted liberally the fact of mixed marriages with Catholics – a common phenomenon among the intelligentsia. Although there were some anti-Semitic feelings, especially against the acceptance of Poles with Judaic religion as docents (a rank lower than a professor), or professors at the university, never did Cracow experience student demonstrations against the Jewish population. In one sense only, the Poles of the Judaic religion were against conversion to Roman Catholicism. They abided by a certain principle: never convert for a career, and especially not for a university career. They were therefore very proud of those Poles of the Judaic religion who achieved the status of professor at the university without converting.

Juliusz's father had great respect for, and involvement in promoting Polish graphic art and founded a firm called 'Salon of Polish Painters.' He owned a beautiful old house in one of the most charming streets of Cracow. The street ran from the old, medieval walls circumscribing the city towards the central place, called 'Rynek.' When you exited this house and looked to your right, you could see, a very short distance away, the famous entrance in the wall called 'St Florian's Porch.' When you looked to your left you could see the Church of the Holy Virgin with its two towers, a splendid example of the Vistula Gothic. Juliusz, who had travelled throughout Europe, used to tell his daughters that this was the most beautiful place to live in, and that he would not like to live anywhere else. Only in his old age would he like to move to Verona.

Dorota's father was a businessman. One of his brothers was a distinguished ophthalmologist, very respected in Cracow; as a medical student he was one of founders of the volunteer medical emergency service that functioned from the end of the nineteenth century until the Second World War. The other brother was a lawyer practising in Cracow. Dorota's mother was from a family whose name was famous in Poland. Her first cousin was an eminent member of Parliament, active in the Polish Socialist Party. Towards the end of Piłsudski's regime, he was put into the concentration camp at Bereza for his socialist views. Dorota's brother was seriously wounded in the First World War and remained in the Polish army as captain. He was mobilized at the onset of the Second World War and came to Lwów in September 1939, after desperately fighting against the Germans with a platoon comprised of remnants of the army.

After the end of the First World War, Poland was free of any occupation. The former Austrian Galicia was now a part of the new Poland. All the inhabitants of this part of Poland were now Polish citizens. The same thing happened in the sections of the country formerly occupied by Germany and Russia.

A great wave of Polish patriotism rolled through the country. Although Poland had only a small coastal area on the Baltic sea, the Poles were very proud of the fact than one of the fourteen points made clear by President Wilson in the Treaty of Versailles was a free and independent Poland with access to the sea.

Like all the Poles, Juliusz and Dorota were happy with the 'resurrection' of Poland, of a country that had suffered so much and so long under foreign occupation. They were full of hope that this new country would be a good mother to all its citizens and that the nation that suffered so much as a persecuted minority in three big empires would come to understand what it meant to be a minority and to respect its laws. This hope vanished very soon after the end of the First World War. In the twentieth century, Poland did not continue the enlightened tradition of liberty, equality, and fraternity.

It was the Polish king Kazimierz, whom history named 'Great,' who extended a helping hand to the Jewish people persecuted and expelled in the fourteenth century by the Inquisition in the Western European countries. The king opened broadly the borders of Poland to the Jewish refugees from these countries and gave them a choice place to settle down, very close to his royal castle. These quarters, named Kazimierz in memory of the great king, became the nucleus of the Jewish quarters in the Middle Ages. In centuries of enlightment there was a migration from these quarters towards the centre of the city, especially by the newly formed Polish intelligentsia of Judaic religion. This intelligentsia easily became assimilated and had the same deep feelings of Polish identity as its Catholic counterpart. It suffered the same humilation and despair when Poland was divided and occupied by its three neighbours, and hailed the 'resurrection' of Poland after the First World War with the same enthusiasm as other Poles.

Soon the Polish intelligentsia of Judaic religion was disenchanted by a wave of anti-Semitism, promoted by some rightist elements as an expression of patriotism. 'Poland for Poles' and 'Jews to Palestine' were their slogans. Economics figured in the campaign, because the post-war period was economically hard and characterized by very strong competition in industry and commerce. It seemed the easiest to blame the international Jewish connection for the economic hardship.

The official attitude of the Catholic church did not help to counter such feelings. On the contrary, very often it was heard in the churches that the Jews were responsible for the martyrdom of Jesus, and therefore that the people of the Judaic religion should be treated with contempt. The anti-Semitic feelings weighed heavily on the souls of the majority of Polish Jews who were, at the bottom of their hearts, Polish foremost, regardless of the differences based on religion. The Jewish minority was not the only group treated in an unfair way in post-war Poland. That experience was shared by the Ukrainian and Belorussian minorities.

It was difficult for Juliusz to continue to function in Poland as a lawyer. The Jagiellonian University produced a surplus of lawyers, planning to supply lawyers to all countries in the Austro-Hungarian Empire. When the enormous possibilities of practising the law anywhere in this Empire disappeared because the Empire itself disappeared, many lawyers in Cracow looked for another way to survive financially. Juliusz was in the fortunate situation of having a father established in the graphic arts. He therefore had an idea that he would establish his own graphic enterprise. There was a great demand from schools for the new graphic art reproductions, reflecting the events of the Polish history.

With this idea in mind, Juliusz understood that it would be very difficult to start such an enterprise without well-educated Polish workers. He decided to bring specialists in graphic art from two German cities, famous for their excellence in this art. He invited for a short stay two specialists from Dresden and Leipzig to instruct the Polish workers in this type of work. He imported as well a special modern machine from Leipzig to aid in the education of Polish workers. The graphic products were soon in great demand from the schools, and Juliusz was able to import two other printing machines and teach a new group of Polish workers. The German teachers from Leipzig and Dresden returned to their homes a couple of months later, leaving very well-educated Polish workers in Cracow.

The results snowballed: the two Polish workers became teachers of many new students eager to learn the art of graphic reproduction. The demand was growing from schools, public and private institutions and there were already six machines and many orders for importing new ones. Very soon the enterprise, named Akropol moved from a small rented house in the suburbs of Cracow to its own building, designed by Juliusz and built on its own lot in the city itself. In association with his younger brother Józef, also a lawyer, Juliusz formed a company: It was Juliusz's task to expand further and perfect Akropol and Józef took charge of all the administration, organizing the office duties of editing, accounting, marketing, distribution and sales of Akropol's products. The company kept the inherited name of Salon Malarzy Polskich (Salon of Polish Painters), and was located in the very centre of Cracow. In less than ten years Akropol had about one hundred workers, proud of being educated in Poland, pioneers in the graphic art of reproduction. Financially, it was also a success. However, Juliusz did not feel happy because of the increasing wave of anti-Semitism. Some articles in the press, although praising the techniques and successes of his factory, labelled this factory as a Jewish business and were asking for a boycott of its products. 'It is better to buy from a Catholic firm, even if it is not as good'; 'Poles should buy from Poles only,' the articles announced.

The attitude of the Polish government was expressed in a slogan: 'We do not condone the fights at the universities with razor blades. However, we say yes to an economic boycott.' This slogan made reference to university students from the extreme right who were cutting the dresses of Jewish students with scissors or razor blades.

Juliusz's daughters had to go, after Matura, to university to study, and he was frightened about their future. Although he felt strong enough to stand up to the anti-Semitic campaign against his enterprise, he was questioning the future of his daughters if, at the university, they faced danger.

With Hitler's coming to power in Germany and with the anti-Semitic attitudes growing daily in Poland, Juliusz began to ask himself if he was right to stay in Poland and not to emigrate to somewhere in Western Europe or perhaps to the United States. Was it fair to his children that his love for Poland, and especially his very strong emotional ties with Cracow, prevented him from taking the dramatic step of emigrating from Poland? However, his respect for the history of Poland and his inborn optimism prevailed, and he decided to maintain firmly his Polish patriotic position, whatever winds were blowing from the right, either in Poland or in Germany. Truth and honesty must eventually prevail – this was his political credo. He was right in essence, but he did not survive to see the defeat of Hitler.

The tragedy of the Polish defeat in 1939 was not only his personal tragedy, it was for him a patriotic tragedy. When he fled from Cracow with Dorota and Karolina, he left not only his personal belongings and the graphic enterprise he had created, but a defeated Poland that was returning to a shadowy existence as an occupied territory. The Soviet invasion from the east reminded him of Poland's tragic partitions among her neighbours. Should this tragedy of history repeat itself, and Poland vanish again for over hundred years from the maps of Europe?

Being in Lwów was, for him, like being caught in a trap. He could not return to the German occupied territory because he heard from his former co-workers that the Germans had pillaged his graphic reproduction factory, taking all the machines to Germany. To stay in Lwów during the bombardments and hear anti-Semitic remarks was torture. Once a young girl said that the Jewish people should not be allowed to take shelter in Polish cellars. The cellars were over-crowded, and Polish people did not have enough space because Jews were coming to the shelters, and the war was caused by the international Jewish league.

Fortunately enough, before Juliusz could say anything, a young Pole, made indignant by these remarks, told her that it was a shame that a Polish woman could have such inhuman thoughts: 'You have forgotten what it means to be a Pole under occupation. You should better remember what it means to be a national minority. Shame on you. You do not deserve to be named a Polish woman, because no Polish woman could nurture such feelings. God forbid but if the Germans enter Lwów, you might find yourself in the situation in which you wish to see your compatriots, who differ from you only in their religion.' Juliusz felt relieved that, in the Polish nation, the righteous survived. He could not stand the contempt that some Jewish people had for all the Poles, labelling the entire nation as anti-Semitic.

After the bombardments a new problem arose for Juliusz. According to Communist doctrine, he certainly was a capitalist, because he owned a big factory. He had to go into hiding and remain unidentified. Having a talent for drawing, he decided to become a 'retoucher' in a small photographic shop and work in the dark. It was, indeed, not a very joyous life in Lwów for a person as active as Juliusz was.

During the days of relative calm, when the German army stopped at the western outskirts of Lwów and the Soviet army appeared from the east, everything seemed to Juliusz like an interval in a theatre performance. The first act ended when Poland was defeated. Very soon, the second act would start, its outcome unknown. The performance had a gloomy uncertainty. He felt very insecure and asked himself again several times about his attachment to Poland. Was his love of Poland's glorious and heroic history, its literature, paintings, customs, music, and nostalgic landscape, more an attachment to the past than a love of contemporary Poland, with all its vices, the most hurtful of which was its growing anti-Semitism? Was he right to expose his own family to such a risky situation, like the current one in Lwów? Was he right to stay so long in Poland before the beginning of war, only for the love of a Poland of the past, if, in modern Poland, he was treated like a second-class citizen only because of his religion? He was not a practising Jew; he was attached only to the heritage of Jewish history. His love for Poland was not reflected in the official and unofficial treatment of Poles with the Judaic religion. What future price would he and his family pay for this unilateral love?

All these thoughts were interrupted by the arrival of the Soviet army in Lwów. Of the two imminent threats, the German and the Soviet invasions, the Soviets seemed to him less dangerous. He had nothing to do with Communism, but liberal intellectuals like himself did not feel any anger against the trials of introducing a new system in Russia. He felt, however, very uneasy and angered by the fact that the Soviet Union made a pact of non-aggression with Hitler's Germany. At that time, it was not yet known that this pact included a clause regarding the partition of Poland between Germany and the Soviet Union.

Juliusz tried to adapt to the new life. It was not easy because he was again a citizen of second class, not only because he was considered a capitalist but because he had escaped to Lwów from the region occupied by the Germans. For unknown reasons, all the refugees from western Poland were treated as potential spies and were issued, by Soviet authorities, passports containing paragraph 11. This paragraph was notorious because citizens with such passports could be deported any time from Lwów to any region in the Soviet Union. Juliusz was to learn this first-hand in the near future.

The majority of the Polish population in Soviet-occupied Lwów were given passports without that paragraph. That did not mean, however, that no one was suspected of being an enemy of the Soviet revolution. Many people were put in prison because of such suspicions. Especially suspect seemed people who formerly were members of the Polish Communist Party or of the Communist Party of Western Ukraine. Juliusz belonged to neither, but he had a capitalist past. Owning a factory meant that he was a blood-thirsty capitalist, exploiting the workers. Therefore, he and his family could be deported to Siberia any time. They spent many nights in Lwów hiding, in cellars or elevators.

His brother, Józef, who had also fled from Cracow to Lwów, was deported under very hard conditions with his ailing, feverish wife and his two small children. Also, other members of his family who fled from Cracow to Lwów were deported to Siberia. Unknown as yet was the fate of some members of his family who stayed in Cracow. Hindsight has shown all tragic consequences of staying in Cracow and, ironically, also of not being deported to Siberia.

Kuba, the brother of Dorota, who was a captain in the Polish army, mobilized at the beginning of the Second World War, arrived in Lwów midway through September after trying unsuccessfully to halt the German army. He arrived in Lwów already in civvies and unarmed after the defeat and joined the family of Juliusz.

Early one morning in November 1939 armed Soviet soldiers knocked at the door of the apartment where Juliusz was living with his wife, two daughters, and Kuba. Karolina, who was always a courageous girl, refused to open the door and argued with them that the Soviet constitution does not allow the police or army to enter a citizen's apartment without a warrant stipulating the reason for such a visit.

The discussion on the warrant was cut short because the officer in command of the Soviet soldiers told her that, if the door was not opened, they would shoot and open it by force. Juliusz opened the door, and about fifteen armed Soviet soldiers invaded the rooms and made a search for arms. It lasted about three hours. They did not find any hidden arms. When they had finished, they declared that the search had been instigated by false information that Kuba was hiding arms. To punish the false informer, they decided to confront him with Kuba, who, they said, would be back very soon. Turning to Dorota, who wanted to give Kuba some food and warmer clothes, the officer said: 'Better prepare for him a hot lunch, because it is cold and he will return hungry for lunch.'

He never returned, and Juliusz and his family could not trace him. They learnt only that, the same night, many Polish officers were taken from their apartments or hide-aways, although they were unarmed. All were deported to an unknown destination.

About three weeks later, a Soviet soldier brought Dorota a small piece of paper with Kuba's handwriting, asking for warm clothes, socks, and cigarettes. The soldier took all these things that Dorota had gathered but did not say where Kuba was, giving only an indication that he was somewhere in prison.

After a couple of days they traced Kuba to the prison of Brygidki in Lwów. Permission was granted to bring him, once weekly, food, cigarettes, and warm underwear but they were not permitted to see him. Zosia, the least suspect person in their view, regularly made the visits. After two months, she was informed that the visits must stop because Kuba had been transferred to another prison whose location was unknown. Although they tried various means, they never could trace him again and, with the outbreak of the war between Germany and the Soviet Union in 1941, any possibilities of doing so were washed away.

One day a Soviet man from the NKVD (the People's Commissariat for Internal Affairs), who was living in an apartment in the backhouse, brought Juliusz an official paper stating that Juliusz's apartment had been allotted to him and his family. Juliusz and his family had to move immediately into this man's apartment in the backhouse. Juliusz asked 'Why?' The NKVD man answered: 'You have always been a capitalist and I, for ten years, a member of the Communist Party. We are building a new society based on principles of justice. You have lived all your life until now in a front apartment with a nice view, and I have been living in a backhouse. Now I will live in the front apartment and you will live in the backhouse with the view of the court. This is the revolutionary justice principle. I am not taking away your furniture and carpets; we are going to share all that with you. You are getting half of the carpets.' Before Juliusz could say a word, the man took out a knife and cut the carpet down the middle – 'Here is your half.' The same principle was applied by him to the number of beds, chairs, armchairs, sofas, etc. Fortunately enough, there was no sharing and cutting in half of the beautiful, antique grandfather's clock. Just in time, Juliusz told him to accept this clock as a gift of friendship.

'I will transfer my family in the afternoon and I will help you with your move.' The man seemed very happy and satisfied with the realizing of the just principles of the Communist revolution. No discussion was possible. To all questions he had only one answer: 'Everything is on the allocation paper.'

In the afternoon, Juliusz moved his family into the backhouse. Being a capitalist he had to look on the courtyard. Justice was done.

Juliusz and Dorota had, in Lwów, many family members and friends, who, late in the afternoon, nearly every day, dropped in to see them and to have an up-date of the present military and political situation and perspectives for the future. Similar meetings happened also in other social circles. Whatever the war communiqués were, even the most victorious from the German point of view, the future was seen always as very optimistic by the Polish population. Even with the German invasion of Paris, even with the lethal bombardments of London, the forecast, in this social milieu, was for a victory of the Allied Forces and a catastrophic defeat of the Germans. At the worst, this triumph would take less than one year, and a free, democratic Poland with no prejudices would soon emerge.

IV

ON 15 OCTOBER 1940, ANDRZEJ, WHO WAS WORKING AS assistant professor in the Psychiatric Department of the Medical Institute, received a phone call from the new chairman of the Department of Pharmacology. The former chairman, who was Polish, had fled from Lwów because he was afraid of the Soviet regime. The new chairman was sent by the Soviets from Moscow. He was well educated and friendly to students. The Polish Faculty members characterized him in these words: 'Although a Soviet and a member of the Communist Party, he is a very decent man.'

The Soviet professor asked Andrzej if he would be interested in a collaboration with the Department of Pharmacology on research concerning the action of psychopharmacological agents. In the Department of Pharmacology they had started to study, using rabbits, the mechanisms of the intravenous injections of the mixture of camphor and oil. Since the outbreak of war, the Soviets had a shortage of cardiazol, and they had started to inject a mixture of camphor and oil intravenously in psychiatric patients needing convulsive treatment. The professor wanted to know the opinion of clinicians on the therapeutic effects of such treatment and on its side-effects. Andrzej knew how controversial this problem was from the clinical point of view and was also interested in the pharmacological evaluation of intravenous injections of oil. Therefore he looked very favourably on the proposal of collaboration. The professor asked him if he could find some time for a visit from one of his students, working in the students' scientific circle on experiments with such injections on rabbits. This student, whom he qualified as a 'polyglot,' could present to him in detail the results of the pharmacological research and could, at the same time, ask him about a bibliography on convulsive therapy. He would appreciate it very much if Andrzej could prepare some reprints from the foreign literature. It would then be possible to discuss some problems of common concern.

Andrzej was prepared to see the student as soon as the next day, at any time in the afternoon, because, on 16 October, he would be on duty for twenty-four hours. The best time would be at about 4:00 p.m., after his rounds. The conversation finished in the most courteous way. Both sides had a scientific interest, the clinicians could be inspired by some theoretical ideas, and the theoretical approach could become more pragmatic.

Andrzej did not know at that time that this phone call would open a new chapter in his life, a chapter that would continue until the end of his life.

For a while he felt uneasy, despite the warmth and courtesy of the Soviet professor. The Soviets in general were badly accepted by the Polish population. Their treaty with Hitler was considered as treason, and their invasion as a stab in the back of Poland. The student, if working with the Soviet professor, might be imported from the Soviet Union. This 'polyglot' was probably as rigid as most of the young people from the Soviet Union and might 'politicize' all conversation in the direction of Stalin's ideas.

On the same day, Karolina, who was a student in fourth year at the Medical Institute of Lwów, received from the same professor an order to consult with clinicians about the experiments she was conducting on rabbits with the intravenous injections of camphor mixed with oil. She had to ask for the details of the patients' reactions to convulsive treatment with camphor mixed with oil, and possible complications and side-effects.

Karolina was working in the Pharmacological Department of the Medical Institute and participating in the meetings of the students' scientific circle. Such circles were a kind of breeding ground for future researchers.

Karolina was admitted to such a circle when the Soviet professor saw that she had a fairly good knowledge of English, French and German pharmacological bibliography. She was with a great pleasure making translations for him and working in his circle. Until the beginning of April 1940 she was not admitted formally to the third year of medical studies, although she was regularly participating – with the knowledge and consent of all the Polish professors and their staff – in theoretical and practical lessons. None of them could help in her official admission because she had a passport containing the paragraph 11. When the Soviet professor arrived, she felt very insecure, fearing that he might forbid her to continue such unofficial studies. When he saw her several times in the library, reading scientific papers in different languages, and asked her about the subject of her interest, she told him her story. He seemed very upset by the injustice of her situation and in a couple of days changed her status from unofficial to official and asked her to participate actively in the scientific circle. He was helpful not only to her, but to all other workers in his department, some of whom also had paragraph 11 passports. He used to offer them refuge at night in his department when they were threatened with being deported to Siberia by the NKVD, and also offered such refuge to Karolina and her family. Apparently he was very influential, being a party member since 1917 and known as very courageous in defending many falsely accused people. She accepted his phone order without hesitation and promised to discuss with the physician, whose name he had given her, the clinical problems of convulsive therapy. She did not know at that time that this phone call would open a new chapter not only *in* her life, but *for* her life. This chapter would last until the end of her life.

The next day was 16 October 1940, Andrzej's twenty-sixth birthday. It was his second birthday during the Second World War. Still, many people held on to the belief that the war would end within a couple of months. By this time, Lwów had been under the Soviet occupation for nearly thirteen months.

Andrzej expected the arrival of the student at 4:00 p.m. It was a very busy day on duty. In addition to his routine tasks he had to prepare a bibliography and several reprints for the Soviet professor. At 3:00 p.m., he started to check the prepared reprints. The nurse on duty, Filomena, was very helpful in accumulating the bibliography and preparing the reprints. She was extremely professional and, at the same time, very warm and had an excellent relationship with the patients. She had no prejudices concerning nationality, race, or religion. She was a nun and, before the Soviet invasion, she had always worn a habit. After the Soviet invasion, she had to change her traditional habit for a civilian nurse's dress, but she remained a nun. Andrzej had worked with her for three years, for nearly two of them as a student volunteer, and then as a physician. He told her that a student of the Soviet professor would be coming to discuss some problems of convulsive therapy.

Exactly at 4:00 p.m., Filomena entered Andrzej's office and announced the arrival of the messenger from the Soviet professor. At once a wave of rancour against the Soviets embraced Andrzej's heart, and he did not feel comfortable about seeing a Soviet student. He was thinking of the terrible moment when, on 17 September 1939, it was announced that the Soviet army had invaded Poland on its north-eastern frontier. And now he had to deal with a Soviet student. Pretending to be still busy with the reprints, he told Filomena that the co-worker of the Soviet professor had to wait at least fifteen minutes. Filomena, who was used to Andrzej's punctuality in keeping the appointments, could not understand why he was suddenly busy when everything had been prepared in advance. She accepted his order none the less and reappeared after fifteen minutes, stating: 'Fifteen minutes have passed. It is now time to see the envoy of the Soviet professor.' 'Is he speaking Russian or perhaps, being a 'polyglot,' he learnt also to speak Polish?' Andrzej asked. Filomena was amused by this remark: 'First of all, it is not him, it is her. It is a girl, a Polish girl, speaking, of course, Polish. A very nice Polish girl, good looking, well dressed, and well perfumed. Andrzej, I think you will enjoy meeting her.'

Andrzej, always very courteous towards the ladies, opened the door amd went out of the office to invite the girl waiting in the corridor into his office. He had always to regret in the future that, because of bad feelings against the Soviet invasion, he kept his future wife waiting those fifteen minutes in the corridor.

Karolina arrived exactly on time for the scheduled meeting with the psychiatrist on duty. It was the first time she had been in this big psychiatric hospital on the outskirts of Lwów. She has found without difficulty the pavilion housing the Department of Psychiatry of the Medical Institute and presented herself to the nurse on duty. The nurse knew everything about her mission and immediately announced her arrival to the psychiatrist on duty. After a while the nurse returned, a little upset by the fact that the psychiatrist was too busy to see Karolina immediately and that she had to wait about fifteen minutes. Karolina was not annoyed. Waiting was something that a Polish citizen knew very well. One could wait many years to be accepted to the Medical Faculty, especially when your religion was Judaic. You always had to wait in offices. Before going abroad, you had to wait for a passport, even though you had paid a lot of money for it. Waiting did not stop with the Soviet invasion. On the contrary, there were many more places to wait. Shopping consumed long periods. Karolina herself waited over six months to be officially accepted as a student in the third year of medicine, although she has finished the first two years of medical studies just before the outbreak of war, at the Jagiellonian University in Cracow. Thanks to the Soviet professor of pharmacology, she was officially accepted in April 1940. Waiting fifteen minutes was nothing for her. The nurse on duty seemed very nice to her, warm and helpful. During the fifteen minutes, they spoke about the tragic situation of Poland in war-time. Karolina also told the nurse about the difficulties of the Polish citizens who were refugees from western Poland and who had lost their homes and were treated by the Soviet authorities as second-class citizens. Because they were issued paragraph 11 passports, they could be deported at any time.

After fifteen minutes of conversation with the nurse, Karolina had the feeling she had known her a long time, and nearly regretted that her wait was over. Immediately after the nurse entered for the second time, the doctor's office, the doctor on duty came out to meet Karolina in the corridor and apologized for keeping her waiting. She got up from her bench and entered his office.

At the first sight of Karolina, Andrzej thought that Filomena was right. The girl seemed to him rather attractive. She was tall and had long graceful legs, and her face was quite pretty. He was struck by the sad expression in her big green eyes. She moved with a certain grace, which – for some unknown reason – made Andrzej think of the famous gait of Princess Berenice. After she entered the office, Andrzej apologized once more for keeping her waiting. 'I am sorry, I made a mistake,' he said, without further explanation.

Karolina looked at him and, in turn excused herself for taking his time when he was on duty. She introduced herself as a refugee from Cracow, where, just before the war, she had completed the first two years of medical studies at the Jagiellonian University. She explained that she was continuing her studies, since the outbreak of the war, at the Medical Institute in Lwów. He liked her low, husky voice. He was being extra courteous to make the girl forget his negligence in making her wait. He said that he had plenty of time, because the nurse on duty was very experienced. After thirty years of work in psychiatric wards, she knew – in his opinion – much more than some young, inexperienced doctors, like himself.

Andrzej did not want to start immediately with the professional side of the conversation because, after all, it was his birthday and the girl seemed attractive enough for a more personal conversation. He asked her about the beginning of the war in Cracow. She told him that the first bombs fell on 1 September 1939, early in the morning, on the open city. She and her parents were hoping that perhaps they could stay in Cracow, after they heard that France and England had declared war on Germany. Later they were influenced by the mass exodus from Cracow by the majority of their friends. On 3 September they could not catch the evacuation train at the Cracow railway station because it was bombed. Her father decided to take a horse-driven carriage and accompany her mother and her to the nearest railway station and then return to Cracow. She begged him not to return, but to go with her mother and her on the last evacuation train, which they caught at the nearby railway station. The three days of travelling in this train under constant bombardment by German planes were terrible because they had to escape many times from it and hide in the ravines. They eventually reached Lwów, where her younger sister, Zosia, was anxiously waiting for them.

He listened attentively and that encouraged the girl to tell him how difficult her life as a refugee in Lwów had been, how she and her family were threatened with deportation to Siberia because of paragraph 11, how she was discriminated against by the Soviet authorities of the Medical Institute and not accepted officially, even though she had all necessary documents. She was grateful to the professor of pharmacology who helped her to be officially accepted. Her story lasted over half an hour and, when the girl looked at her watch, she stopped her narration and apologized for taking so much of his time for her personal story. She asked him for the reprints and had also some professional questions prepared by her professor.

Andrzej asked her to stay for a while: 'Today is my birthday,' he said. 'I will take a short break for the pleasure of conversation with you. I will also tell you my story.'

'I was born here in this city twenty-six years ago, shortly after the beginning of the First World War. Now, for more than a year we have a new war, and our life is not easy. Since the war, I have had no party for my birthday and only my parents have given me gifts. Today, however the Soviets, who in such a treacherous way invaded us, gave me a great birthday gift. This great gift is your visit in this department.' He was always very courteous to the ladies, but, as soon as he finished speaking, he felt that he had 'overdone' it this time.

Karolina was evidently amused and immediately wished him 'Happy birthday, and many happy returns.' She wished also that he have, for his next birthday, a more precious gift than her visit today. She blushed when he complimented her, but her eyes remained sad.

'In my opinion, Karolina, if I may call you so, dear colleague, this visit is a great gift for me. The future will show who was right in the evaluation of this visit – you or me.' Again he felt uneasy about 'overdoing' it. He was afraid the girl might think that he was one of those womanizers, saying nice things to any woman they see. He wanted to offset his tactical error, and continued: 'I like your way of thinking. We have many similar ideas and we have the same evaluation of many problems. I hope that we could become good friends, if you would consent to see me again. If you do not want to know me better, then we could begin immediately to discuss professional matters.'

She blushed again and, looking straight into his eyes, she said in her deep, husky voice: 'You are very kind, doctor. You are talking in a very interesting way – may I say in a very seductive way. But what do you know about me? Perhaps knowing something more about me, you might regret what you said about friendship. Maybe also, knowing you better, I might regret telling you what I am thinking now. You are looking at me and probably thinking 'a nice girl, I would like to know her better.' Your impression is positive, but very superficial, based merely on a visual evaluation. However, I am not a picture, only to be looked at. I have some patterns of thinking, some emotional values that you might not like. Looking at you I have also a positive visual impression. You are a young, handsome man. I know also from the nurse that you are a good doctor, dedicated to your patients, interested in scientific research.'

She paused for a while and then she lowered her head and looked at the floor for a couple of seconds. Her face was now pale. With his knowledge of psychology, Andrzej thought that she might now be more open, that she wanted to tell him something important. He knew that he should not interrupt her. It was quiet in the Office; you could hear only the ticking of the wall clock.

After a while, Karolina looked again straight into his eyes and continued: 'I have to go ahead, even if it is difficult and unpleasant. I do not want to have any deception and I do not want you to be deceived. Being sincere with you, I have to tell you something that might be very important for you. I am going to do it now to avoid any pain later. I am a Pole like you, but I am a Pole of the Judaic religion, or, if you prefer to call it otherwise, a Polish Jew or a Jewish Pole. You are a Pole of the Catholic religion. For me, the difference is not a problem. I have grown up in a totally assimilated family, but I have grown up, at the same time, in the shadow of Polish anti-Semitism. For many Poles, I am not a Pole, I am simply a Jewish girl, without the right to be called a Pole even by myself, with no right to feel like a Pole.

'Many times in my life I have not been accepted as a Pole by other Poles who were born Catholic. Before I started to study medicine, I graduated in another faculty at the same university and then I took a good lesson in Polish anti-Semitism. The Poles of my religion were not allowed to sit in the front benches; a "bench ghetto" was assigned to them by the Polish Catholic students. They called themselves "the future of the country." It is true that there were many Poles opposed to that. I had several Polish Catholic friends who not only did not accept such attitudes but were fighting morally and, yes, also physically with other students from the extreme right. I have seen the same anti-Semitism here during the war, when some Poles expelled people of the Judaic religion from the shelters during bombardments. I still feel this anti-Semitism around me, at the Medical Institute, although in a milder form. There is still a social ghetto, at least among the students. If I survive the war I will face anti-Semitism in this country again.'

She paused again, her big eyes full of tears, but she was strong enough to continue in a low voice: 'For many Polish boys, a Jewish girl is good only for a short physical liaison. I am not making generalizations; there are many honest Poles who are not anti-Semitic and fighting racist and religious prejudices. I do not know what kind of Pole you are. If you do not accept me as I am, tell me at once and, instead of planning a friendship, let us start immediately our professional discussion. However, I will never forget that it was, for me, good to meet you and see somebody so much interested in my personal life. Nor will I ever forget the date of your birthday. Next year I will send you a nice card with "Happy Birthday" wishes. In the meantime, the collaboration between the departments will continue according to the wish of my professor.'

Andrzej knew only one thing: he had never met such a girl, and he liked her more and more. After her outburst of sincerity, he had a feeling for her, different from what he had felt for any girl before. He was ashamed now that he was paying her cheap compliments.

He looked straight into her eyes, smiled and said warmly: 'Karolina, my dear Polish girl, I will not deceive you now and I promise not to deceive you in the future. I and all my family hate any kind of racism, any kind of religious, national, or social discrimination. I was educated from early childhood like that. I am ashamed of Polish anti-Semitism and, when you will know me better, you will hear from other people that I was always fighting anti-Semitism during my medical studies. Many of my closest friends are Poles of the Judaic religion. All of them told me exactly the same stories that you are telling me. They know also that not only me, but many Poles were fighting for equal rights for students and career scientists at the universities, and many workers were coming during students' unrest at the beginning of the academic year to fight with the nationalist students in the name of equality and freedom. I understand very well your bitterness and your sorrow. Thank you for having enough confidence in me to tell me all that, without knowing me better, already at our first encounter.'

At once Karolina's eyes brightened and, looking at Andrzej, she said: 'Thank you very much, doctor. Your nurse, Filomena, told me that you are an excellent therapist. Indeed, for me your words were soothing, and they acted like psychotherapy. Excuse my acting out, or whatever you call such an outburst in psychiatry. Let us return now to another type of therapy and let me ask the questions addressed to you by my professor. How fortunate I am that I might perhaps in the future have an opportunity to discuss more professional and perhaps also non-professional questions with a person who has an outlook so close to mine.' 'May I invite you to have a cup of coffee after our discussion?' Andrzej asked. She accepted with pleasure.

This was the evening of the day on which Andrzej met for the first time his future wife. It was an extraordinary birthday, and he felt a happiness that he had not known before and was looking towards the future of this relationship with great hope. He could not foresee what terrible things would happen in the future and how, all at once, a hell would open upon their heads.

During the next hour they discussed the mechanism of convulsive therapy. Her questions were very clear, and she was also able to engage in discussion beyond the prepared agenda.

Sister Filomena brought them coffee and cookies that the nuns had prepared as a surprise gift for Andrzej's birthday. During this time, Andrzej was trying to find a pretext for meeting with the girl again, and as soon as possible. He did not know that Karolina had the same idea in her head. She would never make such a proposal. At that time, girls were not supposed to ask for a date. They had to wait to be asked. Andrzej knew that. He decided that the most intelligent way to continue this relationship was to show his readiness to answer promptly all the questions of the professor of pharmacology and that the best 'channel,' as he called it, would be through Karolina. Karolina liked his idea. 'Of course, doctor, I could be the right channel. It is my professional duty, and at the same time it will be for me a personal pleasure. Five days a week, I work on my experiments in the Department of Pharmacology, always between 3:00 and 6:00 p.m. In the morning, I have to attend lectures and practical lessons.'

'Thank you very much for this information. May I ask your permission to come and pick you up in the Department of Pharmacology tomorrow at 6:00 p.m. We could then take a walk through the streets and discuss any additional questions that your professor might have.'

'That is an excellent idea. What will happen, however, if my professor has no additional questions?'

'I do not think such will be the case. There are still many complicated and unanswered questions in convulsive therapy, and he is an intelligent man if he understands the necessity of a collaboration between clinical observations and experimental pharmacology. If he does not have questions, I have a lot of them. I am even asking myself whether this is the right method of treatment, if some new, less aggressive methods should not be invented. I heard already of the invention of electric-shock therapy, not yet introduced in pre-war Poland or in the Soviet Union. It is still an aggressive method, but ... Let us leave all the discussions for tomorrow.'

It was completely dark outside. Andrzej looked at his watch. It was already 7:00 p.m. 'I know that you have to go. I am on duty and I am sorry that I cannot accompany you to the tram. Filomena is just now finishing her rounds. Let me ask her to accompany you to the tram stop and see you off. I will have then the feeling that you will arrive home safely.' He kissed the hand of Karolina and said: 'I am not a strong believer. But I believe that only God could send me on my birthday somebody like you, and do it through the intermediary of a Soviet professor.'

Karolina blushed again and said: 'I just wanted to tell you that you are very romantic, and that I could go home unprotected.' Andrzej, in turn, did not want to appear too much to be imposing on her and persuaded her that this was an exceptional day and he was in command because it was his birthday. He did not know at that time that, in the near future, he would have to protect Karolina's safety and life in much more dangerous circumstances, very often exposing himself to the greatest danger. Now, it was only typical Polish chivalry, in general much appreciated by the ladies. Karolina liked it. 'Thank you very much for your courteous behaviour. I will be very pleased to see you again tomorrow at six, at the Department of Pharmacology.'

Filomena returned at 8:00 p.m. Andrzej felt some anxiety over the one-hour delay. 'What happened, Filomena? The walk to the tram stop lasts only ten minutes.' 'Nothing happened. We were so much interested in our conversation that we deliberately missed two trams.' 'I imagine that you were mostly talking about religious matters. As far, as I know you, you did not try to convert her,' Andrzej said. 'You know very well, Andrzej, that although I was and am still a nun, I am open-minded. Nuns in general are much more open-minded than most of the doctors think. No, I did not try to convert her. She does not need to be converted. She is in a perfect contact with God, and her God is the same one that I have in my heart. But if, one day, for any reason, it will be necessary to have her converted, I will be there to help her.' And, after a while, she added: 'And you, doctor, you, Andrzej, I hope you will be gentle with her, will not harm her. She is very vulnerable. She had a hard life until now, and I do not think the future will be easy for her.'

'Filomena, you are a good nun and an excellent nurse. However, you think in the way most nuns are apt to think. Namely, that all doctors, especially the young ones, are very wicked with women. No, certainly I am not going to do any harm to Karolina. Filomena, I am in love with her. I have been since I first saw her. I am going to marry her.' He was speaking in a very emotional way. At once he stopped, looked at his watch, and, in a familiar tone to which she was used, said: 'I have to start my evening round of duty, Thank you, Filomena, for giving me two hours of your free time to accompany my guest to the tram.' 'God bless you, Andrzej,' said Filomena, 'and He will guide your steps.'

V

NEXT DAY, AT 6:00 P.M., ANDRZEJ ENTERED THE LABORATORY of the Department of Pharmacology where Karolina has just finished her work. She took off her white coat and emerged in a very simple and elegant dress with only a single piece of jewellery, an antique brooch. She was all smiles and told Andrzej that the professor was very pleased with the bibliography and reprints. He also wanted to meet Andrzej in person in the near future to discuss with him problems of common concern.

When they left the medical building and its garden, Andrzej said: 'Now, Karolina, we are beginning our journey in the world.' And after a while: 'Now, no more "Doctor," no more "Colleague," please call me Andrzej and I will call you Karolina.' She consented, whispering, 'Yes, Andrzej.' He took her left hand in his right, and when they started walking through the street towards the centre of the city, Andrzej said: 'We are now, as you know, Karolina, on Piekarska Street, a long street leading to downtown. When you look to your left you see some old buildings, more or less beautiful. This is our reality, the one in which we are living at present. Please listen to me and do not look to your right side and I will tell you – if you allow me to dream awake – what might happen in the future, what you could see on your right-hand side.

'With some poetic reverie, I am going to see with you the blue Mediterrean Sea. We are driving in a car, and we are approaching Nice, and slowly climbing the Grande Corniche. The weather is beautiful, and we are feeling very happy. I am looking into your green eyes, as I am doing now. I prefer this green of your eyes to the blue of the sea. We are not wealthy but we have enough money to stop, after approaching the Italian border, for coffee and pastry. You can see now Monaco and the castle on the hill. A little bit farther we are going to pass the Monte Carlo casino on the sea side. We make a small turn to the right, and we are now in Menton. It is a quiet time, no war any more.

'Look always to your left. In reality, we are on Bernardine's Place, with its church. But, on the right, we are already close to the Italian border. You can see yachts sailing on the Mediterrean. it is a beautiful October here, full of flowers, no sign of autumn yet. We will soon cross the Italian frontier and have a nice Italian espresso with pastry in Bordighera.

'Let us return now to the present, because we are just before a nice pastry and coffee shop of Welz in the Akademicka Street, in Lwów.'

During all this walk, Karolina did not say a word. She looked at Andrzej's face and sometimes tried to take a short glance to her right and encountered again and again Andrzej's admonition: 'You have to look to your left and I am describing the future, to make the present more hopeful.'

'Thank you,' she said, 'for this wonderful excursion to the Grande Corniche, and thank you for the still splendid walk through the streets of Lwów. I did not know that you have so many talents – you are a good doctor, a promising scientist, a poet, and at the same a well-travelled person. Have you visited France many times?' 'No, Karolina I never crossed the border of Poland. All I know about the Côte d'Azur I have read in my Mother's French books. Before the war she taught French in a gymnasium and she has an extensive library.'

'Do you think, Andrzej, that it will be possible some time in the future just to cross a street and find yourself in another country? Do you think that the poetic reverie will become truth for us, or will it remain just that, a reverie?'

He stopped for a while and said, 'I want to be very sincere with you, Karolina. I am not very optimistic right now. If I were too optimistic, I could make many mistakes, because I would be not careful enough. During the war you cannot permit yourself to be optimistic. Also you have to be very patient and not lose hope.' And, with a smile, he added: 'The most important thing, however, is to be together. The feeling of togetherness gives you courage and hope. It is easier to suffer together when hard times come. It is more joyful if you can share with somebody your happiness, if you win something in life, you can share it, and if you have to die, it is even easier not to die alone.'

She looked at him and said: 'Thank you very much not only for the journey in future, but also, and above all, for what you said just now, for the last sentence. I have the feeling that I have waited a very long time for such an encounter as we had yesterday. And you have not disappointed me today.' She was evidently moved, and Andrzej has seen again tears in her eyes. But, this time, the reason for the tears was different, and her eyes were not sad. She was smiling.

'I see that we are before the entry to Welz. I have some objections. Everybody feels nowadays rather tight with money, and I do not know if you are wealthy enough to invite me to such an elegant patisserie. Let us leave it for the future – like other things in today's walk, let us leave it on the right side.'

'My dear Karolina, today is a very important day for us because we just started the journey through the world, our journey together, our common journey through the war. Let us enjoy our togetherness. Let us have this small pleasure at the beginning: coffee with cakes. Quiet and relatively safe, just for a while.'

They took a small table in the corner. The place was full of people, many Poles in civilian garb and also many Soviet officers.

'I feel now that I have to tell you something about my family and something more about me. We are now friends, and perhaps one day you will meet my family and my friends.' Then she told him about her father, Juliusz, her mother, Dorota, and her younger sister, Zosia. Karolina graduated from an excellent elementary school and went after it to a gymnasium, where she passed her Matura in 1932 at the age of seventeen. Never in the elementary school or gymnasium was she treated other than as a Pole with the Judaic religion, and always at school and at home she was taught to have very patriotic feelings and pride in belonging to the Polish nation. The anniversaries of the Polish uprisings against occupation in the time of Poland's partition were always remembered as national holidays: the anniversary of the November uprising in 1831 and of the January uprising in 1863, both against the terrorism of tsarist Russia, were reflected not only in Polish poetry and paintings, but also in the vivid memories of festivities at school. These events were called 'Uprising Matinées.'

She knew, however, of the increasing anti-Semitism among the students at the universities and about the difficulties Poles with Judaic religion had being accepted for medical studies. The rationale was the so-called *numerus clausus*, which meant that only a restricted number of such students could be accepted for medical studies.

'I did not even try to be accepted, because I was too proud to have such a deception. I wanted to increase my chances in such a way that I could be accepted, notwithstanding any religious or racial prejudice. I started my law studies in 1932 and, at the end of the year, I was interested very much in it. I was very much encouraged by the fact that my first seminar work, which was on the "Déclaration des Droits de l'Homme et de Citoyen," proclaimed by the great French Revolution, won a prize of honour that came with, at that time, a considerable amount of money. During the second year of studies, I was very interested in the ecclesiastical law, which at that time was taught in the Law faculties. I was also interested in the constitutional laws of big empires, especially of the British Empire.

'I finished my law studies in 1936, with the degree of Master of Laws, and was eager to see how it felt to live in an empire. So, I had decided already in 1935 to go for a certain time to London, to the London School of Economics and Political Science. I met there the most interesting person from the Labor Party, Professor Harold J. Laski. After a couple of interviews with him, I decided that, after receiving the master's degree in laws, I would try to write a doctoral thesis on the constitutional law of dominions. You certainly know what an impact the Statute of Westminster, published in 1931, had on the future of the British Empire. Thus, after obtaining the master's degree, I started, in 1936, to write my doctoral thesis on this subject. I obtained special permission to defend it only one year after graduation with my master's (and not after the compulsory period of at least two years). I defended my thesis at the end of May 1937.

'Then I could see that, whatever I did, there was no possibility for me, being of the Judaic religion, to begin a university career at the Law Faculty. The idea of medical studies, which never left me, entered again my mind. After some consultations with the very liberal university rector (principal) and a professor of forensic medicine at the Medical Faculty, I was advised to compete for admission to the Medical Faculty. I was told confidentially that this is the last opportunity, because of the growing anti-Semitism. The next year, 1938, no Jewish students would be admitted. *Numerus clausus* would no longer apply; instead, there would be *numerus nullus*. It proved to be true.

'I have won the competition, and I could now study something that I could practise anywhere in the world. The situation in Poland was more and more difficult for people with my religion, and I had to take into consideration the possibility, or even the necessity, that I emigrate from Poland. Such a fate was faced already by the German students of the Judaic religion, although most of them were assimilated and considered themselves more German than the Germans themselves.

'You know very well, Andrzej, what kind of discrimination I had to face from the extreme-rightist students, because in Lwów existed the same situation as in Cracow. There was even a case of homicide of a student of the Judaic religion in Lwów. You know also that there were many open-minded Polish students who fought verbally and physically against such discrimination. I had many friends among them. To express their protest they were especially sitting on the benches destined as a ghetto for "Jews" by the rightist students. I felt not only personally humiliated, but humiliated as a Polish citizen, that such things could happen.

'I finished my second year of medical studies after passing all the five exams of the second year in June 1939. And then there was the war, the flight to Lwów, and again difficulties because I was a refugee and I had this terrible passport with paragraph 11. I did not give up my studies and, with the consent and approbation of the Polish professors, I was continuing them unofficially until – thanks to the professor of pharmacology who came from Moscow – I was officially admitted, and all the unofficial period was accounted for. As you see, Andrzej, you can never predict who will help you. The Soviets were generally considered to be "bad" people, and this professor did not change that blanket evaluation, but was considered as an exception.

'This is not my opinion. I believe that in any race, in any religion, in any nationality, you can find people with human hearts and understanding, and people who do not care for anybody. I believe also that human beings can change for the better if they themselves experience hardship. I have seen many Polish rightists changing their anti-Semitic attitudes when they themselves became humiliated here in Lwów by the Soviets. We do not always have the chance to meet people with human attitudes, but there are plenty of them around us.' She looked again straight into Andrzej's eyes and said: 'This is the short story of my life.'

At that moment they noticed the coffee and pastry on their table. 'Let us have some coffee because, if I start my story now, our coffee will have no taste at all and the beautiful cream cakes might collapse.' This was only a pretext for Andrzej, because he wanted to have a short pause, being very much moved by Karolina's story.

After coffee, it was his turn to tell Karolina about himself, his parents, his studies and interests. Both of his parents were teachers, both were also affected by the change in the school system introduced by the Soviets. He was educated in a very liberal way, encouraged to fight any social, racial, or religious prejudices. Therefore, both of them felt, after listening to each other's story, a certain togetherness in their existential insecurity. There was a warm air of understanding and, at the same time, a high emotional degree of feeling close, one to the other.

After a short silence, Karolina said: 'To be sincere with you, I have to be less shy and tell you that I simply want to make this atmosphere full of poetic happiness between us to remain as good as it is now. With all my disappointments and feelings of insecurity, I have not been very happy until this hour in my life. I love my parents and Zosia, I sometimes have struggles with my mother, most probably because of the generation gap, although both my parents are very liberal. I have an extremely good relationship with my father, although I have to fight always with his inborn optimism. I have many friends, from both faculties in Cracow and now in Lwów, but this meeting with you seems to me to be emotionally different. You understand what I mean,' and she blushed.

She continued after a while: 'Since yesterday, I understand what I am really feeling. I am not ashamed to tell you what is in my heart. I know now that, until yesterday, I had not met anybody whom I could like very much, I could ...' She stopped and lowered her head.

After a short silence, Andrzej said: 'Karolina, my dear girl, you told me in a shy way something that I understand very well. Don't be afraid of words, don't be ashamed of your feelings. Love is the most precious human feeling. I have loved you from the very first moment we met. Please, don't misunderstand. I don't want to become your lover. I want to marry you. I respect and admire all that you have done in your life. I am sorry for all your sufferings. I want to be your husband, and I want to face with you all the dangers around us. Together with you I want to survive this war.'

Karolina looked at him throughout this declaration. Her cheeks were now red, and the tears were flowing down her face. After a while, she said in a low voice: 'I love you, Andrzej. I am crying because I feel so happy that it overwhelms me. My love is forever. Pay attention, Andrzej. In this respect I am perhaps very Catholic, like – or more – than the Pope. I can love only once in my life and, for me, marriage is forever. God bless you, my love.'

It was dark already, and many people had left the coffee house. The couple went out on the street, and this time they were not holding hands like children. Andrzej had Karolina's left arm in his right, holding her tight. For a while they could not utter a word. After a while, Andrzej asked: 'Are you a believer, my dear love.' 'Yes, she answered. I believe in God, who is for me the symbol of everything that is good, honest, noble, and beautiful in our world. Life is for me easier and more beautiful with my belief. My God is giving me inspiration and hope. He gave me you. In this unknown city, where I have never been before, in this city where I could not for many months continue my studies, where I was on many nights obliged to go into hiding not to be deported, He had pity on me and finally permitted me to continue my education, permitted me to find the most precious thing in the world, permitted me to meet the man I loved from first sight. It all seems to be like a dream. Or is it a miracle? Will He also permit us to survive this terrible war together?'

She looked at Andrzej: 'Don't you think that it is something that is nearly a miracle? Are you, Andrzej, a believer?' Andrzej was moved by her emotional outburst: 'I like very much your God and I believe in His presence in your heart. When I was a young child, I was a strong believer. At the ages of twelve and thirteen I used to pray very much. Every morning, before school, I went to church to pray for my grandmother's failing health. I loved her so much. But later on, in the gymnasium, we had a very rigid and vicious chaplain who was preaching hatred towards anybody who was not Catholic. He especially hated those who called themselves Poles and were of the Judaic religion. In his opinion, all Jews were responsible for the martyrdom and crucifixion of Jesus.

'Like many other Polish Catholics, I had many colleagues of the Judaic religion who were my closest friends. They were honest, with high moral values. How could he accuse them of bearing the responsibility for crucifixion? How, in general, can you accuse a whole nation for crimes committed by its citizens? In such a way you could find that any nation in the world bears the hideous stigma of crime. When we tried to argue with him, he called us Jewish serfs. As, at the same time, he was teaching us catechism, I slowly started to evaluate many things in a critical way. From my most profound belief, through the stage of not taking seriously liturgic ceremonies, I became one day what might be called atheist. However I am still a believer in God, very close in my conception of God to your conception. I think, Karolina, that you will help me to restore God's place in my heart.'

'I will try to do my best. Don't be afraid, Andrzej. I will not try to convert you. My God is everywhere in the universe, in the souls of all decent people with any religion or without it. I discussed this problem at length yesterday with Sister Filomena, who is a nun. There was no divergence between us on the subject of religion, and belief in God.'

They had reached the porch of the house where Karolina was living with her parents in exile imposed by the Nazi occupation of Cracow. Andrzej took her both hands into his and kissed them.

'See you, my dearest love, tomorrow at the Department of Pharmacology.'

'Yes, until tomorrow, my dearest love,' and she disappeared up the staircase.

VI

THOSE WERE TWO DAYS OF UNBELIEVABLE HAPPINESS, when life seemed to both of them a most beautiful dream. The night that followed those two days was, for both of them, a night without dreams. Both were full of anxiety, of insecurity, of eagerness to face the future as soon as possible – and, at the same time, to postpone the moment that might or might not bring them a disenchantment. Both were mature enough to ask themselves: Is it really love or just an infatuation? They knew each other just two days and, although those two days were full of confessions about the past and the present, many things were left unanswered. Both believed that this was love and that they wanted to marry.

There was around them a terrible war. They had lived through the loss of the independence of Poland. This was also their personal tragedy. They had witnessed bombs and unrest, defeat of the Polish army, very often harsh treatment by the Soviet authorities. Karolina could be deported any time to Siberia; Andrzej could be taken into the Soviet army if the Soviets decided to go to war and participate in the victory of the Germans, who had become their allies. Andrzej's parents had lost their opportunity to teach in the gymnasium, and only one of them was now employed, earning the poor salary of a teacher in an elementary school. Karolina was deprived of her home, her books, and the very special atmosphere of Cracow. Her beloved father could at any time be persecuted as a pre-war capitalist who, as was being said about capitalists, always exploits the working class.

They were asking themselves if it was right, in such circumstances, to make plans about marriage with a person one had known just two days. Were they only enchanted by the physical beauty and poetic charm of words? Was this tragic situation, when many people were losing their lives in the war, the time when people were suffering and dying in concentration camps, the right time for love and vows of marriage? A man in an unknown city for Karolina, a girl from a city occupied by Germans, God knows for how long. Where were they going to live? What were they going to live through? Could they trust each other? Could they trust themselves?

The days were full of romantic poetry; the nights that followed these days were full of reality, showing its sad and cruel face to both of them. Both knew that the feeling of happiness, of something never experienced before, was still there, day and night, whatever threat the future might hold. Only the future could give them answer to their questions. There was strong sense of reality present in the fact that each of them was inspiring in the other this feeling of happiness, never imagined before. This seemed to be the indicator of something unusual, something special, deceiving and dangerous or full of confidence and security.

However, what to do, when so many factors were not dependent only on their characters and emotions? Were they just like autumn leaves, dancing in the streets? Or were they like strong sailors fighting a hurricane on the sea, where only extreme bravery, experience, and mutual help could save them from drowning? Maybe, the insecure situation around them added a special flavour to their encounter, which, in the setting of peace and harmony, would not reach such emotional heights.

Next morning both of them went to work in the same medical institute, trying to concentrate the best they could on their obligations: Andrzej as a doctor, Karolina as a medical student. Both of them were looking forward for the evening meeting.

It was like that, during many days after their first encounter. And each and every day brought this soothing answer: 'Be quiet and happy with every minute, with every hour, that still brings you the feeling of love. And, yes, not only no deception, but growing confidence. Each day brought greater confidence and greater happiness.

'I am going to tell my parents about you, my love,' said Andrzej one evening.

'That's exactly what I am going to do. My parents have to know how happy I am and what we have decided,' answered Karolina.

'They might have objections,' Andrzej said. 'They never lived in Lwów and I am sure they would not be happy that you have decided to marry somebody of whom they know nothing more than that, perhaps more often than other colleagues, I visit you when it is raining and we cannot walk in the streets and parks. Autumn is an unfortunate season for lovers. All love stories are set in spring. And not necessarily in wartime. Your parents will see me as an immature person, and they will forbid you to see me again.'

'I am sure they will not do that. My father liked you very much the first time you came to see me.' Andrzej came very often to see Karolina in the modest dwelling allotted to her family by the Soviet official who had evicted them from their apartment.

'I am more afraid of your parents' reaction. It is wartime. I come from another city. I have been here only a short time. They have not seen me yet. I know very much about them from you and therefore I do not even mention that they might object to your marriage to a girl of the Judaic religion. Although it might be one day – if the Germans continue their victorious march on Europe – a danger; the Germans could invade the territory they have given away to the Soviets. But I am persuaded that this is not a big danger because, before that might happen, the war could be finished and we could be free again. Let us hope that this new Poland will not be anti-Semitic and that you will not have to fight for equal rights for your wife. Still, I am a newcomer here, and you are the only son of a tightly knit family. You are still very young to be a doctor, and they might principally object that it is too early for you to make decisions affecting your future life.'

'Therefore we have to tell them as early as possible, so that they have enough time to adapt to the new situation. I would be married one day anyway, and they know that.'

'Perhaps we will have to concede to their wishes not to go as fast as we would like, but they should adapt to this idea, and we will do everything to adjust the exact date to their wishes. Let us see and feel out their reactions.'

Karolina told her parents what she felt about the young doctor who sometimes came to visit her. She felt for the first time in her life what it is to be in love with somebody. She did not yet mention anything about marriage. She felt that they liked him from the first visits and that they had an inkling of Karolina's emotional involvement. As they were quite open-minded, they suggested she invite Andrzej to dinner so that they could talk with him about different things and not rely only on a very positive, but still superficial, impression that they had of him from his former visits. They were very often absent during these visits and, if they were at home, they never interrupted the conversations that Karolina had in the second room with Andrzej, or with any of her colleagues who came to see her in connection with their studies and preparation for exams.

She felt happy about the invitation and immediately told Andrzej: 'You see how nice they are. You are invited to have dinner with us, and I am sure they will like you very much when they have the opportunity to talk with you.'

Andrzej's parents had been aware for a while that something unusual had happened to him, something different from the meetings with colleagues that he had had during his years as a student and since he became a doctor. He had always had many friends who visited him; he was always telling his parents that he was going to visit one of his friends. They knew most, nearly all, of his friends, boys and girls. They met them with grace, and they were liked by them very much for their kindness and personal charm.

Now, however, something was different. Andrzej was leaving home always at the same time, before 6:00 p.m., telling them, as usual, when he would be back, but he did not mention whom he was going to meet. They did not ask any questions, because it was their custom not to ask if he did not tell them. Between themselves, they spoke about the possibility of a romance or some difficulties at work because they knew that some of his colleagues had problems with the new Soviet authorities. Andrzej felt that he should tell them the whole story, not yet about marriage, but of being in love. He felt he should also ask them about the possibility of inviting Karolina to their home, to introduce her. As a matter of fact, fighting with his own attitude, he felt the necessity to share with them his own feeling of happiness. He was sure they would understand everything; they themselves were very much in love in their youth, and they had married because they were in love.

He told them that he had met a girl who was a medical student in her fourth year, and who was working on a research study conducted by his department together with the Department of Pharmacology. They had common interests; they had met originally because of professional interests. Then, little by little, knowing the girl better, he realized that it was something serious.

'We do not know her at all, is that so?' his mother asked, because she knew nearly all the girls who were preparing for exams together with Andrzej. Their son was not a womanizer, but liked always the company of ladies, and he was very much in demand, because of his courtesy and good looks. They were very proud of him.

He was not surprised and very grateful when they proposed that he invite the girl one day for dinner. Only then did he realize that he had forgotten to tell his parents that the girl was not from Lwów, that she was from Cracow, one of very few medical students refugees.

Two days after this conversation with his parents, Andrzej had such a high fever that he had to stay at home. There was no phone in their apartment, nor was there a phone at Karolina's parents'. Andrzej asked his mother to call in the afternoon the Department of Pharmacology and to tell Karolina that he could not come to pick her up this evening because he was ill. She had also to tell Karolina that she and Andrzej's father would be delighted to have her for dinner as soon as Andrzej got better.

Karolina, however, did not want to wait until then to see Andrzej. If he was ill, she wanted to visit him at once, after work. Would his mother permit her to come and see Andrzej today, in the early evening hours?

'If you are not afraid of catching yourself the flu, you will be the most welcome guest' was the mother's answer. Karolina knew now from whom Andrzej had inherited his courtesy.

'Yes ... no, I am sorry. I am not afraid of flu. Thank you for the invitation.'

'Why should we then wait with the dinner until he gets better. Let us dine tonight together with you.'

Karolina told her parents that she was invited for dinner by Andrzej's parents and that she would return home later, after that dinner. She went to Andrzej's home directly from the laboratory, extremely eager to see his parents. Not only was she delighted to meet people who were specialists in subjects that had interested her greatly at the gymnasium, but these people were Andrzej's beloved parents. She could not dream of better coincidence. At home, she had had long talks with her father about the ancient story of Rome and Greece. Her father taught her the principles of Latin poetry before she was introduced to it at school, and from an early age she had studied French, and then in the gymnasium, she had been especially attracted by French literature.

Andrzej, who still had fever, felt much better in the evening and was proud that Karolina, in her conversation with his parents had showed some knowledge of subjects that his parents taught. At moments, he felt a little bit uneasy because he himself could only with great concentration address the problems that seemed so familiar to Karolina as if she was a linguist. At once it flashed in his memory how dissatisfied he was when the Soviet professor spoke of her as of a 'polyglot.'

Andrzej's mother prepared the best dinner they could afford during Soviet times in Lwów, when food was scarce. There was among this small circle of people meeting for the first time in their lives something particular that made them feel close one to another. Part of it was that, during the Soviet occupation and the war raging abroad, people in Poland felt a togetherness whenever they met, even if it was for a short time. More than that, however, that feeling was created by the unusual warmth and charm of Andrzej's mother and the security and sense of humour emanating from Andrzej's father.

Andrzej's father accompanied Karolina back home. He was enchanted by Karolina's wit and education, and especially by the maturity of her system of values. During this walk home, she told Andrzej's father that her religion was Judaic, but that she had always felt she was Polish. She felt very ill at ease with the Soviets in general, with the exception of her professor, but was still convinced that, under the Soviet occupation, the Polish people would suffer less than under the Germans' Nazi system. She made reference to the scary days in 1939 when people in Lwów did not know who would take the city.

He listened attentively to her. He also felt that, if there had to be an invasion, it would probably be less painful under the Soviets than under the Germans. As for her religious or national identification, to him it made no difference if she was Judaic or of any other religion, or without a religion; of that or other nationality, or just a feeling citizen of the world. The real issue was the moral value of the human being, his or her attitudes towards any other race, nationality, class, or religion.

He seemed to her extremely open-minded, and he communicated his opinions with such a sense of humour that she was eager to listen to him. When they reached her home, he told her something that made her admire him still more. 'If the day arrives – let us hope that it will never arrive, although I am not quite sure, so – if the day arrives that Hitler will invade Lwów, you can be sure, that I, my wife

BEFORE THE LAST SUNSET

and Andrzej, we will do all we can to help not only you, but anybody whom it will be necessary to help.'

At once she had a feeling of security not only for her, but for anybody who could be persecuted by a Nazi invasion. Karolina was so impressed by his behaviour that she immediately told her parents about her visit at Andrzej's home, and she had not enough words to praise their charm, education, intelligence, and, above all, moral stature. Her father told her that, by coincidence, he had met some people from Lwów who knew Andrzej's father and told him that he was a man of unusual integrity. Therefore he did not discount her story as that of a girl in love who sees everything in connection with her beloved as unusual. What she perceived was simply true and, yes, not very common. He could feel only happiness that his daughter has met such people in this city where she had experienced so much sadness over the possibility of continuing her medical studies.

'I understand your enthusiasm. It is well justified. However, I am sceptical about the impression you could make on them. Although I love you and I am proud of you, I do not know if everybody looks upon you with the same feeling. Still I am looking forward very much to knowing better a son of such wonderful parents.'

When Karolina told Andrzej about this unusual feeling of security that she had talking with his father, he understood how important it was for her, after so many deceptions in her life, to meet somebody like his father. She knew from his students that, as a professor, he was very demanding, although he judged their work in a very just and honest way. If he gave her this feeling of security, he reasoned, she probably did not deceive him very much. And, indeed, Karolina was very well accepted by his parents.

A couple of days after the dinner at Andrzej's parents home, Andrzej was invited to the very small and modest apartment where Karolina, her parents, and her younger sister, Zosia, were spending their second year of the war-imposed exile in Lwów. This time Andrzej, whom Karolina's father knew only from very short encounters when they exchanged greetings, met for a longer time with Juliusz. It was an emotional encounter, and it remained like that until the end.

Juliusz was in his early fifties, not very tall. His smile had a great charm, and he liked to smile, because in general he had an extremely optimistic and friendly attitude towards everybody. However, at the time Andrzej met him, although he was still smiling easily, his beautiful, large, dark blue eyes were full of sorrow. Not sadness yet, but sorrow. When he started to talk, Andrzej very soon understood why Karolina called her father an unforgivable optimist. He had a faith in the existence of absolute justice, a utopian idea of a perfect society with righteous people. The war, in his opinion, would end very soon because such an evil as Hitler could not survive for long. For Andrzej, Juliusz was and remained an unforgettable example of how easily real life can destroy people who are overly confident about the righteousness of human nature and in the victory of Good over Evil.

Juliusz knew from the way Karolina had described Andrzej, and also the meeting with his family, that she was seriously involved. For the first time in her life she was behaving as if she was in love. He knew that Karolina had what people used to call a idealized, nineteenth-century romantic conception of love. For her, love was forever, an emotion that you can nurture only once in life. For her, love meant faithful forever, and if it came to giving up life to save the beloved person, she would have chosen dying over a life of safety with no love. For unknown reasons, it seemed to Juliusz that the young doctor, whom he knew just from sight, must have the same ideas in his head.

Karolina's mother, Dorota, was four years younger than Juliusz. Karolina told Andrzej that her mother had beautiful 'ancient gold,' or, as the Germans called it, 'Altgold,' hair long enough to touch the ground. When short hair became the fashion, she cut it, and the hair at once lost its glamour, although retaining the colour. She had a different personality from that of Juliusz. She had always a very liberal system of values, was very much interested in social reform, and, probably after stopping her studies, lost confidence in her professional future. She married Juliusz, who was a faithful chum of her brother Jakub (Kuba), just before the First World War and, at the outbreak of the war, was pregnant with Karolina. When Cracow was threatened by the advancing Russian front, Juliusz managed to transport Dorota to Vienna, where she gave birth to Karolina on 31 December 1914, New Year's Eve, 1915. The second daughter, Zosia, was born in Cracow.

The First World War was a tragic experience for Dorota; her only brother was seriously wounded in his hip and, after a long stay in hospital, walked with a limp. Juliusz was taken to the Austrian army, and she never knew when she might lose him because his courage was close to bravura. Fortunately, his life was spared, and after the difficult post-war period she managed, with Juliusz, to have a nice home. She shared his interest in arts, especially in music. After the First World War, there was a period during which Juliusz and Dorota found at least a couple of hours in the late afternoon each day to play together. He played the violin and she accompanied him on piano. Then, for unknown reasons, most probably related to the difficult atmosphere in Poland after the war, little by little they stopped playing. From time to time, Juliusz, much more often than Dorota, returned to playing.

The outbreak of the Second World War ruined their home and all their hopes for a quiet future. Much more critical about the course of the war and not optimistic as Juliusz was, Dorota lived with terrible anxiety from the outbreak of the war. She was mortally afraid of the Nazis and felt greatly the harshness of life with the Soviets. Not only were she and her family deprived of their nice home, and of most of their friends, but they had to cope with the threat of deportation to Siberia. They lived in a very modest apartment and very often had to leave it for a night when they received warning that deportation – 'Wywozka,' as it was called – was planned by the NKVD. Her brother, Kuba, was imprisoned by the Soviets merely for being an officer of the Polish army. They never saw him again after the night in the fall of 1939 when the Soviets took him away. Until April 1940 Karolina could not officially continue her medical studies, and Zosia had no possibilities of studies because all of them were refugees, with passports carrying paragraph 11.

When Karolina was accepted for her studies in 1940, it was a great relief for all. At least one member of the family could continue life with an eye to the future. But the war was still on, and Dorota did not believe, as Juliusz did, in its short duration.

Andrzej understood later that the smile on Juliusz's face not only expressed his optimistic attitude but was intended to create a more joyous, acceptable, and less ominous atmosphere for Dorota. It may have been the case that Dorota was not at all relieved by this optimism and was aware that a too optimistic attitude might lessen some caution and hence be dangerous.

When Andrzej arrived for dinner, Dorota still had her beautiful golden hair with no trace of grey. She liked Andrzej from first sight, for his courtesy and delicate and kind manners. Some of Karolina's colleagues were not so nice. Karolina knew that Dorota was always hypercritical, as if to balance the optimism of Juliusz.

The younger sister of Karolina, Zosia, was a very intelligent and talented girl. She had a special gift for mathematics, but did not even start studies in the subject. After a serious conversation with Juliusz, she understood that there was, in Poland, no opportunity for a scientific career in mathematics. And Juliusz wanted very much to leave the printing factory to one of his daughters. Zosia was very interested in the graphic arts and accepted the offer that she go for studies in Vienna. At that time, Austria was very much against Hitler. There were some members of Dorota's family living in Vienna.

When the Nazis invaded Austria, Zosia had to interrupt her studies and return to Cracow, where she took practical lessons in the graphic establishment under Juliusz's guidance. Zosia was an extremely shy girl, very much liked by her colleagues, because she was always helpful and modest. She loved Karolina dearly and, being so different from her, was extremely proud of her. It may be that she was, in a way, abashed by Karolina.

The conversation they had during Andrzej's visit with Karolina's parents was typical for Poles in the autumn of 1940. Everybody knew how bad the political and military situation was, and nobody spoke about the sad present. The only topic was an excellent outlook for the future,and here Juliusz was playing the principal role. Already during this first conversation with Juliusz, Andrzej was frightened by his optimism. Karolina felt uneasy in this situation and tried to shift the attention towards their work and the general situation at the Medical Institute.

Juliusz was enchanted by Andrzej, and when the visit came to an end he told him that he would always be the most welcome guest at their modest home. 'Now, we are feeling first signals of coming autumn. Please don't walk in rainy weather with Karolina, don't go to coffee houses, usually full of smoke. Come here, and we will be more than happy to give you a nice cup of tea. I understand that you want to talk with Karolina and not be disturbed by anything. This apartment is small and modest, but certainly nobody will disturb you. The adjacent room is Karolina's working place, and this can accommodate both of you. It is a very warm apartment, and our hearts will warm up when we see you.'

Juliusz was speaking from the bottom of his heart. He told

Karolina later that he would like very much to see Andrzej again. She replied that, if Juliusz met Andrzej's parents, he would like them very much as well. She felt especially happy when Dorota, who was always very critical, joined Juliusz to say how she liked Andrzej, his good manners, his open-mindedness, and his education. It was not easy to gain Dorota's approval, and Karolina knew that.

VII

AUTUMN 1940 WAS COMING TO AN END. GONE WERE THE days of Polish 'golden' fall. Gone were the days of wandering in the streets and parks, looking at the trees gracefully coloured with red and yellowish-red leaves, through which the last sunbeams were shining. Winter was approaching. For Karolina and Andrzej, it meant that they would much more frequently stay at Karolina's home in the late afternoon and in the early evening. Being in love, they would find, even in the very modest apartment of Karolina's parents, a poetic charm heightened by the murmur of the oven fire warming up the interior. It was warm inside, even when there were cold showers outside, and, as usual, towards mid-November you could see flakes of snow. There was a Polish saying: 'Saint Martin is arriving on the white horse.' Saint Martin's Day was on 11 November, and, indeed, by then it had started to snow. Each day Andrzej came in the late afternoon to pick up Karolina after work in the Department of Pharmacology and walk with her to her parents' apartment, located on the same street. It was already too cold to continue the walks outside.

Everyday life in Lwów was difficult and imposed many burdens on people. The official Soviet opinion was that those burdens were unavoidable during the birth of the new social and economic system. 'You cannot expect to give life to something new without pains of delivery. Look at the human being, there are also pains of delivery.' Those pains of delivery had already lasted more than twenty years in the Soviet system, and they mostly consisted of the discomfort of not getting proper food and clothes. The people had to line up to get bread, and it was sometimes impossible to get butter. Shoes and clothes were in great demand with the coming winter, and the supply was never sufficient.

Juliusz worked all day in a dark place in a cellar because he was employed as 'retoucher' at a photography shop. Karolina was busy with her studies. Dorota and Zosia were 'employed' full time in lining up for bread, eggs, meat, and cheese, and, of course, wood and coal. Andrzej and his father were working, and Andrzej's mother was also a full-time employee in the line-ups. Both of them, Andrzej and Karolina, when they could find some spare time, especially on weekends helped their parents in making some provisions. The salaries of Andrzej's father and of Karolina's father were in evident disproportion to the prices. Karolina was getting a scholarship, which was also modest, and Andrzej's salary, combined with his father's salary, was just sufficient to feed their small family. The resources of both families were sufficient only to survive.

Worse than the practical hardships, however, was the general atmosphere, full of suspicion on the Soviet side, and full of fear on the Polish side. The Soviet bureaucracy was poisoning the already difficult life. It became taxing to work out even the simplest problem. The 'dictatorship of the proletariat' meant, in everyday terms, the dictatorship of the party officials, called by the population 'apparatchiki.' The 'class struggle,' another theoretical dogma, meant, in everyday terms, the struggle of 'apparatchiki' to get a better position in the party, and to better exploit those who were called capitalists. Mostly it was the Polish intelligentsia who obtained by hard work nice apartments and houses. Although nobody in any social system would call them capitalists, they were so baptized by the 'apparatchiki,' eager to get something by means of what they called the 'class struggle.'

Andrzej and Karolina, although both were very progressive, felt extremely disappointed looking at all that. Not only was it a treacherous thing to make a pact with Hitler and invade the already dying Poland, but the ideas of the new regime, which partly appealed to some people, showed their cruel side in reality. What was worse was that those ideas were being forced by the Soviets on a population that was practically defenceless.

The only way to raise the morale of Andrzej and Karolina was to talk of their love and make projects for the future. Although they knew that the projects might any time turn into 'castles in the air,' they were young enough and so happy with their love that they liked to forget sometimes the cruel reality that their wonderful love was flourishing in a very tragic moment of history.

During their conversations with Juliusz, Andrzej very soon understood that Juliusz's optimism was a projection of his own honesty onto other people. Juliusz was educated in German philosophy and literature. He often spoke of the fight between Good and Evil. The momentous victory of Evil was just a short gap in the history of mankind. Very soon Good would prevail in the souls of the majority of people. He was a strong believer in God's justice. The rites of the Judaic religion were not observed by him, with the exception of the anniversary of his parents' death. That was the only time in the year when he went to synagogue for a special Judaic prayer for those who passed away. He experienced God as something noble in his soul and presumed that everybody had weighed Good against Evil, regardless of race, religion, or nation.

The theory was appealing, but it was as Goethe would say 'grey' ('Grau ist jede Theorie'), and life in this period was not joyous. The present situation was absolutely in discordance with Juliusz's philosophy. On both sides, it was the victory of Evil: with the Germans, it was the victory of racism, considered by Juliusz as betrayal of the German culture; with the Soviets, it was the victory of a rigid bureaucracy combined with paranoiac hatred of people who wanted to be free. This again was considered by Juliusz as treason against the high ideal of social democracy.

One day, when discussing with Andrzej and Karolina the question of patriotism, Juliusz gave them his evaluation of the German nation and its fascination with Hitler: 'Mein Kampf and the skill to make speeches impressed the masses, creating, unfortunately, in the Germans a feeling of national superiority, a kind of a cruel 'patriotism' that is opposed to true patriotism, which respects the dignity of any human being. This cruel patriotism, despising any other than the German nation, was unfortunately accepted by the majority of Germans because Hitler was democratically elected.'

Hitler's Germany was seen by Juliusz as a gigantic experiment proving that false nationalism and cruel patriotism could be nurtured by hatred and convert human beings into 'beasts.' This day Juliusz looked very tired and extremely sad. He did not sleep at night, and rethinking his philosophy he came to a conclusion: 'If this human depravation, which started before the war and was one of the reasons for the military invasion of Poland, if this depravation has to last longer, I would not like to continue my life. I still believe in the prevailing of the Good in human values. If I would be unable to see this soon in my life, I would prefer to die earlier. To witness how the human being is turning into a brutal beast would be so much against my philosophy of life. I would prefer to pass away and be at peace with my God. But up to now I still have confidence in human values and I hope that Hitler will not be able to morally destroy the great German nation that has given to humanity so much inspiration in philosophy, literature, art, and music.'

Andrzej was touched by his sadness and wished Juliusz to be right in his optimism, but he still was unconvinced that the end of 'Evil' would come soon. The situation might build eventually to a war between the Germans and the Soviets, and perhaps that would be the end of Hitler. Juliusz looked at him and said: 'With such a poor Soviet army, with so badly trained soldiers, with no modern equipment, I doubt very much that Hitler might be finished. The excellent armies of the West, of France and England, could do nothing but surrender, how could you expect that Stalin could defeat him?' There was no place for further discussion because, this day, both felt pessimistic.

In January 1941, Andrzej and Karolina decided that it was time to tell their parents about their marriage plans. Andrzej has chosen a day when Karolina would be absent, and Dorota and Zosia were invited somewhere. Juliusz was alone in his apartment. Andrzej thought that the proper thing to do was to proceed in a traditional way: to ask for 'the hand of Karolina,' as was the custom in Poland. Feeling a little bit shy, Andrzej started his speech: 'I have proposed to Karolina and she has said that she accepts and, as it is a custom to ask the father to give away his daughter, I am asking you for your blessing. I have also to add that my religion is Catholic. For Karolina, it was no problem, however I would like to hear your opinion on that before you give your consent and blessing.'

Until that moment, religion as such was not a subject of discussion between them. When Andrzej has finished, Juliusz rose from his armchair and advanced to hug Andrzej and kissed him warmly many times. Then he sat down again and said: 'God bless you, Andrzej. I give my consent with a great feeling of happiness. I feel happy for Karolina that she has chosen you as the man of her life and I know that you will be happy with her. Whatever is your religion, the most important thing is what kind of human being you are. I know and feel that you are an honest man with a very decent system of values, a great sense of responsibility, and extreme courage. I would not dare to ask you who is your God, by what religious channel you communicate with Him when He is speaking to you. God is God, like Good is Good. There is only one God, and your God and Karolina's God are the same. I will pray to God to protect both of you, to protect the divine part of human nature. Never abandon this greatest treasure existing in your souls.'

He turned his face away to hide the tears that had appeared in his eyes. 'There is one thing, however, that I have to ask you, to be fair with you: You are pessimistic about the duration of the war and you think that the Germans might invade Lwów. Do you realize that, if you marry Karolina now, during the war, you will have a wife of the race that has to be exterminated? This will be for you a mortal danger. Are you aware of that?' He looked at Andrzej with a sadness in his blue eyes.

'Yes, Juliusz, I am aware of that, and I will never abandon Karolina. I will do everything to make possible our survival, and if it is impossible to survive together, we will perish together' was Andrzej's answer.

Juliusz rose again from his chair and hugged Andrzej. 'Do not worry, Andrzej, my dear. We will not be under the rule of Hitler. In one year I will prepare in Cracow a beautiful apartment for you and Karolina.' He smiled again, but his eyes were still full of sorrow.

'As you will have a wife of Jewish extraction, I would like to give you some personal remarks concerning some Jewish problems.

Jewish religion teaches the Jews that they are a chosen nation. I do not share this opinion, because God, as I believe in Him, is too just to make preferences among the nations. All nations are equals among equals. We know from history that the Jewish nation was never particularly happy. The first diaspora was a time of Babylonian exile in the sixth century B.C. After the destruction of the rebuilt temple of Solomon came a second diaspora, almost two thousand years ago, when thousands of Jews had again to leave Jerusalem. The Jews were dispersed all over the world.

'In some countries, during some periods of history, they lived in peace. Very often, however, they were violently persecuted during outbreaks of anti-Semitism. Nevertheless, many Jews tried to assimilate, to consider as their home the country to which their ancestors emigrated and where they were born. For many generations, this trend towards assimilation was so strong that they considered themselves as genuine members of a given nation. They have contributed to the sciences and to art and culture in a great number of countries. Some of them made eternal contributions to humanity, like, for instance, Einstein. There were various difficulties with assimilation, because there were some prejudices bound up with their race and religion. As you know, not only in Poland, they were treated as second-class citizens. Life of an assimilated Jew was not always easy.

'You know probably that one of the assimilated Jews was Herzl, who initiated the movement called Zionism. Herzl was so impressed by the affair of Dreyfus that he has lost his confidence in the possibility of the assimilation of Jews and therefore has initiated the movement, which has easily found followers. Many Jews belong to this movement, and I wish them to have in the nearest future their own country. This country should be a model state for all the world, a treasure, an example of freedom, justice, and tolerance. A nation that suffered for such a long time so much from lack of freedom, of justice, and of tolerance, should be able to impose and enforce the ideas of tolerance.

'My family, for many generations, was assimilated in Poland. We always considered ourselves as Poles with Judaic religion. My family and the family of Dorota have contributed very much to Polish culture and art. I believe that the Poland that will emerge from this war will be a free democratic country. My wish is to live in this country and to die in this country. It happens that sometimes I am afraid that I may be wrong and that staying for such a long time in Poland instead of emigrating was the biggest mistake in my life. And then I ask myself: how could you live somewhere else than in your beloved Cracow?

'The Jewish people who dream of establishing, or rather re-establishing, their homeland in Palestine are against assimilation. Many of them are very religious, educated in the Torah. Religion is a very important factor in their feeling of unity and in their political reasoning. It is very difficult to make a connection between religion and politics. The Catholic church has given discouraging examples of such dogmatic connections during the time of the Inquisition. However, I am full of hope that Zionists will avoid this kind of deviation.

'Some Jewish people in many European countries, fighting with injustice, racial discrimination, nationalism, and anti-Semitism, are convinced that only Communism can solve these problems. They expect that the Soviet Union, as a homeland of the working class, will solve problems of humanity. Seeing what is going on here in Lwów under the Soviet rule, I am not sure that this is the case. I am afraid that humanity will pay a high price for this kind of Communism that we are witnessing now. I may, however, be wrong.

'I could not tell you where the best solution for the Jewish people is to be found. The more I think about it, the more insecurity is growing inside me. Certainly the assimilation solution did not prove to be the best in Germany, or in Poland. There is still a social non-acceptance of assimilated Jews among the intelligentsia in France and in England, and in the United States and in Canada. They remain a kind of social pariah, even when they achieve high degrees in science and art. Unless they become famous all over the world, because of their achievements, they very rarely cross the social barrier, instead remaining among themselves. Of course it is not a general rule; there are many exceptions.

'There is also a quite frequent phenomenon of mixed marriages here in Poland. Dorota and I, we have in our families such examples. There will be another one after you marry Karolina. It will probably be the first example in your family, Andrzej, won't it?'

Here Andrzej interrupted him: 'No, it will not. Lucien, the beloved only brother of my mother, married before the First World War a girl of the same race and religion as Karolina, and they lived happily until the outbreak of the Second World War. They have a daughter, Alice, who is now studying medicine here in Lwów. And they live in Warsaw. My uncle is doing everything to protect my aunt Madzia from the racist persecution.'

'And he succeeded until now?' asked Juliusz. 'Yes,' said Andrzej. And in the eyes of both men were apparent changes. Juliusz had much less sadness in his eyes. The luminous blue eyes of Andrzej were now dimmed and full of sorrow.

VIII

SPRING WAS ALREADY IN THE AIR IN THE SECOND HALF OF March 1941. Snow on the sidewalks was easily thawed by the sun, much higher now in the sky. Andrzej and Karolina could, on such sunny days, resume their walks in the streets of Lwów and look at the trees in the parks, on some of which buds were already visible. On one such walk, Andrzej told Karolina: 'Do you know, my dearest love, that we are engaged nearly one year? Do you realize that you have been my fiancée for nearly one year?' She looked at him, astonished: 'I remember very well that we met on 16 October 1940. It is just the sixth month since our first meeting, how did you count that as one year?' He smiled and replied: 'Because the years of war count double and because I want to marry you before summer arrives and have a honeymoon with you not later than this summer.'

At that time Andrzej did not even imagine that the years of war will count much more than double for both of them, and that every fifth Polish citizen would not survive this war.

Karolina felt very happy with his proposal, and they started at once to make plans for the wedding and honeymoon. Andrzej knew well the picturesque surroundings of Lwów; Karolina was not that familiar with all that because she and her family, since the beginning of the war, had not travelled out of Lwów. She wanted to see on the map the location of the various places mentioned by Andrzej and tell her parents as soon as possible about the plans for an early wedding.

They returned home quickly. They had both chosen as their preferred place a small town called 'The Valley' (in Polish, 'Dolina'). They waited until Juliusz returned home, and then they announced their plans to Karolina's parents. Consent was given, although the parents preferred to make the celebration more sumptuous after the war. It was agreed that, as soon as Karolina passed her fourth-year in medical studies, they would be married.

The same consent was given by Andrzej's parents. An approximate date was settled on – the third week of July – and had to be adapted to the possibility of getting a two-week stay for them in a so-called Kurort (under the Soviet regime no private hotels were available). Karolina worked out all the details in the Kurort office, chaired by a physician whom Karolina knew from before the war.

The personal plans for the wedding and honeymoon were badly synchronized with historical events. In April 1941, Hitler invaded Yugoslavia, which was soon divided among Germany, Italy, Hungary, and Bulgaria. At the end of April 1941, the Greek mainland was in German hands, although the heroic resistance was still alive. In May 1941, Crete had fallen. Stalin took the office of prime minister of the Soviet Union. Everybody could feel that the war between Germany and the Soviet Union could not be avoided. It was, in fact, imminent. At the beginning of June 1941, war erupted between Finland and the Soviet Union.

On 22 June 1941 began the last act of the greatest world tragedy. The invasion of the Soviet Union by the Germany army was so fast and powerful that Lwów was occupied only a few days after the Germans crossed the frontier at the river San.

Karolina consented to Andrzej's proposal to be with him in the Department of Psychiatry, to be protected better than in the city itself. Her parents and Zosia had chosen to stay in their apartment, although Andrzej wanted to arrange the same shelter for them. Most of the time between the beginning of the war and the German occupation of Lwów was spent by the population in cellars. Andrzej and Karolina were staying in the shelter of the Department of Psychiatry with patients and the medical staff. The city was under heavy bombardment, the trams did not function. During the first three or four days, it was possible to get a phone connection from the suburbs to the downtown area. Andrzej and Karolina could at least in this way, using intermediary channels, communicate with their parents. Afterwards the hospital in the suburbs was completely cut off from downtown Lwów.

The Polish population was aware that the most difficult time had come and that the retreat of the Soviet army could be the beginning of the full victory of the cruel and perverse dictator. At night, in the cellars, people could not sleep, and discussed the situation. Filomena, who was in the shelter with Andrzej and Karolina, was doing everything to relieve the anxiety of Karolina.

The best way for both of them to avoid Hitler was to leave Lwów with the retreating Soviets. It was, however, impossible for each of them to leave their parents, especially Karolina's parents. Karolina often cried silently at night and had moments of great depression. Andrzej hugged her in his arms, kissed her eyes and her hands, and spoke words of comfort to relieve her great depression.

The noise of bombardments and explosions caused great anxiety and fearful excitement in patients. Andrzej and other doctors in the department had a great amount of professional work to do to calm the patients down.

After five days, the medical staff knew that the German army was very close to Lwów. The Soviet associate professors and assistants left the hospital. Before their departure, they came to say farewell to their patients and to the medical staff. They were very sad and evaluated the situation as very, very difficult, but they were convinced that, after many sacrifices, the Soviet Union would win the war.

One of the next nights, Andrzej and Karolina were sitting on a long bench with the Polish associate professor, his parents, and some young patients. Opposite, on long benches, were sitting about fifty other patients, with nurses and doctors. It was close to midnight.

For an hour it had been much quieter; the explosions were not so loud and seemed to be far away. Close to Karolina was sitting a young peasant girl who was being treated in the department for a deep depression. She turned towards Karolina and asked: 'Don't you think that the war is over? It is much more quiet.' Karolina looked at Andrzej, and he answered: 'I don't think that it is over yet, but anyway we have one day less of the war. Tonight it will be quiet, and very soon you will go to your bed and have a good night's sleep. The morning will bring nice sunny weather. Please, don't worry. We will take care of you.'

Indeed, after one hour, all the patients and the medical staff left the shelter and went upstairs. Andrzej and Karolina went to Andrzej's office.

He invited her to sit down on the same chair opposite his desk that she had used when they had met for the first time. He sat behind the desk. They sipped coffee prepared by Filomena. Filomena was making up a sofa for Karolina to sleep on, and, for Andrzej, a stretcher used for physical examination of patients.

There was a silence in the background. Sporadically a noise of explosions from far away cut into it. The fighting was going on now far from the city, probably in the east.

Filomena finished her work and turned towards Karolina. She hugged her warmly, kissed her forehead, and, turning to Andrzej, wished him goodnight and asked when they would like to have breakfast.

'Please don't worry about our breakfast, Filomena. You worked very hard during all this time, taking care not only of patients but of virtually everybody. You have even found time to prepare small gifts for the departing Soviet doctors. I know that you will be on duty until tomorrow morning at 7:00. I will see you then for a while because I will leave with Karolina very early in the morning, before 8:00. We have a long way to go to see her parents, and afterwards my parents. I will be very busy in the coming days with my personal arrangements. I guess that you know, Filomena, what kind of problems I have to deal with. I made already some arrangements with our associate professor. He will stay here in the department all the week with his and my patients. He is afraid of going to his apartment downtown. I am going to take a short leave, just for one week, and he will replace me in an emergency.' Filomena nodded with understanding and left with: 'God bless you, Andrzej, and you, Karolina.'

There was silence in the office, measured by the ticking of the wall clock. Andrzej and Karolina were sitting opposite each other and sipping coffee. After a while Andrzej said: 'Karolina, my love, the Soviets left in defeat and the Nazis are now occupying the city. Fighting is still going on, but many kilometres far east of Lwów.'

And there was again silence. Karolina was looking straight into the eyes of Andrzej and, after a while, she said, with a voice full of tears: 'I know, Andrzej, the Nazi army is now in the city. It could be so nice if we could sit here and talk about our happiness, our love and plans for future, about our marriage and honeymoon, about you, my first and my last love in life. And now the Nazis are here. Tomorrow I and all my family will be nobody, with no rights. We will be deprived of all human rights only because of our race. Even religion does not mean anything. The Nazis say: 'Jud oder Christ ist einerlei, in der Rasse liegt die Schweinerei.' The people of my race will no longer be human beings. We will be dirty Jews, fated to be destroyed. I read the Nazi bible *Mein Kampf*, and I have no illusions like my father.' She was crying now, the tears were flowing down her face. After a while, she continued in a low voice: 'I am scared, I am full of fear. First of all because of you, my only love. What would happen to you, Andrzej? Being with me, being my husband, you will also be a nobody. You will be treated like a Jew. Your parents will be treated like parents of a Jew. What is my love offering to you? You would be, because of me, in a tragic situation. What Hitler is imposing on me and my family, I would impose on you and your family: a constant fear of perishing and a constant fight to survive.' She stopped again. She was unable to speak for a moment.

Andrzej looked at her with enormous love. He did not interrupt her. He knew that she was going to make a confession from the bottom of her heart. He knew that it would be very painful for her, but he knew also that it was better for her to speak up, to say what she had wanted to say for a couple of days.

She continued, crying bitterly: 'Andrzej, I will not marry you. I love you too much to kill you. We have to delay our marriage until the end of the war. I will survive or perish. If I survive, I will come to you and ask you to marry me immediately after the defeat of Hitler. I know that you will wait for me. If I perish, I will perish thanking God that I could, during my life, know what love is, and I will pray God to let me wait for you in heaven. I will keep in heaven a place for you. You will be honoured very much there above, because you are an extraordinary, noble, and good human being.' She stopped and hung her head.

Andrzej knew that it was enough. She had finally told him what she had wanted to say since the beginning of the German invasion. He rose from his armchair, approached her, and dried her cheeks and eyes with his handkerchief. He took her face into his hands, kissed her eyes, her cheeks, and her lips. Then he sat on his desk, on her side, very close, and began to talk to her.

'Karolina, dearest, now you listen to me. I do not accept your plan, I reject it at once and forever. Our dreams began in this office here. Nobody and nothing can change our love, and our dreams will come true. Be reasonable, be quiet, be strong. We met in a difficult time. We met to be always together. Our love is stronger than our life. You told me many times the true love is when you love the other person more than yourself. I do not see any price for our love. Even the price of our lives would be not too high. The ties that bind us together are like steel – even Hitler cannot destroy them, he can destroy only our lives. But we will do all that is necessary to survive. This is my decision, my final decision, and you have to obey me. You will have to obey me all the time during the war. And, after the war, when I will be a little tired, we will change our roles. I will obey you.

'Now you will pray and I will fight. I give you always the more difficult task. You will have a potent ally, your God. And here on earth we will have also very good allies – my parents, my friends, and some other honest and good people. I feel that the most important person in this battle for our lives will be my father. He told me already one week ago how he is going to help us. It was just before Hitler's invasion on the frontier of the Soviet Union. In two or three weeks, I will marry you and I will find the best, the safest, and the most decent way to do this. Hitler's visit did not change our plans. Our program is for life, for better and worse.'

He got up from his desk and stood close to her chair. She was in his arms, and he kissed her for a long, a very long time.

Andrzej spoke in a highly convincing and quiet way. His decision was firm, and nothing could change it. What he was saying was coming from the bottom of his heart, and he meant what he said. His main goal was not only to convince Karolina but to instil courage in her mind and to hide his own fear of the future.

There were moments when a terrible fear raged inside him, and there was only a spark of hope. He was not a hero without fear, and he certainly did not feel like a fearless hero.

After a while, Karolina opened her eyes and said in a very warm way: 'Thank you, Andrzej. Thank you for teaching me what love means. I am convinced that you are right. I will wait for your orders. I will obey you always, not only during the war. You are for me all the world. I will do my best to be a good and courageous companion.'

She tried to smile, but it was difficult for her. Her eyes were again full of tears.

PART TWO

—

TIMES OF CONTEMPT

And when the thousand years are ended,
Satan will be loosed from his prison and
will come out to deceive the nations
which are at the four corners of the earth,
that is, Gog and Magog, to gather them to battle;
their number is like the sand of the sea.
And they marched up over the broad earth
and surrounded the camp of the saints
and the beloved city; but fire came down
from heaven and consumed them,
and the devil who had deceived them
was thrown into the lake of fire and
brimstone where the beast and
the false prophet were,
and they will be tormented day and night
for ever and ever.

The Revelation to John
20:7

Là-bas . . .

Ils ont égratigné les murs des fours crématoires
　en dernière instance d'être et de savoir.
Leurs cris ont tissé des fleurs atroces
　que nul printemps ne revandiquera.
Leurs regards ont fui les rivages iniques
　que nul humain ne pourra contenir.
Leurs gestes ont égaré la promesse trahie
　que nulle terre ne pourra accueillir.
Mes frères, mes soeurs,
　mes élus du martyre sans pareil!
Vous avez égratigné les murs des fours crématoires
　en dernière instance d'être et de savoir

PIERRE MATHIEU

I

KAROLINA AND ANDRZEJ DID NOT SLEEP DURING THE FIRST
night after the German army occupied Lwów. She was lying on the
sofa, and he on the stretcher prepared by Filomena. They did not
talk. Each of them wanted to be silent and give the other the
opportunity to sleep, even for a short time.

Andrzej was thinking of all the dangers of their future life and of
all the ways to avoid them. The dangers were multiple, and the
possibilities of organizing a safe life were very limited. Until now
they have planned to have a civil marriage. Now, under the German
occupation, such a marriage would be suicide. They would have to
present to administrative authorities, under German control,
Karolina's birth certificate from Vienna, with the Judaic religion
indicated on it. Looking desperately for a solution, he came to the
conclusion that Karolina had, for safety reasons, to change her
religion and marry him in the Catholic church. They badly needed
help from the Catholic church. He remembered the talk he had had
with his father, on the night just before the outbreak of the war
between the Germans and the Soviet Union. His father was a highly
respected professor in the gymnasium in Lwów and, for a certain
time, held also a very important position in the teaching administration for the colleges in the three provinces of south-eastern Poland.
He had many professional and social connections. He was himself
not a believer, but he was always full of respect for people who were
believers, and for all the religions. Hence he had excellent contacts
with some priests. He knew personally one of the bishops of the
diocese of Lwów. Andrzej felt that the most important help will
come from his father.

Karolina prayed during this long, tense night. She asked her God
to look at their love and offer some guidance about how and where
they should seek help and protection, and she felt that the God
listened to her. Faith in God was a great relief for her in difficult
times. She had stayed with the religion in which she was born, never
even considering converting to assist her career. She appreciated
very much the historical and cultural background of her religion, but
did not care very much about the religious rites. Some of those rites
had for her a historical charm, but the same charm she found in
other religions. Faith was the corner-stone of her religion, and the

possibility of communicating with God from the soul. The soul was the house of God.

Thinking about all that, she knew that to change her religion now might make their situation less tragic. Showing that she followed the Judaic religion was not only dangerous for her, but for her future husband and his parents. For the safety of their love, she had to make the situation a little less dangerous, and she was sure that the God would not see her as a traitor. She would simply communicate with God through another channel. It was not easy for Karolina to make this decision and ask to be baptized. She was a distraught human being, a victim of a cruel, historical moment. All that she wanted was to save her love and not condemn the man she loved and his family to suffering, and most probably to death.

In the pale light of dawn, Andrzej could see that Karolina's eyes were open and that she was looking at him. When she saw that he was awake, she started to talk to him in a low voice: 'Good morning, my dearest. You know, Andrzej, that, for the first time in our life, we have spent the night in the same room. And during this night I prayed, and for me it was a splendid night of love.

'I have spoken with my God of our love, of all that you have told me last evening in this room. With his inspiration, I have decided to convert to Catholicism. My faith will be always in the same God, but the rites will be different. I want you to know that this is my personal decision. Nobody on earth influenced me, nobody could convince me. God is with me, as He always was.'

She looked straight into Andrzej's eyes and tried to smile. Andrzej knew how difficult this night was for her. And, she called this night 'a splendid night of love.' He knew that one thing was splendid – her love – and that she was doing this for their love.

After a while, Andrzej said: 'God is really generous and I am full of respect for Him. He understands us. I have nothing else to say than that I am staying with God who is in your soul. Thank you, my God; thank you, Karolina.'

They dressed and prepared to leave the department early, at seven o'clock in the morning. Andrzej left the office to see the associate professor, who was of the Judaic religion and terribly afraid to go out. He had given Andrzej the keys to his apartment and asked him to bring him and his parents some small personal things. When Andrzej returned to the office, Filomena was already there, speaking with Karolina in the corner of the room. Breakfast waited on the desk. After breakfast, Filomena accompanied them to the porch. 'God bless you both,' she said. 'I will pray for you.' Her face was sad and her eyes were swollen.

The trams were not functioning, and they had to walk 8 kilometres to reach downtown. The city was full of military trucks with German soldiers. An enormous German army, fully motorized, was crossing the city on its way to the east. From time to time personal cars with German officers passed. They sat stiff on their seats, in their elegant uniforms. Some of them wore monocles. Their posture was much more suited to a parade than a war. However, the sounds of explosions coming from the east were reminders that this was an army in wartime.

The sidewalks, which had been full of people before the German invasion, were practically empty. The German soldiers were not looking at the few people on the sidewalks. They were looking at the monuments, at the houses and other buildings. The officers were looking straight ahead, probably seeing the 'Lebensraum' they were conquering.

Karolina and Andrzej did not see any Germans getting out of their cars or trucks. During their long walk, Andrzej held Karolina's arm. After two hours, they reached the house where Karolina's parents lived.

Juliusz was evidently restless, walking back and forth in the small apartment. Dorota and Zosia were sitting in the corner of the room. They had tears in their eyes. Juliusz was trying to console them: 'Sure, life will be difficult, with many restrictions, but I believe that there is a certain limit to atrocity, even for the Nazis.'

Andrzej has taken Juliusz aside to tell him that, in the near future, he wanted to marry Karolina. The wedding would be arranged in such a way that it would give them as much safety as possible. Juliusz did not ask about the details. Andrzej told him also that he and his parents would do their best to help Juliusz, Dorota, and Zosia. He advised Juliusz to be very careful, and not go out in the streets. Although, at the moment, only the invading German army was in the city, very soon the Gestapo would arrive and the terrible machine of Hitler's administration would take over. Andrzej promised to return in the evening, bringing them food and other necessities.

At this moment, they heard on the radio, for the first time, the German announcement of a compulsory curfew from 7:00 p.m. until

6:00 a.m. Nobody from the civilian population would be allowed in the streets between those hours, and the curfew would be enforced by the death penalty. Andrzej looked at his watch. It was already 11:00 a.m., and he had to see his parents, talk with them, go to the apartment of the associate professor to pick up things for him and his family, return to Karolina, and once more make the journey to the home of his parents.

Karolina accompanied Andrzej via the backyard balcony to the staircase: 'Tell your parents of my love and admiration for them. Tell them also of our conversation last night and of my own, personal decision. I want them to know that my love for you is stronger than the fear of perishing. Therefore I told you last night that I will wait with the marriage until the end of the war, not to expose you and your family to a mortal danger. Tell them how you understand that love is stronger than fear, and stronger than life. Tell them that I am fully aware of the heroic effort made by you and them. Tell them also about my absolutely personal decision. I love and admire them, and my love and admiration are the only things that I can offer them.' She kissed him: 'Take care. Don't rush. You look so tired and I can do nothing to help you.' He kissed her warmly, told her not to worry, and disappeared down the staircase.

The day was very warm, and Andrzej was already tired after the long trip from the hospital to downtown. He rushed to his parents' house, fortunately in walking distance of Karolina's apartment. Alone now in the street, he felt an enormous fear. It was much easier to reassure the beloved person than to reassure oneself. It was easier to appear to be a 'hero' than to feel inside that he was one, a man without fear. Love had taught him already to behave like that, and he was listening to an inner voice in him, repeating an old verse from the Bible: 'Who is saving one life is saving humanity.'

The long-expected only son arrived eventually at his parents' home. After very moving greetings, they immediately started to talk. His parents were both very sincere, warm, and prepared for this conversation. They wanted to do their best to save Karolina. They knew that her life was, at the same time, Andrzej's life. Both of them had to make an effort to save sinking people, even though they might themselves sink with them.

Andrzej's mother said: 'My dear son, more difficulties provoke more efforts to solve them. We will be with Karolina, which means with you and Karolina, all the time.' Her eyes were full of tears.

Andrzej understood her well. Her only son would be exposed to a mortal danger constantly during Hitler's occupation. It was not a question of coping with one difficulty and doing away with the mortal danger. The danger was not only mortal, it was persistent and could descend from anywhere. Andrzej's parents knew well the value of love from their own experience. They loved Karolina, and they had fully accepted her for good and bad times.

At the beginning of the conversation, Andrzej's father said: 'You have decided to marry Karolina, and never abandon her. Your decision will not be discussed, because you will never be a traitor to your love. What we will discuss now is, how to organize a safe, possibly safe, future for both of you. I was thinking about it during your absence, and now I will discuss with you the framework and work out the details.'

After three hours of discussion a more detailed plan was set out. Andrzej's father decided to ask the next morning for an audience with Bishop Baziak from the diocese of Lwów, whom he knew personally. He would outline for the bishop the present situation and ask for counselling and help. He would tell the bishop that it was the personal wish of Karolina, made independently, to be baptized and have a Catholic wedding in the church as soon as possible. He would ask also for advice and instruction as to how to prepare the documents concerning the baptism and marriage to secure relative safety for his son and his bride.

They decided that the newlyweds would stay with Andrzej's parents and be given one room in their three-room apartment. It would be a temporary arrangement because Andrzej's father was advising that they all leave Lwów as soon as possible and relocate to a place where nobody knew Karolina's former religion. He was already at that time afraid of informers, especially in a city with mixed Polish-Ukrainian population where many people knew Karolina from her studies. In his plans, Andrzej and Karolina should move first, possibly to the countryside, where there might be a need for a doctor. Andrzej's parents would very soon move to join them, making a kind of a family frame for Karolina, who would thus be not only with her husband but within the nucleus of a Polish Catholic family.

At the end of the discussion, Andrzej's father said: 'When I see Bishop Baziak, whom I know to be a very open-minded man of goodwill, I intend also to discuss with him the situation of Karolina's parents and her sister. I am sure that the bishop will advise me what the church could do for them, without any religious obligation on their part.' He smiled and looked at Andrzej: 'Be quiet and very, very careful, my dear son. I am proud of you, even if I and your mother are very afraid of the situation. In all my life I held in greatest esteem honesty, fidelity, and love. Therefore I am proud of you.'

After lunch, Andrzej's mother prepared a small parcel of food for Karolina and her family. Food was already scarce in the city, but his mother had always been driven to share, and nothing could stop her generosity. She said: 'Don't forget to kiss Karolina for me. This is from the bottom of my heart.'

When Andrzej returned to Karolina, after a short visit to the apartment of the associate professor to pick up some of his and his parents' belongings, he met Filomena at Karolina's place; she had left the hospital immediately after them. She was dressed already in her traditional nun's habit with the medieval 'corner hat' of the Sisters of Charity. She brought some food for Karolina and her family. Her convent was not far from Karolina's apartment. She intended from now on to pay frequent visits to Karolina, and had asked other nuns to be of assistance to them. Her organizing was already evident as nuns from the convent of Holy Sacrament had brought fruit and vegetables from their garden to Zosia. They, at once, took a great liking to her and promised to bring fresh fruit and vegetables every day. Before Andrzej's second visit on this day, Filomena had a chat with all the members of Karolina's family, and she fully understood their sufferings. She came to comfort them and diminish their isolation.

Karolina had already told her of her decision to convert to Catholicism. Filomena brought her some books so she would be prepared for questions that the priest might ask her in the pre-baptism lessons. As Andrzej never told her of Karolina's former law studies, she was astonished by Karolina's excellent knowledge of ecclesiastical law, of all the canons, of the sources of this law, and of the organization of the Catholic church.

'When I heard what she knew, I was happy to see that not only did she have God in her heart, but that she was, from all the points of view, prepared to be baptized.' She continued: 'Karolina is my dear friend. I have spoken with her many times since we first met, and I appreciate her faith and her love for you. I never tried to convert her, because in my conviction it was not necessary. But now, in this dangerous situation, I will do my best to help her with her baptism and your marriage.'

She was very moved emotionally. At the end she added: 'The Evil entered today this city, but our God will not abandon it. He is in the souls of many of us and we will win, if we keep Him in our souls.'

Andrzej took her hands and kissed them. Karolina did the same.

He told both of them all the details of his conversation with his parents. Karolina's eyes were full of tears. When Andrzej finished there were no questions. There was a long, deep silence in the room. Then Karolina approached Andrzej and said: 'What more can I say? God is indeed in this city. Thank you, Andrzej, and take with you my words of greatest gratitude, love, and admiration to your parents. I will never forget what they are doing for me.'

Then Filomena said: 'My God, what kind of people are your parents, Andrzej? Now I understand better why you are as you are. God is in all of you, whether you believe in Him or not. The essence of religion is: "Love the other human being as yourself." Some say that "all the rest is only a commentary."'

It was already late afternoon, and the hour of curfew was approaching. They entered the other room to speak with Juliusz, Dorota, and Zosia. Andrzej had time to tell them only the general plan outlined by his parents. Karolina promised to tell them all the details. She was anxious that Andrzej reach his parents' house before curfew.

Andrzej took his leave from Karolina's parents and told them that he would come early next morning. Standing close to Filomena, he said: 'Please, sleep quietly. You see how many devoted friends you have.' He left with Filomena to accompany her to the convent. He was so tired that he hardly could walk. For three nights, he had had no sleep.

In the streets with empty sidewalks, he saw the German army, still marching to the east.

II

NEXT MORNING, ANDRZEJ AND HIS FATHER LEFT THEIR apartment together. Ludwik was on his way to the diocese of Lwów, Andrzej to see Karolina.

It was not easy to move in the city. The German army was still crossing the city in its victorious march towards the east.

The presence of the German secret police, the Gestapo and the SS, was already visible in the city, Everywhere – on the walls of the houses, on billboards – were posted the first orders of the German military command of the city. It was declared that the population of the city was obliged to obey all the orders published by the military command and that disobedience or negligence would be punished. Under martial law there was only one punishment: death. The Jewish people were obliged to carry on their left arm a white armband with a blue star of David. Further orders would be published. It was stated that under the command of 'Der Führer,' the great German nation was on its way to victory. 'Das Deutsche Reich' would be the superpower for a thousand years.

'The tragedy is coming very fast,' Ludwik told Andrzej, reading the announcements. 'I have to rush and try to see the bishop as soon as possible. If necessary, I will wait all day. I am a very patient son of a Polish peasant. I waited seven years in Siberia to return to my wife and to you, my son. You have also to be very patient, Andrzej. World wars do not end in months; they last for years. Take care of yourself now, and I hope to bring some good news.' With that, he went in another direction, and Andrzej continued his walk to Karolina's place.

Juliusz knew already the contents of the military order from his neighbours. He was prepared for such news, because the same orders were given in Germany after the beginning of Hitler's rule in 1933, in Austria after 'Anschluss,' and in the part of Poland occupied by the Nazis in 1939.

The rules were intended not only to humiliate the Jews but especially to isolate them from the rest of society. All Jews were persecuted, but this did not mean mortal danger, in Juliusz's opinion. 'It means that we will be persecuted; however, it does not mean that we will be killed, if we obey such orders. The death penalty is only for those who disobey. I, Dorota, and Zosia, and also

Karolina, will obey those rules.' Here, Andrzej interrupted: 'As regards Karolina, please don't let her go out in the streets with the armband until my father returns from the bishop. I would also prefer that all of you stay home until then. I will bring you all food and whatever you need. Just wait here in your apartment until I come with the news from my father, who is trying now to see the bishop.'

Karolina told Andrzej that Juliusz had accepted without discussion her decision to be baptized and be married in the church. As a matter of fact, the change of religion and marriage in the church were never treated by him as treason, except if they were done to further a university or social career. He was very grateful to Andrzej's parents. He understood that it was necessary to change the story of Karolina's past, to create for her a new biography to protect not only her, but also Andrzej and his parents. He understood why Karolina should therefore not go out with an armband. It could put somebody on her trail after the marriage and lead to terrible consequences for Andrzej's family. Nor could she go out without an armband before all the documents were prepared for her safety, because, if discovered to be a Jew, she risked the death penalty.

Andrzej then went to pay a visit to Karolina's uncle, who lived in the front apartment of the same house. This apartment belonged to his sister-in-law, who had invited them to stay with her during their self-exile from Cracow.

The uncle was seventy years old and had been very sick for a long time. He had stomach cancer with metastases, and suffered terribly. He knew Andrzej from his former visits. He had heard of Andrzej from his son, even before Karolina met Andrzej. His son was a psychiatrist trained before 'Anschluss' in Vienna in one of the very reputable and famous neuropsychiatric departments. After his exile to Lwów, he attended all psychiatric scientific gatherings, and there he met Andrzej, whom he respected very much. This young psychiatrist was, like his father, very progressive and involved in social movements. For a short time, he was a member of the Polish Communist Party (KPP), but withdrew from it, disenchanted by Stalin's 'great political purge.' He was again downcast by the treaty between Stalin and Hitler in 1939 and by the actions of the NKVD in the parts of Poland occupied by the Soviets.

Karolina's uncle greeted Andrzej, as usual, with great joy. He was happy that Karolina's fiancé was the doctor of whom his son had spoken with high praise.

The old doctor's sister was living in Vienna, and he had had news from her until the outbreak of the war. The news was very sad after 'Anschluss,' and he knew what Hitler's occupation meant. He knew also that he was mortally ill with terminal cancer. He told now Andrzej: 'My only wish is to die in my bed before the Nazis can kill me. I don't care about myself. But I am full of sorrow and despair when I think of the future of my wife, of my son, and all of you under the Nazis.' He was very brave, he never cried, but when he spoke of his family his eyes became wet.

After this sad visit, Andrzej returned home, promising Karolina to return as soon as his father was back from the bishop's office. On the way home, Andrzej thought constantly of the tragic situation of the old doctor and his family. Nobody could help them now because the old man was too weak to get up from his bed, his wife would never leave him to go into hiding, and his only son was going to wear the armband and might be chased in the streets by Nazis and taken to a concentration camp.

If a ghetto was imposed on Lwów, what were they going to do? How could anyone help them? All the perspectives were grim. These human beings were in a mortal trap.

Ludwik entered the building of the diocese with great hope and a strong will to do everything to keep his son out of danger. In his most hopeful dreams, he could not imagine how open-minded, understanding, and helpful the bishop was. Although very busy, when he heard Ludwik's name he quickly found time for an audience.

He knew Ludwik, from former discussions with him, to be a man of rare integrity, and although he did not share his opinions on teaching religion in schools, he respected him very much and was considering his advice on how to proceed in some delicate problems of religious teaching. He greeted Ludwik very warmly, saying that he would do his best to help. He asked his secretary to take notes and, with a smile, told Ludwik: 'All that is written here will immediately be burnt after we take care of the matter.'

He listened to Ludwik's presentation of the situation with no interruption. After a while, he said: 'I promise you, professor, that I personally, and all the priests under my jurisdiction in this diocese, will make all the efforts to secure the life of the young couple. I say "couple", because your son, Andrzej, according to the Nazi doctrine, will be exposed to the same danger as his future wife. In the laws imposed by Hitler, there is no place for religion. Baptism alone will not protect her from the persecution of racists. Marriage in a church and a sophisticated set of documents could be of great help. We will pray to God to give the young couple the chance to survive this atrocious period. Are you aware, however, that if your intention is to keep them with you, you and your wife would be exposed to the same danger, as if you all were Jewish?'

'Yes, I am well aware of that. This is my only son, and I accept his decision, knowing what might happen to all of us. And I know what is love and what is faith.'

The bishop continued: 'We have to proceed at once, before the German administration, the Gestapo, organizes here their cruel machine of persecution of Jews. They are quick, and afterwards it will be very difficult for Karolina to disappear, to move from one place to another and to change her name. All the Jewish population will be registered and classified, and the German administration will keep the names and addresses in their files. For the past two years I have been in constant contact with the priests in the part of Poland that, since 1939, has been under the German occupation, and I know their methods and the speed of their operations.'

The bishop discussed with his secretary the choice of the priest who would be the best person to baptize Karolina, marry the couple, and, after the wedding, have them under his constant vigilance to advise them what to do in the case of imminent danger. After a while, they agreed on one of the priests from the Bernardine Monastery. His name was Father Aloisius (Alojzy), and the secretary promised to arrange an appointment with him for the couple next day at 10.00 a.m. in the office of Bernardine Monastery in Lwów.

The bishop added: 'Father Alojzy will take care of all the documents that will be needed. He is a very courageous and shrewd person. In the fight against Evil we have to use sophisticated methods and act quickly to save decent people. He knows how to fight and what methods are appropriate. He is under my jurisdiction, and I will personally watch over your situation and always be of assistance.'

Ludwik did not know how to express his gratitude for the help for his family and Karolina.

There was still the matter of protection for Karolina's family. Encouraged by the bishop's attitude and by his question: 'Maybe there are other problems in which our church could be helpful?' Ludwik said: 'Karolina has parents and a younger sister. They all are here in Lwów because they were lucky to avoid as refugees deportation to Siberia. Now I see that perhaps some of the deported refugees might easier survive in the cold of Siberia than under Nazi persecution. They need help now. What would you advise me to do for them?' The bishop thought for a while, and said: 'Tell them that my best advice is to hide all three of them: the father in one of our monasteries, the mother and Karolina's sister in a convent with nuns. We could proceed with this immediately, or as soon as they can manage. The sooner, the better. Any day something might happen to them. Therefore, dear professor, you should immediately transmit this message. They will be protected by all the means available to the church. Of course, the means are not unlimited, and our greatest concern is that we cannot help all people who need protection. Our help is unfortunately a drop in the big ocean of human needs. This help has to be kept in strictest secrecy. One false step and everybody might be lost.'

He paused and then continued: 'Do not forget to tell Karolina's parents that we do not expect them to convert. Nor will we exercise any pressure in this direction. Although the mission of the church is to expand the Catholic faith, above all our mission is to help, in Jesus's name, any needy human being. As I just told you, our greatest concern is that we can do it only for a limited number of people who, in this country, are in grave danger.'

At the end of the conversation, the bishop added: 'We consider the Nazis' anti-Semitism as racism and crime. It is the result of nationalism pushed to craziness. The German nation was educated to feel superior to all the nations of the world. In general, any anti-Semitism, not only theirs, is considered by us to be against the teaching of Jesus.' His voice was very sad now: 'Unfortunately, some of our priests before the war preached in a way that was not always consistent with the conception of love for all human beings, whatever their nationality and religion might be, not in a way that Jesus taught us.'

'Now, before you leave with my messages, I wanted to tell you how much I respect you for your courage in this dangerous situation, for all your heroic endeavours to diminish the sufferings not only of your son and your future daughter-in-law, but of her close family. Thank you for showing the confidence in our church. Thank you for coming to me. God bless you, professor, and your family.'

In the early afternoon, Ludwik came home, where Andrzej waited for him. He told Andrzej immediately about the most gracious meeting he had with the bishop and gave him all the details of the bishop's message: 'You cannot imagine how warm, open-minded, and courageous Bishop Baziak is. I come here not only with his messages, but with his blessing for both our families.'

Once more in his life Andrzej had seen how decent, honest, and courageous his father was. In such principles, Andrzej had been educated from early childhood. Now his father had given him another practical lesson on how to behave in life. He kissed his father many times, thanking him for all the inspiration and for all that he was doing.

'Hurry up now, Andrzej. Take these messages immediately to Karolina and to her parents. Each hour, each minute, counts here.' He did not have to repeat this twice, as Andrzej was already at the door.

In the early afternoon, Andrzej was at Karolina's place, delivering the message. She was very moved, tears running down her face. She spoke through her tears of her admiration for Ludwik and for the bishop. On Karolina's suggestion they agreed that it would be better if Ludwik himself would tell Juliusz about the bishop's proposal concerning hiding in the monastery and convent.

'I know the optimism of my father, and I think that he will accept this offer more seriously if it is presented by your father, rather than by you. He sees you as a romantic dreamer, overly protective when your love seems to be in danger. He has great respect for you, and he has loved you from the first moment. However, I think that he will listen much more seriously to your father.'

Andrzej therefore told Karolina's parents and Zosia only the news concerning Karolina. They were full of admiration for the bishop's attitude, for his open-mindedness and honesty and for the way he criticized anti-Semitism. They felt admiration for Ludwik, who was doing everything to organize the wedding as soon as possible. He showed quite exceptional courage in these hard times when a Jew in the family meant a terrible threat for all. They were aware of the fate Andrzej was imposing on himself and his beloved parents to save his love.

Andrzej himself was thinking about the feelings of Karolina's family. He understood how complicated they were. Karolina, the beloved daughter and admired sister, was entering a more secure position. It was for them a certain consolation in those tragic moments. They knew that Andrzej and his parents would stand up for Karolina and had decided to share her fate, and that they would do everything to make that fate less threatening. However, at the same time, Karolina's departure was creating in them nostalgia mixed with joy. This very special feeling is common in parents whose daughter leaves home to create her own family.

In these terrible times, this mixture of nostalgia and joy was combined with many other complex factors. Her family were themselves facing an unknown future, with all the dangers of wartime and the Nazi occupation. In this future, Karolina would not be with them, and they would miss her protective presence, warm emotions, and very realistic advice.

Karolina felt deeply the emotional situation of her family. To bring a moment of relief, she told them that they could expect next morning a visit from Ludwik, who had some good news from the bishop for them that could make their situation more secure. Andrzej assured them that the ties between the two families would be close, although caution must be exercised to prevent the tracing of Karolina's whereabouts.

Juliusz tried to make some optimistic remarks, tried to smile when speaking of their extraordinary love. However, it was evident that he was sad, and that it was difficult for him to hide his emotions.

Dorota and Zosia were sitting in the corner, preparing white armbands on which they had to sew the star of David.

How could Juliusz not be sad?

III

NEXT MORNING, ANDRZEJ WENT WITH KAROLINA TO THE office of Father Alojzy in the Bernardine Monastery. Father Alojzy was a man in his late thirties and had a warm, charming smile. When he looked at them with his understanding blue eyes, they felt at once a peculiar atmosphere of confidence. He held Karolina's hands in his for a while, telling her that she should feel quite secure here and that everybody in the monastery would do everything to make her future as secure as it could be in wartime. From the first moments of this encounter he seemed like a real father to them.

Andrzej presented to him all the details of their story. When Andrzej finished, he said: 'We will help you and your fiancée. I think' – and he turned to Karolina – 'that your father is right to believe in God's presence in all people of goodwill. It is an obligation of such people to fight against Evil, which is the greatest enemy of humanity. In this fight we have to be very cautious and shrewd enough to anticipate some of the enemy's moves. We have to organize as early as possible all the details of our actions. Fortunately enough I have had for two years excellent contacts with the monastery in Cracow and I know what they were doing to save people in a situation similar to yours, Karolina.

'You, Karolina, have only two things to do: thoroughly prepare to be ready to be baptized and then marry your fiancé. Before your baptism, you have to become familiar with the principles of catechism. Father William [Wilhelm] will discuss this with you. Do not think we are enforcing unnecessary formalities if you are asked to learn all the details of liturgic rites. Such knowledge will enable you to understand the essence of liturgy. At the same time, knowing Catholic prayers, the principal rites, and catechism, you will be able to behave as if you had been baptized in your infancy. Father William will explain all that to you. Andrzej will work out with me the framework for the necessary documentation because, as you know, baptism itself, Catholic religion itself, is not sufficient for somebody born like you to avoid Hitler's persecution.'

Father Alojzy spoke quietly and with warmth, and Andrzej and Karolina felt that he believed that it was his duty and his mission to take the dangerous burden entirely on his shoulders. When they thanked him for his attitude, he said: 'Thanks are due to God. I am only his humble servant.' He rose from his chair, hugged each of them, and kissed their foreheads.

Then, he explained to them that the certificates of baptism and marriage had to be written on old forms; that of baptism on a form used in or around the time of Karolina's birth, the certificate of marriage on a form used before the Second World War. In the Lwów monastery, they had neither form. He knew that they still had the marriage forms in the village parish about 20 kilometres from Lwów. Andrzej would have to go there with a message from Father Alojzy, and bring the forms to him.

It was much more complicated to get the form for baptism. Each baptism was entered in the parochial books of baptism. In addition, at the end of the calendar year, the parson sent a register of all baptisms in his parish to the archdiocese, where each baptism was entered in the archdiocesan books. Both the parochial and the archdiocesan offices were, at the same time, offices of the civil state, providing data on the population to state registers. Therefore, even with the access to the archdiocesan books, it was dangerous to enter Karolina's name into them because it could be easily discovered that her baptism had not been registered in the parochial books. To avoid this danger, it was necessary to find a church in which the parochial books of the period close to her birth had been destroyed, burnt during the First World War, between the two wars, or at the beginning of the Second World War. Father Alojzy had heard rumours of a parsonage that had had its books destroyed. If Andrzej could go to this parsonage and ask for a certificate of baptism, the parson would tell him that he could not provide such a certificate and that he had to ask the archdiocese to make an extract from its books. Based on this extract the parson could then deliver a certificate of baptism for this person. Father Alojzy would be informed in two days of the exact address and the name of the parson. Andrzej, who was on a one-week leave from the hospital, was ready to go there.

After making appointments for the next morning – Andrzej with Father Alojzy, Karolina with Father Wilhelm – the couple went to Andrzej's parents' house. Andrzej wanted Karolina to meet again with his parents. He knew that, to relieve Karolina from her anxiety, it would be useful to have her with his parents for a while. The courage, calm, and experience of his father and the warm charm of his mother would have a beneficial effect on Karolina's feelings.

After a lunch prepared by Andrzej's mother, they went with Ludwik to Karolina's house. Ludwik was full of hope that he would be able to convince Juliusz to accept the spontaneous proposal of Bishop Baziak to hide them in the monastery and convent. Karolina, knowing the optimistic evaluation of the current situation by her father, was rather sceptical.

On the street, Andrzej held Karolina's left arm and Ludwik her right. They were walking through small side streets, hoping to avoid any dangerous encounter. Father Alojzy had warned them about those who, for money, were informing the Gestapo about Jews who were hiding or those who were disguised and walked in the streets without an armband bearing the star of David.

Karolina was walking without an armband, although she did not yet have the necessary documents. The situation was extremely dangerous not only for her, but also for the two men at her side. Ludwik was apparently calm, and his courage was of great help to them. He taught them, before they went out, how they should behave, namely, not to look around with fear and to adopt calm, indifferent postures.

When they were crossing a larger street, they were witness to the Nazis' cruelty and crimes. An old Jew, wearing an armband and with a cane in his hand, was slowly moving on the sidewalk. He did not see that an SS officer was approaching him from the opposite side. The old Jew did not step aside quickly enough. The officer of the SS slapped the old Jew's face. The poor old man started to cry loudly, which served only to increase the aggressive behaviour of the officer. He knocked the old man down to the sidewalk, then took out his revolver and shot him. The street was full of military trucks, but nobody was interested in the assassination of the old man. The officer put his revolver back into his pocket and continued his walk. Andrzej, Ludwik, and Karolina would not believe their eyes. They were so terrified that they could not utter a word.

At this moment, Andrzej felt for the first time in his life the hopelessness of the situation. For the first time, he thought that the best thing was to return home with Karolina, take poison with her, and die together in peace. What kind of life could they have, he thought, in such an incredibly cruel world? Even if they survived, how would they be able to live after being surrounded by such cruelties. Karolina was so pale that he was afraid that she might faint. Ludwik was still holding her right arm and continuing to talk to them: 'This is an example for us to remember that our adversaries are simple criminals. Do not cry, do not show your reaction, do not stop, continue walking. We have to continue this walk to help your father, Karolina. Do not show any reaction, my dear child. The criminals are looking at us.' He kissed Karolina on her cheek.

After a while he continued: 'Tell me, Karolina, why are you afraid that your father will not accept the proposal of the bishop? It would be easier for me to convince him if I know his motivation. I know that it is very difficult for you to speak now, but we have to learn how to dissimulate our emotional reactions in the presence of enemies. The streets are full of informers, and they might be looking at us. If you talk to me, Karolina, your behaviour on the surface should appear quiet. Don't show the fear that is inside you, my dear.' He pressed her arm to show her that he would stay with her whatever happened.

The behaviour of Ludwik was so encouraging and reassuring that Karolina answered after a while, turning her head towards him as if they were conversing about mundane things: 'I am afraid that my father, in this dangerous situation, will not want to separate himself from my mother and Zosia and leave them in a totally alien situation. It does not mean that he does not have confidence in the church.

'The fundamental problem of my father is his optimism, his faith in the victory of justice. At the bottom of his heart is deeply implanted the conviction that all that is going on now is temporary, of short duration. He believes that this is a momentary, short and tragic imbalance in moral values, and that the victory of noble human feelings is imminent. From this conviction irradiates the invincible hope that he and my mother and sister will survive to see the moment of victory. I am afraid that this philosophy will kill him, my mother, and Zosia.' After a while she added: 'Therefore, we asked you to present personally this proposal to him. If presented by Andrzej, he might evaluate it as a romantic solution seen by a young, inexperienced man. I know that he has great respect and confidence in you, and if somebody could convince him it would be only you. But even with your best and most logical arguments I am afraid that the battle against his optimism might be lost.'

When they reached the porch of Karolina's parents' apartment, they witnessed the most tragic conversation of their lives.

Juliusz and his family greeted Ludwik with great joy and grati- tude for the arrangements made in preparation for Karolina's baptism and the wedding. Ludwik explained that he came to present to Juliusz and his family a proposal made spontaneously by the bishop, and concerning their fate under the German occupation. At the outset, Ludwik mentioned that he did not wish to make Juliusz feel that he, Ludwik, was imposing on Juliusz or forcing his acceptance of this proposal. However, in Ludwik's opinion, it was an extremely clever and safe proposal, and his advice was to accept it as early as possible. It would create a quite new situation for Juliusz and his family. They could survive the war in much safer conditions. He finished his presentation of all the details of the proposal with these words: 'As somebody who went through a very difficult childhood and very harsh years, as somebody who spent seven years as a prisoner of war in Siberia, during the years of war and revolution, and, first of all, as the future father-in-law of your daughter, I am asking you from the bottom of my heart to accept this proposal for the safety of yourself, your wife and Zosia, and also for the sake of Karolina, who is our common treasure.'

Juliusz listened attentively, without asking any questions. He was evidently moved, and after a while he began his most tragic answer:

'Thank you very, very much for your concern and devotion. I am deeply touched by the fact that, as the future father-in-law of Karolina, you are by any and all means trying to help all of her family. I will never forget it. However, it would be very difficult for me to change my life, to hide in a monastery and to separate myself from my wife and daughter for maybe a long time. It would be also very difficult for me to be a burden to many unknown people. Although I hold in the highest esteem the generosity and courage of the fathers in monasteries and the nuns in convents, I don't see myself in this situation. You are right: our situation is awful, very dangerous and stressful. But we are not the only ones in such a situation. There are millions like us. In Poland alone are three million Jewish people. There are some excesses; there are cases of brutality; the possibility of a tragedy is much, much higher than in the time of peace. I will go through this difficult interval in my life together with my wife and my daughter. I will protect them until my last breath. Good people like you are around us, and they will help us. Above all, there is God, who will help us. He knows that we are honest and He will not forget us. In need, He will not leave us without help.

'Thank you very much for all the pains you have taken to convince me to accept this proposal, and to describe its details. Please tell Bishop Baziak how very grateful I am for his generosity, courage, and dedication. We will keep this proposal in our hearts in greatest secrecy.'

While Juliusz spoke, Dorota and Zosia remained silent. Towards the end, they began to cry. Zosia said in a low voice: 'Father, don't you think that we should not reject this proposal at once? We should think about this generous offer, discuss it again and again over the next few days. It might afterwards be too late for such a discussion.' A burst of tears washed away her words.

It was now Dorota's turn: 'I think that Zosia is right. We should not turn down the proposal but ask for a couple of days to think about it, and I am sure that the bishop will understand that we need some time to think it over. Juliusz, please do not say no to this generous and, I believe, very clever proposal. In this time of misery, people change their minds. You might change yours. Please do not decline at once.'

Juliusz was sitting in silence, his head lowered. He closed his eyes to concentrate better. He understood that his decision might be crucial not only for his life, but also for those of his wife and daughter. He was against the bishop's proposal because, in the depth of his soul, he did not believe that the Germans would be mass murderers and that they would exterminate millions of Jews. The idea seemed absurd to him in light of the treasures of the German cultural past. His attachment to this past was distorting his evaluation of the present.

Karolina was convinced that the proposal was like a gift from God. When she first heard of it from Andrzej, she considered it as a miraculous message and she would accept it with no hesitation. She had no delusions about the future.

She decided to use all her arguments to convince her father: 'Father, you do not know if, in the future, such an offer will be possible. Now, at present, you, mother, and Zosia can simply leave this apartment and go – of course, under protection – to a convent or monastery. Very soon it might be too late. You know that the Germans are organizing ghettos. One day such a ghetto will be organized in Lwów. You, my mother, and Zosia will be imprisoned in such a ghetto. The decision you are making now may become irreversible in the near future. You know that some decisions can not be withdrawn.'

She stopped and looked at her father. He was extremely sad, his head still down. He said: 'Karolina, you are a very good girl. You are very young and speaking under the influence of anxiety. I have my own life experience. I understand the danger, but I have hope. I have always hope that good will prevail in the not-too-distant future. My dear daughter, would you like to be hidden in a much safer place than the apartment of Andrzej's parents, in a convent, and leave Andrzej without you until the end of the war? You certainly would not. Why, then, do you insist that I behave in such a way? Don't you understand that it is for me impossible to be hidden in a safest place, but at the same time without direct contact with your mother and Zosia. No, I cannot accept such a situation. Such a solution would be acceptable to me only in the case of imminent danger to life. And I do not see that at present. I am in the same situation as millions of Jewish people are now. If you want to tell me that all the Jews will be exterminated, I think that this is an unrealistic exaggeration. We will suffer, but we will suffer together. I will do everything to alleviate the sufferings of your mother and Zosia, and we will survive together.' He stopped and, after a while, added: 'If I am wrong, I don't want to survive this war. I don't want to be witness to and perhaps a victim of the extermination of millions of people, I prefer to die than to live in a hell. If you are right, this earth will be a hell.'

There was silence in the room. Then Andrzej said: 'There is a great difference, Juliusz, between your and our evaluation of the situation. You believe that mass murder is impossible. We think that extermination of some nations, first of all of the Jewish nation, is in Hitler's program. If the war will last longer, he will have enough time to realize his program. The current military situation indicates that the war will not end soon. We are all discussing the life of your family and your own life. How can you compare a separation that is a very dramatic event with a situation so tragic that your lives will be in jeopardy? There will be nobody close to you to help you and your family, for instance, if something happens in the ghetto. We are not panicking; we are not exaggerating. But, dear Juliusz, don't you think that it is safer to exaggerate than to underestimate? The separation certainly is a drama in itself, but it is temporary. To know that the killer is close to you and that you are unable to prevent or avoid the danger is a tragedy. Think about the bishop's offer many times again before you definitely reject it.'

Juliusz looked at Andrzej and said with a sad smile: 'I am not a crazy man, my dear Andrzej. I want very much to survive this war and I will do the best to protect my family. I will think over the proposal. You can be sure that I will think it over again.'

And, turning to Ludwik he added: 'Thank you, thank you very much for all your care, devotion, and love. God bless you, Ludwik.'

For Andrzej and Karolina, and also for Ludwik, it was clear that he wanted to end this conversation. He was simply convinced that he was right. If he promised to think it over, they had to wait and hope that he would accept the proposal.

Karolina was sure that he would eventually reject it. She had the feeling that a day would come when he would deeply regret his decision, and it would be already impossible to avert a tragic fate. She therefore asked Ludwik to tell his wife that she was invited to tea with Dorota and Zosia next day. She wanted Estelle to influence Dorota and Zosia to stand firm on the issue, and in the meantime she wanted to talk with Juliusz in another room without any witnesses. She asked Ludwik to wait some time before conveying Juliusz's answer to the bishop's proposal.

In the next days, they tried to convince him several times. The same was done by Dorota and Zosia, to no avail. Andrzej and Karolina knew that if Ludwik, whom Juliusz held in great esteem, could not convince him, there was no possibility that anyone else could.

After telling the bishop how grateful Karolina's family was for his generous offer, Ludwik asked for a short delay before giving a definite answer. After a lapse of two weeks, he went to the diocese with a negative answer, carrying the message of immense gratitude of Karolina's family and trying to explain the attitude of Juliusz. The bishop was sad, but not surprised: 'Unfortunately it is not the first time that we have seen such an attitude. We will pray for them with the hope that they will accept our offer and that when this happens it will not be too late. Sometimes just one hour, one minute, means life or death. As long as there exists such a possibility, our doors stay open for them.'

Andrzej and Karolina understood that, since the evening when Ludwik could not convince him, Juliusz had chosen a direction from which he did not want to return. On their way home, Ludwik and Andrzej could not talk, they were in such despair. Karolina could not sleep at night. She knew that her father would go with strong convictions towards a tragedy that was unthinkable for him. He was, in this respect, not alone.

IV

THE MORNING AFTER THIS TRAGIC CONVERSATION, ANDRZEJ went with Karolina to the Bernardine Monastery for a lesson with Father Wilhelm. At the same time, Andrzej had an appointment with Father Alojzy to work out details of his two trips for the necessary forms.

Father Wilhelm was a young Bernardine monk, very shy and, at the beginning, not very eloquent. After a while, he felt very at ease with Karolina and, when he started the catechism lessons, one could see how seriously he was taking his task and how happy he was when Karolina started to ask questions. Knowing that Karolina was a medical student, he had asked her some questions related to his important work with various personalities. They were both so much interested in the discussion of catechism that, when Andrzej reappeared in the door of Father Wilhelm's office, Father Wilhelm and Karolina could not believe that the lesson had gone on for more than two hours.

Father Alojzy, during those two hours, explained to Andrzej how to get to Glinna Nawaria, a small village about 20 kilometres from Lwów. He instructed Andrzej to present himself as a messenger from Father Alojzy to get the forms printed before 1939, for the parish in Lwów. After this journey, Father Alojzy assumed, Andrzej would need one to two days of rest. Afterwards, Andrzej would have a very difficult task – to travel by train about 150 kilometres and then go by foot about 10 kilometres to another small village. Father Alojzy had an unconfirmed report that the parish in this village had been destroyed towards the end of the First World War and that all the documents had been burnt. Andrzej had to present himself under another name and ask for a duplicate of his 1915 baptism certificate. If the documents had indeed been burnt, the parson would be unable to do that and would tell Andrzej how he should proceed in such a case. The point was to get confirmation of the destruction of the documents. Further action would be taken later.

The tasks Andrzej faced were not easy. Travel was dangerous in these times. The trains were overcrowded, and there was practically no regular schedule because civilian and freight trains had to give way to military transports. If there was no direct connection, the passengers had to wait, sometimes for many hours, to change trains. A special German police 'Schupo' supervised persons going by train, looking, in particular for Jews who might travel to find a place to hide. As the Jews were, in general, not permitted to travel by train, the Schupo was on the look-out for people who either were suspected of being disguised Jews or had been reported by informers. The Schupo was also looking for people from the resistance who might transport either arms or secret messages and documents. A rail traveller was exposed to danger from anywhere and at any time.

Father Alojzy instructed Andrzej to behave in a very cautious and circumspect way. Both Father Alojzy and Andrzej knew that there was no other way to get the documents that would play a vital role in the life of Karolina. All this had to be done as fast as possible. During Andrzej's absence, Father Alojzy would go to the archdiocese to study the registers of baptisms during the First World War and of weddings before the outbreak of the Second World War, to find the proper spots to enter those two events in Karolina's life. He would also supervise Karolina's comings and goings to and from Father Wilhelm for catechism lessons. She would be accompanied on her way to and from the monastery by one or both of Andrzej's parents or by one of the nuns who were their friends. Father Alojzy blessed Andrzej for his journey and offered him hope that all would go well, despite the stresses of travelling.

Early the next morning, Andrzej took the two-hour walk to the railway station as the urban trams were not yet running. Crowds of people were waiting, sitting on the benches and on the floors of the waiting rooms. The Gestapo was patrolling the station, looking for suspects. Those suspected of being disguised Jews or smugglers of arms or documents were brutally pushed out into waiting police cars.

Andrzej waited about three hours for a freight train going in the direction of a small village close to Glinna Nawaria. At that time, freight trains were very often used as means of transportation for the civilian population. After one hour in an overcrowded train, Andrzej arrived close to his destination. From there he had a half-hour walk to the parish.

The parson welcomed him warmly when he mentioned that he had been sent by Father Alojzy. The parson was in his seventies but still in good shape and agile. He handed Andrzej baptism and marriage forms printed before the outbreak of war in 1939. He did not ask any questions, but, as he passed to Andrzej a bunch of forms, mentioned: 'Father Alojzy might need more. God bless you, young man. Take care when travelling.'

Andrzej was happy to take all the forms. Others could be helped by them and spared the dangers of travelling. He returned to the local station. There was no information about the arrival of a train headed in the direction of Lwów. After waiting for one hour, he decided to go by foot to Lwów.

It was just past noon, and he had to reach his house and the monastery before curfew. It was a brisk walk lasting five hours, and a stressful one because, all the time, German military cars were passing him. What if one of them stopped and questioned him about the purpose of his walk? He had his identity papers on him, documenting that he was not a Jew, but he also had the void baptism and wedding forms. He felt a terrible anxiety. If they searched him, he would be lost at once. 'No,' he reasoned, they will not do that. I have the certificate stating that I am a physician. I carry my small physician's bag, and I will tell them that I have to hurry to a patient who has a heart condition, or, better to a woman who is bleeding from an abortion. I will manage to convince them. Most important, I must not show that I am afraid.' And afraid he was.

He reached the Bernardine Monastery in a state of great physical and psychological exhaustion, and at the same time, with a feeling of relief that the forms were now in a safe place. After a short conversation with Father Alojzy and a couple of minutes' rest, he went to Karolina; he knew that she was waiting for him with great anxiety. She greeted him with tears of joy. She bore the guilt that she was responsible for his exposure to all the dangers of travelling. She saw how extremely tired he was, and he promised her that he would take one day of rest before the next journey, which might last at least three days.

Next morning, Andrzej came again to take Karolina for her catechism lessons at the monastery. He wanted also to discuss the details of his next journey with Father Alojzy. Father Wilhelm told Andrzej that he was very satisfied with the progress Karolina was making. In his opinion, she would very soon be ready for baptism.

Andrzej accompanied Karolina on her way home, but this time she insisted on his early return to his parents for a better rest before the long, difficult, and dangerous journey.

Next morning, Andrzej woke up in a state of great anxiety. He was afraid to leave Karolina for three days, he was afraid of all the dangers of travelling, he was afraid of the Germans altogether. Nobody could help him in this situation. He concentrated on his love for Karolina and on his faith in the future, repeating to himself that only strong will and love can make survival possible. Strong will and love.

He dressed carefully, took again with him the small doctor's bag, and took the same walk to the railway station in Lwów he had taken two days earlier.

The journey to the village situated 150 kilometres from Lwów lasted a whole day. He had to change trains four times. The trains were so overcrowded that he had to stand all the time. He was able to sit down only on the floor of the railway station when waiting for the next train. When he eventually arrived at the last railway station, he had to walk 10 kilometres to the parish. It was already near sunset when he arrived. When he told the maid to announce that he had come for the duplicate of his baptism certificate, the parson came out immediately to see him and invited him into his office.

He was a good-natured man and, when Andrzej asked him for a duplicate of the certificate of baptism from the year 1915, was immediately sorry. 'The parish,' he said, 'does not have the registers of baptisms for this period. Towards the end of the First World War, all the documents were destroyed during a great fire, in 1918. I realize how important it is now to have the certificate of baptism. The only thing to do for people who were baptized in this church at that period is to ask for a copy at the archdiocese in Lwów. Each year the archdiocese was informed in detail about every baptism given in our church.' Thus, Andrzej received the information he needed so badly.

His return journey to Lwów lasted more than a day. The train was expected next morning, and Andrzej would have to sleep on the floor in the waiting room.

Fortunately, the train destined for Lwów was a passenger train and not a freight train. Although he was able to travel in better conditions, it turned out that this journey was a terrible experience for him. At once a young woman sitting in the compartment went up, opened the door, and said loudly to a man standing in the corridor: 'What are you doing here, Mr Goldman? You are a Jew. Don't you know that, at last, the Jews are not allowed to travel by train. You are on the train, and, on top of that, you aren't wearing the armband with the star of David. You are not obeying the existing rules. You have to be punished.' At the end of the corridor, a male voice announced: 'They have found a Jew. We have to make an example of him. Jews caused the war.'

The old man cringed in fear and whispered to the young woman who had betrayed him: 'Mary, why did you do this?' But it was already too late. Somebody had put out an alert, and the German police, patrolling the train, arrived. One of the policemen brutally grasped the collar of the old man's and asked him: 'Are you a Jew?' 'No,' answered the old man. 'Yes, he is a Jew,' said the young woman who had first recognized him. 'I know him. I worked for him. He had a shop in my town. Yes, he is a Jew,' she repeated with satisfaction. The policeman slapped the old man's face and said: 'We are going to check you in the toilet. Follow me.' After a while, they emerged from the toilet. The face of the old man was bloodied. He was crying desperately. The policeman announced in an official tone: 'Yes, he is a Jew. And he is without the armband with the star of David. And he is travelling by train. He does not obey the orders of our Führer. He will be punished at the next stop of the train.' While making this statement, he was beating the old man with the butt of his gun.

After a short time the train stopped in a small railway station. The policeman kicked the already unconscious old man out of the train and shot him.

There was silence, full of fear and terror, in the train. Even the informer did not say a word. After a while, when the train began to move, a peasant in the corridor between Andrzej and the informer asked: 'Why did you do this? How could you be so cruel?' 'Shut up,' she shrieked. 'I will ask the policeman to check you. Perhaps you are also a disguised Jew.' The peasant did not say a word and moved towards the end of the corridor. The train was moving slowly, leaving on the platform the body of the massacred man.

The informer returned to her compartment. Opposite her sat a young priest. After a while, he said: 'God will never forgive you. You, and not the policeman, you yourself killed this innocent, poor man. Even when, after confession, some priests might absolve you and forgive on this earth, I can assure you that God has condemned you already for ever. You will suffer for ever, because you are not a human being. You are an Evil. For Evil there is only one place – hell.'

The young woman started at once to cry. The priest returned to his breviary.

V

AFTER RETURNING TO LWÓW, ANDRZEJ IMMEDIATELY informed Father Alojzy that the parish register of baptisms up to 1918 had indeed been completely destroyed. Hearing this and knowing from Father Wilhelm that Karolina was already well prepared for baptism, Father Alojzy decided to work the next Sunday afternoon with Andrzej on the documents of baptism for Karolina and on the document of marriage. He had received from the diocese permission to forgo the bans, and Karolina could very soon in the coming week be baptized and married.

In the meantime, Andrzej had to return to work at the hospital. His week of leave was finished, and he had accomplished his task. He also wanted to help his associate professor and his family.

Karolina was going outdoors only in the company of Andrzej's parents, Filomena, or Andrzej. Each time she went out she was taking a risk, walking without an armband.

In the city were many Ukrainian and Polish informers. Various nations in Lwów were always living in discord and hatred. It was very dangerous to stay in a city where many people knew Karolina. As long as they stayed in Lwów, she would be restrained in her ability to take walks outside.

The atmosphere in the city was very tense. Soon after the German army occupied Lwów, the Gestapo has taken many university professors from their homes, among them thirteen professors in the Faculty of Medicine. Their families were informed that the professors were being transported to Germany, where they would have all the possibilities of better professional and research work. After they were taken, nobody ever heard of them. Only after the defeat of Hitler, was it known that, immediately after being taken by the

Gestapo, they had been shot in hills surrounding Lwów (Wzgórza Wóleckie).

The university was closed; the Medical Institute did not exist any more. The Department of Psychiatry had been incorporated into the psychiatric hospital. One of the Ukrainian doctors was now general director of the hospital. The majority of psychiatrists who were working in the hospital were dismissed. Others were told that the same fate awaited them. With the small numbers of doctors and all medication resources cut, all active methods of treatment had to be abandoned.

Andrzej was now the only member of his family who was working. His father lost his job because the Germans closed his school. Since the German invasion Juliusz could not work. Karolina lost her scholarship. Both families had very limited financial resources and were on the verge of poverty.

The situation grew worse daily for the Jewish people. Somebody walking on the street with an armband with the star of David could be picked up by any Nazi and taken to do any physical work. Some of those picked up did not return from their 'special work.' They were either shot by the Gestapo or taken to the concentration camps. Jewish people who dared to walk in the streets without armbands were taking the risk of being blackmailed by informers, most of these were the scum of society, the refuse of humanity. They were 'hunting for Jews' to make money from extortion. They were looking for people with Semitic features and asking them for money or simply forcing them into the porches of houses to check if they were circumcised. If they found somebody who had been circumcised, they blackmailed him. Some of those blackmail victims were known to the informers as 'loaded,' and they were blackmailed many times, although they had been promised they would never be attacked again. If they could not pay, they were denounced to the Gestapo and killed.

There was also another kind of informer – anti-Semitic racists driven by hatred, aggression, and cruelty so intense that they were committing crimes against humanity.

Seeing all this during his walks to and from the hospital, Andrzej could hardly wait for the coming Sunday afternoon to start the work with Father Alojzy.

It was early afternoon on Sunday when Andrzej arrived at the Bernardine Monastery. As advised by Father Alojzy, he brought a small bottle of India ink and various pens. They intended to mix the India ink with water and normal ink to make the writing look as though it had been done long ago. They chose a pen that would produce writing similar to that in a book dating from the year 1915. Father Alojzy has already found and prepared a space in the register of baptisms for 1915, held in the archdiocese of Lwów. Everything had to be changed in the newly created certificate of birth and baptism – the place of birth, the names of parents, grandparents, god-parents. The date of birth and of baptism of Karolina, now Karolina Anna, was entered in the archdiocese book by the hand of Andrzej, who, under precise instructions from Father Alojzy, had changed his handwriting and used an appropriate pen and the 'antiqued' ink. Father Alojzy had entered an abstract of this entry on the pre-war form brought by Andrzej from Glinna Nawaria. Karolina could show it as authentic Aryan paper (AP) because it was written on an old form printed before the Second World War.

The date of marriage was entered in the register of weddings in the archdiocese of Lwów for the last day of December 1938. That was the only available place in the wedding registers of the period before the Second World War. The date corresponded with the date in the Bernardine parish, where the entry was made by Father Alojzy. He considered that it was much safer to date the wedding in the period before the German invasion; he knew that the Germans had access to all the registers made under their rule. Thus, before her wedding, which was to take place at the end of July 1941, Karolina had a proof that she had married Andrzej just before the Second World War. Another document required to validate Karolina's civilian status was the certificate of marriage written by Father Alojzy on the original pre-war form brought by Andrzej from Glinna Nawaria in the bunch handed to him by the parson.

Father Alojzy worked with Andrzej for about three hours, trying various combinations of ink and writing. Now, any time next week Karolina could be baptized and married.

Andrzej went to Karolina and her family with the good news. Filomena was there visiting them and, as usual, had brought fresh fruit and vegetables from the convent garden. They spent an hour together – the most optimistic hour since the Nazis had occupied Lwów.

But the Evil did not sleep. Two days before Karolina's baptism, the

Gestapo came in the early morning to the house where Juliusz was living with his family. They asked the janitor, Dmitro, a middle-age Ukrainian, to mobilize for them all young Jewish people, boys and girls, living in this house. They needed them to clean their military barracks. Dmitro gave them the apartment numbers, with an indication of how many young Jewish people could be found in each apartment. Thus, Karolina and Zosia found themselves on the Gestapo's list. For the first time, Karolina had to put on the armband with the star of David, and together with Zosia and six other youngsters, she waited on the porch for orders from the Gestapo. 'If you work fast and efficiently, you will be back here for lunch,' shouted Dmitro, who was watching them when they left under the command of the Gestapo.

Karolina and Zosia were indeed back home at noon, but nobody else from the group ever returned. What occurred in that lapse of time between the early morning hours and noon on that July morning is the history of two sisters: a victim saved from death and her saviour. From that July day, the lives of the two sisters continued: that of Karolina, so close to death, was to last many, many years after the war, with her heartbeat always close to Andrzej's; that of Zosia, the saviour, did not last a year.

All the young girls and boys from this house were taken by the Gestapo to clean the military barracks, floors and toilets. They worked as efficiently as they could under the supervision of the German officers.

Karolina was trying to wash the floor with a rag. She was bent over her task when she heard the supervising officer shout at her. She stood up straight and at once felt the cold metal of the revolver on her left temple: 'Forget about the past. You might have been a student or a secretary. Perhaps you never washed a floor, but all this is finished. You are finished. You are a Jew, a nobody, at the mercy of the great German nation. If you don't work properly I will shoot you.' In a blink of eye, Karolina heard the voice of Zosia quite close to her, speaking in her perfect German to the officer in a calm and dignified manner: 'Jawohl, Herr Oberst. Sie wird es sofort schön und sauber putzen.' In a second, the cold metal was removed from Karolina's head.

Zosia, an extremely good-hearted human being, but always very shy and silent, had had the courage to speak to the officer. Her immediate response had saved Karolina's life.

Now Zosia took command: 'First of all, bend your knees. Nobody cleans the floor in a standing position, as you did. Do exactly what I am doing. We are going to work together. Follow me. He has probably never seen anybody cleaning the floor without kneeling. He will not do you any harm if you don't talk and don't show any fear.'

Both girls were working very hard and very professionally as if they had done nothing else all their lives. After a while, Karolina heard the voice of the officer. He was not shouting now, but speaking in his commanding voice with a Prussian accent: 'Now it is better. If you continue in such a way, I will not shoot you ... today.' Then he walked away, to the other end of the corridor.

When he was gone, Zosia tried to reassure Karolina: 'I know them. They like to scare people to death. They did the same with my friend in Vienna. Continue to wash on your knees and move with me in the direction of the staircase. Be 'tüchtig' – don't rush and don't show any fear.'

They were already close to the staircase, on their knees washing the corridor floor. After washing the first step down, they moved slowly to the second step, the third, and so on, until they reached the lower floor.

Zosia stood up and so did Karolina. She followed Zosia, who approached another officer, this one of a lower rank. Zosia told him in her excellent German: 'Der Herr Oberst dort oben hat uns befohlen die Treppe sauber zu machen und danach sofort nach Hause zu gehen.' 'Befehl ist Befehl,' answered the officer. 'Move out. Raus.' He did not need to repeat this command. They exited so fast that they had no time to dispense with the rags they were holding.

Outside, the lime trees were in bloom, their buds just opened, and the air was sweet. The sun was shining through the leaves, and the two sisters, still holding dirty rags in their hands, could hardly believe that they are again in this world. They were suffering from physical exhaustion and psychological stress and wanted to sit down for a while and rest. Seeing a nearby church, they entered it.

It was near noon, and the church seemed empty. After a while, two old women approached them. They noticed that the girls were very dirty and wearing armbands with the star of David. One of them said: 'Get out of the church. Jesus does not want to have Jews in His holy church. Leave immediately.'

After a fifteen-minute walk, they arrived home. None of the other six youths taken with them was home yet. Their families would wait in vain for a long, long time.

In the afternoon, on his way home, Andrzej came as usual to see Karolina and her family. Karolina and Zosia told him the details of this terrible experience. All the family was in a very sad mood. Andrzej at once realized the danger of the situation. Seeing his concern and anxiety, Zosia tried to diminish it, without changing the facts to disguise the situation: 'The officer did not mean what he said. He would never shoot her. They do not shoot people working for them in military barracks. I was in Vienna during the Anschluss. There they also took people to work, and I never heard that those people were shot. I know, however, that such things happened in concentration camps.'

'No, Zosia,' Karolina said, interrupting her. 'This is not like the Anschluss in 1938. It is July 1941, and we are at war now. The beast has grown, and they will do all that Hitler wants them to do, to win the war.'

Hearing this, Andrzej begged Juliusz once more to accept the proposal of Bishop Baziak. However, even in such a situation, Juliusz was convinced that the danger was overdramatized: 'Andrzej, don't you see that the girls were taken to clean military barracks and they returned tired but safe, and much earlier than they had anticipated. We did not even have time to worry about lateness. The other youths taken from here will certainly return in the late afternoon. The threat of being shot was a terrible experience for Karolina, but, you see yourself: it was only a threat.'

Andrzej decided to act immediately. He was afraid that, next morning, the Gestapo might return. He told Juliusz that he had decided to marry Karolina next day and asked him to permit Karolina and Zosia to spend the night in the convent of Sisters of Charity with Filomena. Andrzej promised him that the girls would return home after the morning hours during which the Gestapo hunted for Jews from house to house.

Andrzej went then immediately to the Bernardine Monastery. On the way there, he stopped for a while at Filomena's convent and asked her to wait for him at Juliusz's apartment. He told Father Alojzy about the tragic events of the morning and asked him to baptize Karolina and marry them next day. Father Alojzy agreed immediately. Karolina would be baptized in the morning, and they would be married in the afternoon in the Chapel of St John of Dukla in the Bernardine Church to avoid the crowds that might be in the principal nave of the church.

When Andrzej returned to Juliusz's apartment, Filomena was already there. Karolina and Zosia had told her about the tragic events of the morning, and she wanted to take the girls immediately to her convent and return with them later next morning.

Saying goodbye to Juliusz and Dorota this evening was short and heart-breaking. The curfew hour was approaching. Filomena left with the two girls; then, Andrzej returned to his home.

Juliusz and Dorota, who had been looking forward to having Karolina with them the two nights before her wedding, understood that she would never again live with them. From now on, she would be under the care of Andrzej.

VI

THE BAPTISM OF KAROLINA WAS ARRANGED FOR 10:00 A.M. This time was recommended by Father Alojzy as the safest because the streets were relatively empty and there would be few people in the churches. At 9:00, Filomena left the two girls in the convent and went to Juliusz's apartment to see if all was in order and if there was no threat of another visit by the Gestapo. All seemed to be quiet. Karolina's parents had spent a difficult night, full of anxiety about their daughters, and the visit of Filomena was a great relief for them.

Andrzej was waiting for Karolina and planned to accompany her and Filomena on the journey to the church. Andrzej's parents were waiting for them at the street corner. They were to be Karolina's godparents. Karolina went out, accompanied by Filomena in her nun's habit. Andrzej and his parents followed them. All of them entered the church with no trouble. Father Wilhelm was waiting for them in the sacristy. Karolina was given Anna as second name, and was baptized in the empty chapel of St John of Dukla. For safety reasons, Father Alojzy was watching, from the door of the sacristy, the entrance to the church. After the baptism ceremony, he blessed Karolina and hugged Andrzej. In the sacristy, Karolina received from Father Alojzy her certificate of baptism.

All of them went now to the apartment of Andrzej's parents. Filomena helped to make order in Andrzej's room, which had to become after marriage 'their' room. She put a bouquet of roses in a vase. These roses, brought from her convent's garden, were for the bridal bouquet. Then she went with Andrzej to Karolina's parents to bring some clothes and things for Karolina. Juliusz was very sad, because none of the sons and daughters taken by the Gestapo the preceding day had returned home.

The wedding was scheduled for early afternoon. Andrzej, his parents, and Karolina were accompanied by Filomena to the church. On the way, they picked up Juliusz, Dorota, and Zosia, who were taking a risk walking out for the first time in the street without armbands. To make the situation less dangerous, they formed small groups. Filomena, in her nun's habit, went with Zosia, Andrzej with Karolina, Ludwik with Dorota, and Juliusz with Estelle. Filomena was carrying the bouquet to avoid drawing attention to Karolina. They arrived with no trouble at the church. The Chapel of St John of Dukla was again completely empty.

The wedding ceremony was very fast, and, after fifteen minutes, all of them were in Father Alojzy's office. He hugged Karolina and Andrzej and wished them the best, with tears in his eyes: 'God bless you both. He will guide all your steps and accompany your journey in this world. All of us in this monastery will pray for both of you. Come to visit us and keep us informed of your plans. If you need help, don't hesitate. We will do all that is possible.' He greeted warmly Karolina's parents and Zosia: 'God is also with all your family. I know that the bishop wants to help you. Please, listen to my advice: do not reject his proposal. There might not be a better solution.' He had very warm words for Andrzej's parents, whose courage he admired. There was a special blessing for them.

Then the two families, with Filomena again carrying the bridal bouquet, went in the same order to Andrzej's parents' apartment. All were full of anxiety because this journey was much longer. They arrived with no trouble, and sat down to a modest dinner prepared by Andrzej's mother.

During this dinner everybody tried to introduce a note of hope; Juliusz talked about the honeymoon journey that he promised to organize for them immediately after the war. It had to be to Italy, where he had gone on his honeymoon with Dorota. He knew all the best places. His story was for them like a dream that might or might not come true. Nobody was sure that Hitler would be defeated soon.

The war was all around them. They were under Nazi occupation. The bride had only yesterday been exposed to mortal danger. The bridegroom could any time lose his job. The family of Juliusz had to bear the stigma of being branded as out-laws. Ludwik's family was risking their lives to save the wife of their son. There was no end of suffering, current and future. Even if they tried to think about a brighter future, the shadow of danger darkened it. What would happen this very evening, on the way back home? What would happen tomorrow, next week, in the next hour? The wedding, in essence a joyous event, was overshadowed by fear.

The duration of the wedding reception was limited by the curfew. Karolina's parents and Zosia were accompanied home by Ludwik, Andrzej, and Filomena. Karolina stayed at her new home with Estelle. Juliusz was accompanied by Andrzej in this walk. 'Andrzej, my dear Andrzej, you have shown us what true love is. Thank you for that. I love you as if you were my own son. I know that you will do your best to protect Karolina and I will do my best to protect Dorota and Zosia.

'I took a great liking to Father Alojzy. He is praying to his God, I am praying to my God, and both of us know that it is always the same God, unique and universal.' For a while he analysed some spiritual problems. This seemed to relieve him and to allow him to forget for a while the tragic situation.

They worked out how they would make contact in the future. A tragic and difficult question. Juliusz and his family were forbidden to walk on the street without armbands. Karolina could walk on the street without an armband accompanied by Andrzej, or one of his parents or Filomena. Many people knew Karolina, and Andrzej was afraid of informers. If a link would be detected between Juliusz's apartment and that of Andrzej's parents, Karolina could be easily traced and identified. For Karolina's family, to walk outside without an armband was mortally dangerous; for Andrzej's family, to receive people with armbands was equally so. Therefore, Juliusz and Andrzej decided to have personal contact only in the apartment of Juliusz. Andrzej promised to drop in as often as possible on his way to or from the hospital and to visit them with Karolina in the evenings before the curfew. Andrzej's parents were willing to visit Juliusz and his family often, with or without Karolina.

After accompanying Juliusz and his family, who were not wearing armbands, safely home, Ludwik and Andrzej returned to their own home.

This night was a night of love, mutual dedication, and total devotion. It was incredible how was it possible to feel simultaneously happiness without limits and terrible fear that this love could be destroyed at any moment. Mixed feelings of happiness and fear were to persist in their hearts until the defeat of Hitler.

Early in the morning Andrzej left for work at the hospital. It was exactly three weeks after Hitler's army had occupied Lwów.

VII

KAROLINA MOSTLY STAYED AT HER NEW HOME WHILE Andrzej worked at the hospital. She helped Estelle in her household work. She had, however, to go out shopping with Estelle from time to time. Estelle informed the neighbours that her son had recently married Karolina, who was one of the refugees from the western part of Poland. Her parents were far away, in the part of Poland occupied by the Nazis since 1939. Karolina was since that time alone in Lwów, because the university where she studied medicine was closed by the Germans and she wanted to continue her studies. The Medical Institute in Lwów was the only opportunity for university studies in the divided and occupied country. As the Germans had also closed the Medical Institute in Lwów, she had had to discontinue her studies. The information conveyed by Estelle should prevent gossip and speculation as to what Karolina was doing in Ludwik's apartment; Karolina's going out more often was evidence that she was not hiding for any reason.

The food supplies in the city were very scarce and fast declining. There was also a black market, but its prices were outrageous and it was dangerous to deal with as it had formally been forbidden by the Germans. At the beginning of the German occupation, there was plenty of food in the countryside, but very soon the Germans imposed the so-called contingent, forcing the peasants to sell meat and grain to German authorities for extremely low prices. They used these supplies to feed their enormous army. The civilian population was suffering hunger. Bread was rationed, and so were potatoes and other basic foods.

As a working physician Andrzej was allowed to buy twice weekly an additional ration of potatoes from the hospital garden. It was for him very difficult to carry it, walking the great distance from the suburbs to the downtown. When trams began to function, it was easier to handle the burden he had on his back. Always on the way home, he dropped in at Karolina's parents' to share with them the ration of potatoes. Andrzej's salary was too small to buy food on the black market. His parents had to sell some furniture and carpets to buy or barter for food. Their former maid was helpful in those exchanges of 'lard for carpet' because she knew some peasants eager to obtain such necessities for their houses in the villages.

Autumn was approaching. The nights were getting colder, and there was no supply of heating materials such as wood and coal for winter. Andrzej and Karolina were alone with their love, and it was giving them the strength to lead this difficult life, taking one day at a time. Ludwik and Andrzej, however, were spending more and more time, thinking about how to leave the city.

Juliusz and his family had the same problems. Great help was given to them by Filomena. She became their frequent guest, always bringing vegetables and fruit from the convent garden. Some other nuns, from the nearby Convent of Sisters of the Holy Sacrament, were also bringing food from their garden. Andrzej never learned who had told them about Juliusz's family, whether it was Filomena or Father Alojzy.

Juliusz had some golden coins, kept for the 'black hour.' He could not sell them himself, because he could be exposed to blackmail by the trader. He could do it only through his Catholic friends. One of them, Stanisław, was so courageous that even Juliusz was afraid that he might be taken by the Germans for his loud criticism of the current circumstances.

The situation in the hospital grew more and more tragic from one day to the next. The food given to patients was insufficient. The mentally ill patients were deprived not only of medical treatment, but also of the basic nutrients required for survival. Some of them were already showing swelling in their bodies. In the period of four months since the German occupation, over 25 per cent of the patients had died of hunger.

After some weeks the Germans organized special wards for Jewish patients, a kind of ghetto inside the hospital, where the food was worse and distributed in a smaller quantity than the already small rations given out in other wards. In some Jewish wards, only Jewish doctors were employed; they were obliged to wear the armbands with the star of David. One of them was Andrzej's former superior, the associate professor.

The Nazis were not directly killing the mentally ill patients in Lwów. They did not use the same procedure of extermination there as they had in many other psychiatric hospitals in Poland since 1939, for instance, in Kostrzyń, close to Poznań, or in Chełmno Lubelskie, close to Lublin. The population around Lwów, in the south-eastern part of pre-war Poland, was mostly Ukrainian. Those Ukrainians were, in the majority, nationalists, expecting that Germany would help them to form an independent Ukrainian state. For that reason, very often they collaborated with the Germans. The Germans did not want to jeopardize Ukrainian support by openly killing members of their families in hospital. Therefore, they had chosen to kill the patients by starvation.

In October 1941, on the walls of the houses and on billboards, were posted orders of registration for all Jews. It was announced what constituted a Jew, according to the Nuremberg legislation. Any disobedience would be punished by death. It was also announced that, after the end of the registration, the Jews would be obliged to move to special quarters in the city, completely isolated from other quarters.

This was the beginning of the organization of a ghetto in Lwów.

Juliusz was prepared psychologically for this event. For a long time, he had been convinced that the worst solution was to stay in a big city, and the best, to move to a small village. He had decided to leave Lwów and avoid the isolation in a ghetto. He was seeing in a very optimistic light the move to a small village. There would be less problems with food; the Gestapo would not come to a small village; and the Germans would not be especially interested in Jewish families living in the villages. Certainly, they would not order a ghetto for each village. The Gestapo would concentrate on enforcement of their orders in the cities and would have no time before Hitler's defeat to persecute every single Jewish family in a village. The more he thought of this solution, the more pleased he was with it. He was good-natured and easily struck up a rapport with people, and he could easily make friends among the peasants.

Karolina and Andrzej did not share his opinion, although they were afraid to have all three of them relegated to a ghetto. However, the idea of going to an unknown village did not seem acceptable; in doing so, Juliusz and his family could one day find themselves in a trap. Being at the mercy of unknown people, isolated from friends, seemed to them extremely dangerous. They discussed with him many times the proposal of Bishop Baziak. Ludwik went again to see Juliusz and told him that the proposal was still valid. But Juliusz did not revise his former decision, especially now, when the idea of 'a safe village' had entered in his head. Why should he go into hiding and be separated from his wife and daughter, who would be hiding in another place, if it was possible to be with them, in the open, only having to wear armbands. 'A Polish village is a quiet place, and, in some villages, the people are very kind and helpful. They would do no harm to him and his family because they were against Hitler.' Such was his reasoning. 'Anyway, this is the best place for a short time, because the defeat of Hitler is imminent,' he used to add.

Now he was concentrating on how to get out of Lwów to go to this small village of his imagination. He knew that it was forbidden for Jews to travel by train in general to move from one place to another. He could do it only in an illegal way, via secret agents. They could, however, take money from him and do nothing other than blackmail him afterwards. Then, at once, the solution came to him.

A medical student, a colleague of Karolina's, who was a Polish Jew, told him that he also wanted to leave Lwów because he was afraid of being incarcerated in a ghetto. He had already gathered information, based on various sources, that there was a small village in the sub-Carpathian region, approximately 150 kilometres from Lwów. The name of the village was Orelec. A young Polish teacher from this village had characterized its population in a very positive way. The population was Polish and Ukrainian. There were only three Jewish families living there. The relationship between the Polish-Ukrainian population and the Jewish families was very good. The Jews were obliged to wear the armbands with the star of David, but they could move anywhere in the village and its surroundings. The nearest small town was within a distance of 15 kilometres. The nearest railway station was within 10 kilometres.

In a matter of few days, this small village became for Juliusz the symbol of an oasis of peace where he could stay with his family until the end of war. He was obsessed with the idea, and could not think or speak of anything else.

From the outset Andrzej had disliked this idea. Juliusz was, in his eyes, a romantic dreamer, hoping against hope, unrealistic against cruel reality, always believing that Good would prevail, and very soon. He was too honest to imagine what an inhuman machine of terror Hitler could invent, and that it might start to run very fast.

Very soon after the announcement of compulsory Jewish registration, Juliusz told Andrzej that he intended to speak with an agent who could organize the transport of his family to Orelec. Andrzej was in despair, hearing the news, and tried once more to convince Juliusz to accept the proposal of the bishop: 'I beg you to accept the proposal of Bishop Baziak. Do you realize that there is nobody, absolutely nobody, who could guarantee you that the existing situation in the village will last for a long time? It is wartime, and things change from day to day. The bishop's proposal gives you and your family the best security, even if the war lasts a long time, longer than you think. I will organize a system of reciprocal communication among you, Dorota, and Zosia. Each of you will be constantly informed about the others. We talked about that in detail with Karolina. You saw how efficient the help given by the church to Karolina was.'

Juliusz was very touched by his words. He deeply appreciated the generosity of the bishop and knew how strong was the love shown to Karolina by Andrzej's family. Nevertheless he was deeply convinced that he was right: 'My dear Andrzej,' he said, 'I really do not see the necessity of being hidden in a monastery and being separated from my wife and daughter for a long time. A small, quiet village close to the mountains will remain at peace long enough for Hitler to be defeated.

'Very soon, the Russian winter will halt the German troops; this winter will not be easy for Hitler's army. The story of Napoleon will repeat itself. And the Russian front is only one of those on which Hitler's army is fighting. With France and Britain at war, and with help from the United States, the cold of the coming winter will defeat the Nazis. Don't you see that the United States is being drawn closer and closer to war by the force of events. The worst is already behind us. I am going to leave Lwów. I don't want to be relegated to a ghetto. I will live in relatively good conditions until Hitler's defeat.

I am not a dreamer. I am realistic and am taking into consideration all the elements of the current situation.' He smiled, kissed and hugged Andrzej. 'I love you,' he said. That was the end of the discussion.

When Andrzej returned home and told Karolina about this conversation, she had the feeling that she was losing her parents and her sister: 'My father is too honest and too naïve to survive such depravity of human nature. My God, why do you allow the Evil to prevail? Why have we to suffer so much?' They could not sleep at night. Nobody could convince Juliusz. Knowing that there was another possibility, a 'miraculous' possibility, as Karolina called the bishop's proposal, Juliusz's decision seemed to them more tragic than anything. After that sleepless night, Andrzej went back to work extremely exhausted, and Karolina was restless all morning.

Two days later, Karolina and Andrzej heard from the second room, where they were sitting together in Juliusz's apartment, the conversation that Juliusz had with the man whom he called 'an agent' and who was to organize the transportation of Juliusz and his family from Lwów to Orelec. Andrzej did not want to be present in the room in which the conversation took place, but he wanted to hear what was discussed. He feared that the 'agent,' whose name was unknown, might discover his link to Karolina, and thus trace her. On the other hand, he wanted to know the details of the deal, so he could warn Juliusz before he decided on this dangerous course. When he heard the voice of the 'agent,' he knew at once. He had heard this voice many times. It was that of a Ukrainian physician who was working in the general hospital and was known to all the medical students. 'Thank God,' Andrzej thought, 'that he has not seen me.'

They both listened to the deal proposed to Juliusz. A German military truck would drive Juliusz, Dorota, and Zosia, and some of their belongings, to Orelec. They would be hidden inside the truck and not allowed to get out of it at all. Juliusz would pay the driver a certain number of gold coins only after arrival in Orelec. Of course, he mentioned at the end, Juliusz would also pay a number of such coins to the agent because he had to be remunerated for his 'generosity in helping the Jewish people.'

Juliusz listened without interruption to this proposal. At the end they negotiated an agreement. The date was settled for morning three days hence. The driver would receive the coins in a closed box after arrival at the village. The 'agent' would arrive in the same truck to be present at the departure from Lwów. Just before the departure, he would receive from Juliusz 'the present for his generosity.'

When the 'agent' left, Juliusz opened the door to the adjoining room and told Andrzej and Karolina that he was satisfied. The 'agent' had given the impression of being from the intelligentsia; his manners were correct, and his vocabulary was that of an educated person. When Andrzej told Juliusz that, to become a doctor, you had to have a certain degree of education, Juliusz would not believe that he had been dealing with a physician.

This did not however discourage Juliusz. Anyway, it was already too late; he was at the agent's mercy.

Juliusz hugged and kissed them both, and said: 'The day of our departure is close, and very soon the war will be over and we will return to Cracow. I promised you a honeymoon journey to Italy, and you will go there. I don't want to impose on you, Andrzej, but I would be more than happy if you decided to move with Karolina and your parents to Cracow. I will find a beautiful apartment for you and another beautiful apartment for your parents. Our families have so many cultural interests and so many moral values in common. You will not refuse me, Andrzej, when I ask you to accompany on the piano my violin playing.' And he turned to Karolina: 'You have to follow all the advice given to you by your husband. He loves you so much, and is completely devoted to you. I love him as if he were my third child. God bless you both, and Andrzej's parents. From now on they are your parents, Karolina. Be obedient to them, more obedient than you were to me.'

The last two days in Lwów, Juliusz, Dorota, and Zosia were busy with packing. Estelle accompanied Karolina to help in this very sad and tiring work. They had to pack their personal belongings and bedding. No furniture could be taken. The truck had to come early in the morning, not to attract any attention, perhaps even before the night curfew was over. It was a military truck, and curfew did not affect it.

The last afternoon before the departure, Karolina waited for Andrzej with Ludwik and Estelle in Juliusz's apartment. They did not talk about the departure, and to lighten the atmosphere Juliusz spoke about Italy and Greece and the excursions that he would organize after the war for both families. Greece was the country of dreams for Ludwik, and Italy, for Juliusz. They had common interests in ancient Greek and Roman culture and poetry. Dorota and Zosia were exhausted physically and mentally, and he was doing all he could to diminish the tension in the atmosphere. Karolina was doing all she could not to burst into tears.

When Andrzej arrived from work, he discussed with Juliusz all the details of communication between both families. It was necessary to keep secret Karolina's whereabouts; letters could not be sent to her new home. It was agreed that the letters would be addressed to the apartment of their aunt and uncle, who were living together with their son in the same house as Karolina's parents. On his way home, Andrzej would visit them and pick up the incoming correspondence. Their address would be used as the return address on mail sent to them by Karolina. Andrzej was already frequently visiting the old, sick uncle of Karolina and had taken a great liking to all of the family. Estelle, who was extremely good-hearted and in necessary moments very courageous, had started to visit this family and was very helpful to them.

Andrzej promised Juliusz that, as soon as possible, he would come to visit them in Orelec and stay with them for one or two days. They should, however, again for Karolina's safety, keep secret his real link to Juliusz's family. He should be presented as the former employee of Juliusz, bringing him news from Cracow and the graphic factory.

Curfew hour was approaching, and they had to return to their home. Ludwik and Estelle, Andrzej and Karolina hugged and kissed Juliusz, Dorota and Zosia. It was a heart-breaking farewell. Andrzej hoped that, very early next morning, he would be able to see them again before the departure.

That was the last evening that Karolina would see her parents and Zosia. Never in her life did she see them again.

It was mid November. Snow already covered the streets. They could not sleep at night, and in the early hours of the next morning Andrzej was already dressed, waiting for the first minute after curfew. He rushed to Juliusz's apartment for the very last farewell in Lwów.

It was already too late. They had left before the curfew was over. Karolina's aunt, living next door, told Andrzej that she watched from her window their departure. It was very quiet and had been accomplished with no trouble.

Next week, Karolina's aunt received a letter from Orelec, informing her that they had arrived safely, without any obstacles. There was one room and a small kitchen prepared for them. From the beginning the population was very friendly. There was a very nice teacher, who was extremely helpful. Juliusz, who was allowed to take his violin with him, had already started to play, and that made him very popular among the villagers. 'They like very much Mendelssohn's "Lieder ohne Worte."'' Such were the last words of the first letter. As agreed, Karolina's name was not to be mentioned in any letters.

VIII

ANDRZEJ HAD NOW KAROLINA AS HIS WIFE, LIVING WITH him at his parents' house and formally protected by documents that appeared to be authentic. All that did nothing to diminish Andrzej's anxiety about Karolina. Each morning, when he left for his work at the hospital, he thought of the danger that could come from the informers. All the time, his thoughts were with her. At the same time, he had to concentrate on the fate of his patients.

The situation at the hospital got worse daily. The food rations became smaller and smaller. There was no medication available to treat the patients, and the number of doctors and nursing staff was greatly diminished.

It was worse on the 'Jewish' wards, where Andrzej's former superior, the associate professor, was working. Andrzej visited him on this ward each and every day to relieve his isolation. During one of those visits, the associate professor told him that he intended to leave Lwów very soon, in an 'illegal' way. There was an opinion among the Jewish people at that time that one of the best solutions was to have the so-called A.P. (Aryan papers), i.e., certificates indicating that they had been baptized very soon after their birth, and to live as a non-Jew in a big city, such as Warsaw. The associate professor intended to go to Warsaw, where nobody knew him. He could not function as a non-Jew in Lwów because many people knew him. He asked Andrzej to take his books and manuscripts and keep them in his apartment. He did not yet know the exact date of his departure to Warsaw; all depended on the 'agents' organizing such transport from Lwów. If, one day, he did not arrive at his ward, it would mean that he escaped happily.

Such a day arrived before the ghetto was organized in Lwów. Andrzej and Filomena were relieved a little, because, in their opinion, the ghetto in Lwów carried the promise of death.

One week after the associate professor's departure, Filomena arrived at Andrzej's ward in tears: 'They have denounced him in Warsaw. Somebody has informed the Gestapo that he is a Jew without an armband. The Gestapo checked, and shot him in Warsaw.'

A couple of days later, more tragic news shocked Andrzej to the marrow of his bones. One of his close friends, a brilliant student and scientist working in biochemical research, was informed on and shot in the streets of Lwów. His wife, a beautiful, charming, and very talented younger colleague, was not Jewish. She was, at the time of his tragic death, organizing a place to hide him because she was afraid that the Gestapo might trace him to their apartment. He left their apartment in her absence, without her knowledge, leaving only a short note: 'Have to see my parents for a while and did not want to increase your anxiety. Don't worry, will be back soon.'

Since the day her husband was murdered on the way to his parents', she was cut off from life. She could not sleep; she could not eat; she was unable to do anything, unable to continue her life. Father Alojzy, who knew both of them, tried everything to alleviate her pain – to no avail. The poor woman died about ten months after her beloved husband's tragic death.

There seemed to be no end of tragic news. The associate professor of biochemistry, an eminent scientist, who was a Polish Jew, was in such a state of anxiety and tension that, afraid of being followed in the street by informers, he swallowed a cyanide tablet and died instantly in the street.

Amid such tragic news, Andrzej and Karolina became increasingly anxious. Each minute of Andrzej's journey home from work was full of fear for Karolina. When she was there, at the door, he had a feeling that she has been spared imminent death. He would hug her and cover her with kisses, thanking God that she was there, alive.

If all this was not enough, the noose around their necks began to tighten. One day, Karolina, accompanied by Estelle, met an older woman from the neighbourhood. She stopped to chat for a while with Estelle, who introduced Karolina to her as her daughter-in-law, and said: 'Nice meeting you. Funnily enough, you resemble very much a girl that I knew before the war. But she was Jewish. I don't think that you are Jewish.. You don't carry the armband with the star of David.'

Karolina was clever enough just to smile and not to engage in the conversation. Estelle reacted immediately in a kind, but very determined way: 'I am sorry, but you are wrong. Karolina is my daughter-in-law, and her parents have been our friends for twenty-five years. All the family is deeply Catholic, and Karolina is the most devout person in our two families.'

Estelle was a very shy person, but when it came to a fight she was extremely courageous. She fought for her and Andrzej's survival during the seven years when Ludwik had been a prisoner of war in Siberia. The old woman apologized for her mistake.

It was very important, from now on, to change nothing in Karolina's behaviour in order not to raise any suspicion. She went out with Estelle or Ludwik, or with both, shopping and chatting with the neighbours, making friends with them – all this to kill any gossip. They knew how dangerous gossip could be. The nights and days were nevertheless full of terrible fear and anxious tension. Some nights they could not sleep at all.

It was not easy, however, to kill the gossip. One week later, another neighbour, also an older lady, asked Estelle in a confidential tone if Karolina was of Jewish origin. She told her also that some neighbours were discussing this problem. The neighbours were not informers, and were friendly, but gossip itself could be dangerous as it could reach the ears of an informer. Slowly the gossip died down, and Karolina's behaviour was a convincing confirmation that she could not be Jewish.

However, for the always watchful Ludwik, who had excellent foresight and an instinctive understanding of how to avoid danger, it was a signal that it was impossible to survive in Lwów. They started to discuss where and how to move. Their decision was accelerated by the fact that Andrzej was informed by the director of the hospital that he would be dismissed at the end of the year: 'The number of patients has so much diminished that we have to dismiss many doctors and also cut down our nursing staff' was the announcement made at a meeting. The director, an Ukrainian doctor, appreciated very much Andrzej's dedication to his work and to sweeten the dismissal told him: 'I will make you a small Christmas present. You will work only until Christmas but I will pay you until the end of the month.' Without Andrzej's salary, their financial situation became too hard. It had been difficult enough to survive on Andrzej's earnings.

The general situation in Lwów became very dangerous. With the registration of Jews and the organization of the ghetto, the number of informers increased. They were literally hunting for Jews who did not register or who were not wearing armbands. Chances of Karolina's survival would be much better in a place where nobody knew her. Andrzej could practise as a family doctor and provide a better financial situation for the family.

The crucial question was: where to go – a small town or a village? The question was dealt with by Ludwik in his very straight and ingenious way: 'Why should we go to an unknown place with no friendly connections? Let us think rather of the region where I was born, where everybody for generations has known my name, where my sister lives.' His sister, whose name happened to be Karolina, was a widow with five sons and two daughters, all of them living not far from one another and not far from Ludwik's birthplace. Some of her children were already married; the youngest son was ten years younger than Andrzej. Before the Second World War, Ludwik had always had excellent relations with his peasant family. He was proud of his peasant roots, and his family was extremely proud of him. He was very respected and loved by all of them. He was a college professor and he was 'one of them.'

Before the war, when Andrzej was still a child, Ludwik and Estelle took him for short visits to Ludwik's family village in the Carpathian mountains, about 100 kilometres from the village where Juliusz had moved with his family. It was also hidden in the mountains, remote from the big centres. The nearest town was Sanok, at a distance of about 25 kilometres. Ludwik's sister, Karolina, owned a small farm with a couple of cows and one horse.

Encouraged by Ludwik, Andrzej wrote a letter to his aunt Karolina – called 'Karolcia', by her family and friends – asking if there was a possibility that he could settle down in the village as a family doctor and how he would be accepted by the population of the village and its neighbourhood. Would it be possible also to move his parents after a while? Everybody was starving in Lwów, and many of his colleagues were considering a move to the countryside. He mentioned also that his wife was a medical student who was not able to finish her studies because of the war. If the answer was positive, he would come for a couple of days immediately after Christmas to arrange the details and formalities with the district doctor.

The letter was mailed at the end of November 1941, and the answer arrived in two weeks. Everything sounded very encouraging. The peasants in the region badly needed a family doctor because a couple of weeks previously their family doctor had moved to a town where it was more comfortable for him to live. The population of Karolcia's village was very poor. The peasants were obliged to furnish to the Germans 'contingents,' a specified quantity of grain and meat. The peasants had no money, but a doctor could live relatively well, being paid for his services with food. They would pay him in butter, sour cream, eggs, chicken, and sometimes with clandestinely prepared veal. Karolcia's letter was very kind and full of joy that her beloved brother Ludwik, of whom all the family was so proud, was going to join them, with his family. Karolcia assured him in her answer that, at the beginning, she would help them with food. She had already some ideas about where to find a house suitable for the office and residence of a doctor. Ludwik, who had master-minded the idea, was very happy with her answer.

On 23 December 1941 Andrzej's work in the hospital ended. There was no medication to treat the patients, and it was obvious that the Nazis had decided to exterminate the patients by starvation. The death rate among the patients was increasing from day to day, and nobody could change this situation.

With no work to do, Andrzej decided to go immediately after Christmas to Karolcia's village.

Christmas 1941 was the first one that Andrzej and Karolina spent together. Although it was a very modest Christmas from the culinary point of view, it was very rich emotionally. Andrzej could spend three days with Karolina and his parents at home in relative safety.

The political news was very encouraging. After the tragedy of Pearl Harbor, the United States and the Commonwealth of Britain declared war on Japan. Within a few days, Hitler, together with Mussolini, had declared war on the United States. The population of the European states, occupied by German and Italian troops, was again full of hope that the war would end very soon with the defeat of Hitler and Mussolini. The bitter Russian winter was taking its toll on the German army. 'The General Cold,' called by the Russian 'Generał Moroz,' once more since Napoleon's defeat was one of the principal factors in stopping the march of the German army towards the east.

The German offensive stopped not very far from Moscow, and the Soviet army started a counter-offensive.

Ludwik and his family at last were looking to the future in a more optimistic way. They believed that this was a turning-point in the war, and that a new, happier chapter of their life was beginning. There was also encouraging news from Juliusz, brought to them by his good friend, Stanisław.

After three days of relative peace and of new hope in their hearts, Andrzej had to leave for the village of his aunt. He has planned also to visit, on his way, the village of Juliusz. With practically no existing time-table of the departure and connections of the trains, his absence might last six to seven days. It was the first time he and Karolina would be separated for such a long time. Karolina knew that travelling was not without danger, even for people who were not suspected of being Jewish. It was also dangerous to go by foot the long way from the railway station to Juliusz's village.

The visit to Orelec was planned to last two days, and the stay in the village where they had intended to settle down would also last two days. In addition to renting a house, Andrzej had to find a room and kitchen to rent for his parents. He had also to make an official visit to the district doctor to get permission to practise in the village, and was taking with him all his professional credentials.

Karolina's birthday was on 31 December. Knowing that, at that time, he would be absent, he gave her a small Christmas gift as a token of his love and devotion. 'I will all the time think of you, my dearest wife, and I am sure that everything will work out in a very positive way. I will see you again in the first days of the coming year, 1942. Happy Birthday and Happy New Year, my darling dear.' He tried to show how optimistic he was, but his voice was full of tears. 'Let us hope that the New Year will be really a happy one for you and me, and for your and my family.'

IX

AFTER THOSE OPTIMISTIC DAYS, ANDRZEJ LEFT VERY EARLY in the morning to get as early as possible to the railway station. The official time-table indicated that to get to Uherce, which was the nearest railway station to Orelec, he had to change trains twice after leaving Lwów. Boarding the train in Lwów about 6:00 a.m., Andrzej expected to arrive to Uherce at 4:00 p.m.

The trains from Lwów and the connecting trains were so over-crowded that Andrzej had to stay in the corridor. The trains were late because they had to give way to military transports.

Andrzej arrived in Uherce at midnight. The station was small and empty, and there were no houses nearby, only a dark forest. It was scary to walk at night, but from Juliusz's letters he knew in what direction he should travel. After about twenty minutes of walking, he saw the small thatched huts of a nearby village. Orelec was still a distance of 10 kilometres away. He was so tired that he decided to stop and take a night's rest in one of the huts. He knocked at the door of the first hut. Nobody answered. It was late and, during the war, nobody would open the door to an unknown person at night. The people reasoned that if it was the Gestapo or SS, a knock at the door at such a time would signal that they were coming to kill you, whether or not you opened the door. Ordinary bandits would leave and try their luck somewhere else.

Seeing a flickering light in another hut, Andrzej tried his luck again, and knocked at the window, so that he could be seen. They were not sleeping because one of the children was very sick. A middle-aged man opened the door. Andrzej asked him for per-mission to enter and lay down on one of the benches in the kitchen and rest until dawn. The peasant looked at him with suspicion, but no fear. When Andrzej told him that he was a physician, visiting one of his friends in the region, that the train was late, and that he was extremely tired after standing for the fifteen hours of his journey, he let him in. Andrzej was so grateful that he promised to examine his child in the morning, before taking his leave. When Andrzej heard the peasant's story, he had the impression that he visited hell on the earth.

The peasant was extremely poor. His hut consisted of one kitchen. On one bed were sleeping three children, on another his wife with a fifteen-year-old daughter. The daughter was sick, extremely emaciated, and coughing all the time. The peasant showed him a bench on which he could sleep. Andrzej was so tired that, as soon as he lay down, he fell asleep. This sleep did not last long. At once he woke up and saw that the candle was still burning, and the girl still coughing. The mother was now standing close to the bed and listening to what her daughter was trying to say. The peasant was sitting at the table with his head down, snoring heavily.

Andrzej approached the bed and told them that he was a medical doctor and could examine her. After a short examination, it was clear to him that the girl has serious damage to her lungs and was suffering from advanced tuberculosis. She had a high fever. The girl asked him if he could help her, she wanted so much to live and was afraid to die, like her older sister who had died two years earlier and who had also been weak and wracked with coughing. Her illness had lasted several months, and they had no money to pay a physician. The poor girl clung to Andrzej as if he were her last straw of hope.

The father woke up, and Andrzej took him outside so as not to speak in the presence of the girl. In the cold winter dawn, Andrzej told the father that his daughter was very sick and that he diagnosed tuberculosis. She should be taken to a hospital as soon as possible. The father answered that he had no money for the hospital and that his older daughter had died of the same disease two years ago.

Then he began a monologue: 'We, the people, we cannot fight with destiny. All is in God's hands.' The parson came from time to time to visit his family, and the parson told him that it was impossible to fight God's will. If somebody has a miserable life here on earth, he certainly would be rewarded in heaven. It was better to have hell for a lifetime on the earth because then it would be possible to enjoy eternal happiness in heaven, close to God. In such a way, this peasant understood the teaching of the church, and he accepted God's will. He, therefore, was not at all attached to the life on earth, and he would like as soon as possible to move with his family to heaven. Whether the village belonged to Austria, to Poland, to the Soviet Union, or to Hitler, his fate was the same. He heard that the Germans were killing many people. That did not scare him, because it brought him closer to heaven. Andrzej asked him if anyone had tried to help him. He looked at Andrzej with astonishment and said: 'Never.' After a short silence, he looked at Andrzej for a long while and finally said, with tears in his eyes, 'Anyway, thank you, doctor, and God bless you.'

It was time for Andrzej to go. The sun was already above the horizon. It was a beautiful, sunny, and cold winter day.

Andrzej walked two hours to reach Orelec. When he arrived at the school in the village, it was already nine o'clock. The teacher was a nice, pretty Polish girl with a pleasant attitude towards people. She told him that Juliusz and his family were very well accepted by the peasants, Ukrainians and Poles. Andrzej identified himself as a former employee of Juliusz from Cracow. She knew from Juliusz that such an employee would visit him very soon, and she showed Andrzej how to get to the house.

After a ten-minute walk, Andrzej was received with great joy by Juliusz, Dorota, and Zosia. Juliusz was in a very good mood. The situation on the military front gave him a new hope. He was sure that the great military power of the United States would very soon break Hitler's stranglehold and end the war.

'I am very satisfied with my decision to come here,' he told Andrzej. 'I live much better here than in Lwów. The village is far away from the Germans. You do not see them here; you do not feel their presence. The people are very friendly and helpful. We don't feel isolated or rejected. There is no problem buying food. They bring us home-made bread and when they clandestinely kill a milk-fed calf they never forget to bring us some veal. I can go wherever I wish, and I can play the violin. They often visit us to listen to my violin, and we have very friendly and refreshing conversations with them. There is only one thing: this armband' – he showed his arm with the blue star of David on a white armband' – that reminds me all the time of Hitler.'

For the first time since the German occupation, Andrzej saw Juliusz relaxed. His blue eyes were less sad, and his optimism had now a realistic foundation. He had not enough words of praise for the young Polish teacher who was very helpful to them. He liked very much the long discussions with her about the future of Poland.

He was helping in the household, making small repairs, trying to improve the very modest interior with his drawings. He was splitting wood and taking long walks in this very nice village at the foot of the Carpathian mountains.

Dorota and Zosia were also in a much better shape. Dorota had no problems getting bread, butter, eggs, and poultry. Zosia was helping her. They had befriended the young Polish teacher, who was lending them books.

All the family was extremely happy with Andrzej's visit. They talked all the day, eager to have news from Lwów, from Karolina and from his parents. They liked very much the project of Andrzej and Karolina moving to the small village where Ludwik's family lived and his working there as family physician.

Juliusz asked many questions about Karolina. He wanted to know everything: how she was spending the days, was she indeed helping them in the household, did she speak often about him, Dorota, and Zosia. He was full of admiration and respect for the courage of Andrzej's parents and for their attitude towards Karolina. Juliusz had not forgotten the proposal of Bishop Baziak and, although he was sure that his solution was better, he told Andrzej that he would never forget the generosity of the bishop and the help given to Karolina with her baptism and wedding. He asked also after Dorota's uncle, aunt, and their son. The news was sad, because the health of the uncle was still deteriorating. They had difficulties obtaining food, and their son, the young psychiatrist, had been dismissed from the hospital, but was still giving medical treatment to many needy people, and declining remuneration. The news from Juliusz's friend, Stanisław, was encouraging, although Andrzej was concerned that Stanisław was taking risks, going out after curfew, talking loud in the streets about the approaching defeat of Hitler, and not taking seriously the danger of informers. He was always like that, Juliusz told Andrzej with a smile. During the Soviet occupation, they were afraid to talk with him on the streets because he was shouting that Stalin is Evil, without fear that the NKVD might hear him.

The young teacher arrived in the evening. She was open-minded, interested in political and social problems. She hated the Nazis and was convinced that they would lose the war, but was realistic enough to see that victory might not come soon. She was afraid that the Nazis, feeling that their position was threatened, might take revenge on the occupied population. If the war lasted a long time, they might have time to organize in detail their cruel machine of terror. Her judgments had a moderating effect on Juliusz's optimism.

Andrzej spent the night at Juliusz's house. He left the next day to resume his journey to Karolcia's village. Juliusz had hired for Andrzej a country wagon so that he could reach the railway station in more comfort. It took Andrzej about four hours to reach Sanok because he had to change trains. In Sanok, he went to Albina, the daughter of the shoemaker who had given Ludwik a room during his years in the gymnasium. Władek, one of Karolcia's sons was waiting with a country wagon to take Andrzej to Karolcia's village.

It was a lucky trip. Everything seemed so easy. After three hours, they arrived at Karolcia's home. She greeted Andrzej with great joy. She had known him since his childhood from the short visits he had made during vacations. Now he was in her arms, the son of her beloved brother. And this son was a doctor and was going to settle in their 'nest.' Karolcia was a simple peasant without any education, but had an inborn intelligence and capabilities and a tremendous wit and sense of humour. Like Ludwik, she was very well organized, very decent, and helpful. She had lost her husband just before the war. He had cancer and was treated in Lwów. As peasant families had no health insurance in Poland before the war, Ludwik had paid all the expenses for the hospital treatment of Karolcia's husband.

After her husband's death, Karolcia became the head of the family. And what a family it was: five sons and two daughters, six of them waiting in her house for Andrzej to greet him; the seventh, Władek, bringing him in the country wagon. One of the daughters was married to a driller, working in the neighbouring oil field; the other was an unmarried country teacher. Of the five sons, only one had a profession; he was a reputable saddler, very much in demand, for the quality of his work. The other four were working on their small farm under the direction of Cesiek, the oldest. All of them wanted to help in finding the best conditions of life for Andrzej, his wife, and his parents.

At the beginning, they would help him and his wife with food; later, Andrzej would have food from patients but hardly any money, because the peasants had no money to pay for medical services.

Andrzej told them that he had married Karolina shortly before the war in a church in Lwów, that she had finished four years of medical studies, and that her parents were living in Cracow. He said that Karolina had had to interrupt her studies because of the outbreak of war. He did not mention a word about her origins because she had to come to the village without her real past. When he described her as a nice and likeable person, Karolcia cut in, saying: 'Of course, she is nice, because you love her. She is your wife; she is a member of our family. You don't know, perhaps, Andrzej, that, for a Polish peasant, family is a sanctity. We quarrel sometimes, but we never forget what family means. Karolina is an educated person, but I will teach her how to make bread in a kitchen oven and how to cook. Besides, she is my namesake, and there will now be two Karolinas in our family.'

Karolcia was, above all, delighted with the idea that her beloved brother would come to live in her village during the war. She had already found a house suitable for Andrzej and Karolina's residence and office, and close to it, in a very clean neighbourhood, a room large enough for Andrzej's parents, where they could also use the kitchen. She was looking forward very much to the arrival of Ludwik and Estelle. She had not seen them or heard of them since the beginning of the war in 1939, because they were separated by the frontier on the river San. The village was on its left western bank, belonging to the part of Poland occupied by Germany, whereas Lwów was occupied by the Soviet Union.

Andrzej spent three nights in the village. On Karolcia's advice, he rented the house she had chosen for his residence and office, and reserved a very nice room in one of the neighbouring houses for his parents. He presented himself to the most important persons in the village: the parson, the head of the village, the head of the hamlet, and four teachers.

Władek drove him to the office of the district physician, to whom Andrzej presented his professional credentials. He was a very nice, older Polish physician, who was delighted to see a new physician arriving to replace the one who had left. The district physician wrote Andrzej an official permit to practise as a family physician in the village. He advised Andrzej whom to contact in Lwów to obtain a permit to move from Lwów to the village. The drive to the office of the district physician took Władek two hours, but, as it was not far from Sanok, afterwards he drove Andrzej directly to the railway station. Andrzej was in a great hurry, because he was anxious about Karolina. It was already six days since he had left her in Lwów.

X

ANDRZEJ ARRIVED IN LWÓW IN AN OPTIMISTIC MOOD. Karolina and his parents were very happy with the news he was bringing. Karolina was especially happy with the news from her parents and Zosia. Like Andrzej, she was now full of hope that the new surroundings, where nobody knew her, would be much safer. However, when they started to plan in detail their move, they realized what perils they might face.

They had to choose between a train or a private truck. Neither method of travelling was safe. Andrzej had had a recent experience of how dangerous travelling by train could be. He had witnessed the killing of a Jew who was travelling without an armband and who was denounced by an informer on the train. Travelling by private truck seemed still more dangerous, because such trucks were operated by agents, usually in contact with the police and frequently attracting the attention of the Gestapo.

After a very detailed analysis, they decided that the least danger-ous means would be to travel by train at night, diminishing in such a way the possibility of being recognized by an informer.

Before choosing an exact date of departure, Andrzej had to attend to certain formalities imposed by the German occupation. On the basis of the permit from the district physician to practise in the village, he had to apply in Lwów for permission to move to the village from Lwów, where he was registered. The application had to be accompanied by various professional and personal documents. Among them, he had to present his own and his wife's certificates of birth and baptism, and their wedding certificate. This was the first time these certificates had to be presented to the German authorities. All this caused sleepless nights and discussions about whether or not to move. During the deliberations, they learned that the certificates had to be presented anyway, because the new laws on permits to practise medicine required that each physician present such certificates. Andrzej had made copies of the documents and presented them in the 'Ärztekammer' in Lwów. To obtain the permission to move, he had to wait about four to six weeks, because it was necessary to contact the general 'Ärztekammer' for the occupied territories, which was in Cracow. This information only increased their anxiety.

To perfect his preparation for the duties of a country doctor, especially in obstetrics, Andrzej worked, during the waiting period, as a volunteer in the maternity ward of the hospital in Lwów.

The financial situation in Lwów was extremely difficult. The parents had to sell part of their furniture. Karolina sold, through the intermediary of Stanisław, a precious painting given to her by Juliusz as a wedding present. Stanisław was holding some gold coins given to him on deposit by Juliusz immediately after the Nazi occupation of Lwów; it was forbidden for Jews to hold gold. From time to time, in a way arranged by Stanisław, he sold one or two coins and sent money to Juliusz, using clandestine, confidential channels. The last 'channel' by which Stanisław sent money to Juliusz was Andrzej on his way to Karolcia's village.

This winter was extremely harsh. People were hungry and freezing. It was so cold in the apartment of Andrzej's parents that the bottle of water left in the living room cracked when ice formed in it. Andrzej's parents were worried about the health of the young couple; the young couple was worried about the health of the parents.

During warmer days, Ludwik and Karolina were, like many other people, collecting the fallen branches of trees to add more heat in the kitchen, which became the only place they could sit down and relax without freezing. Bread often was not available. Estelle was now buying grain and grinding it in the coffee mill to make hot patties. They were tasty, with a paste made of beans and onions. Potatoes from the shop were often frozen, and only the centre was usable. They were looking forward very much to their move from this city to the countryside.

At the end of January 1941, letters arriving from Juliusz and Dorota were less and less optimistic. They did not write about actual events but the situation was clearly becoming worse. Andrzej decided to take a couple of days' leave from the obstetric ward and visit Juliusz again at the beginning of February. He was given some money for Juliusz from Stanisław, and had obtained from him permission to use his address to receive letters from Juliusz, just in case Dorota's uncle and his family were transported to the ghetto in Lwów.

This time the trains were running much more efficiently, and Andrzej arrived at Orelec in the early afternoon. Seeing the face of Juliusz, he understood at once that something grave must have happened. Juliusz told him that, during January, the Polish police, called at that time, 'navy police,' after the colour of their uniforms, had established a garrison in the next village. Since then, they visited three times the Jewish families in the village, among them also the house where Juliusz and his family were living. The 'navy' police told them that the German police, located now in a small town a distance of 15 kilometres away, wanted to have regular information about Jewish families in the villages. They were preparing special orders for this population. They warned Juliusz that, from now on, he would not be allowed to walk beyond a radius of 500 metres from the limits of the village. They ordered him to stop playing the violin, to deposit it in their garrison, and to stop immediately all social contact with the non-Jewish population. At the same time, the Polish and Ukrainian population was ordered by the police to stop all contact with the Jewish families. 'I do not blame the population. The Germans want to isolate us completely from the peasants,' said Juliusz.

Juliusz changed very much during the last month. His face was thin, his smile practically disappeared. He looked much, much older. Sometimes he had a feeling of being in a trap. Gone were the optimistic predictions. He was now deep in philosophical, moral issues. The fight between Good and Evil was more important to him than the war between the Axis and the Allies.

The Soviets had enormous reserves, but the turning-point was still far off, and the war in the Pacific, in its first phase, was proving disastrous for the United States. This was the reality. But entering into the world of mystics, Juliusz could find hope that the balance between Good and Evil would be restored in a miraculous way. Such was his internal mechanism of defence against reality.

When Dorota and Zosia went out for a while, he told Andrzej that he saw now that his decision to decline the offer of the bishop was wrong. He realized with horror that it was too late to return. Such thoughts were like thorns in his soul; he could not remove them. The fate of Dorota and Zosia was his responsibility. There were times when he believed that they would survive in this remote village. Some days were better, some worse, some terrible. On the terrible ones he saw no future for anybody. The issue of responsibility for the lives of Dorota and Zosia plagued him. He now held his head down, to hide from Andrzej the tears in his eyes.

Andrzej felt the tragedy of the situation. He knew also that there was no way for them to get out of this village, being already registered by the police and watched day and night. For the first time in his life, he did not tell Juliusz the truth. It would be too cruel and quite useless. He wanted only to comfort him, to diminish his anxiety, his terrible fear. What he was telling him was like a shot of morphine to a terminal patient.

'Juliusz,' he said, 'I understand that the present situation is worse than it was a month ago. Nevertheless, this remote village is much better than Lwów, where the Germans are organizing the ghetto. They are much more cruel in the cities. Let us hope that the Germans will have not enough time to further persecute the Jews in remote villages. They have already, and will have, more and more troubles on their fronts.' He was talking to him in a reassuring way, giving examples of how Jews in the villages were in general more secure than those in big cities. For instance, in the village where he intended to move, they were indeed isolated socially from the population, but were able to move freely within the village. And it was already the third year of occupation. There was never talk of organizing a ghetto.

With all his efforts, Andrzej was not convinced that Juliusz was taking his words seriously. He was probably aware that Andrzej was making an effort to calm him down. At the same time, Andrzej felt that, even now, Juliusz was hoping against hope.

At the end, Juliusz said: 'Perhaps I worry too much; perhaps the situation on the fronts will slow down the operations of the Gestapo in the remote villages. Perhaps the attitudes of the local population will be better than in big cities. Perhaps God has more space in their hearts and is deeper implanted. But, in all my deliberations, there is always 'perhaps.' All is very uncertain, and I feel very insecure. Please, do not tell Karolina that I am a little down now. Do not tell her in detail about the changes of our life here. I do not want to increase her sadness. You both have enough troubles now. I know how dangerous it is for both of you to make your way to your village. Kiss her for me many times, and tell her that she is, as always, the apple of my eye. Convey to your parents all my admiration for their courage and love.'

Dorota and Zosia returned after a while, bringing food for the evening meal. In the late evening, Andrzej again saw the young teacher, who, under the cover of night, was clandestinely visiting them. Juliusz asked her to hire a country wagon for next morning to drive Andrzej to the railway station. On the advice of the teacher, the country wagon had to be boarded by Andrzej in front of the school and not outside Juliusz's house, for safety reasons. She also brought some food for the family because the shopping by Dorota and Zosia in the village had been very meagre.

Andrzej stayed at night in great secrecy in Juliusz's house. They spoke long into the night. They were interested in the moving of Andrzej and his family to the village. The news from Stanisław was encouraging, and Andrzej, this time, abstained from any criticism of Stanisław's optimism. The news from Dorota's uncle and his family was sad, as always.

Early in the morning, Andrzej left Juliusz's house and went to the school. The teacher was already in the classroom, although it was empty. She was reading and preparing some notes. She stood up and asked Andrzej to sit down with her for a while on the bench for a short talk. 'I wanted to tell you something that I would not say in the presence of Juliusz and his family. You know probably already from Juliusz that the situation in the village is tense. We are afraid that the Jewish population will not only be isolated in the ghettos and persecuted, but that they might be exterminated, killed by Nazi murderers in the forests. It has happened already in some regions of Poland. The Polish resistance is too weak to save thousands of Jews. The number of arms in the resistance forces is unbelievably small, and all are reserved for military actions, like blowing up military trains. The situation of Juliusz and his family hurts me very much personally. They are my dear friends. I will do my best to help them.

'When you come again to this village, do not go directly to Juliusz. The situation might sometimes be dangerous, with the unexpected visits of the police. Always come here first, to the school. I am all the week, with the exception of Saturday afternoons and Sundays, sitting after class hours in a small room adjacent to the class. The best time is late afternoon. I will always accompany you on your way to Juliusz's house, if the situation is safe enough. You can rely on me. I am a Polish girl who hates the Nazis. I tried to fight them and I am ready to perish in this fight.' She looked at Andrzej and added after a while: 'My father was in the Polish army and was killed on the second day of the German invasion in 1939. You can trust me.'

She looked through the window: 'The country wagon to the station is waiting for you. And I am waiting for the Ukrainian and

Polish children that I am going to teach. The Germans want to have slaves who just know how to write and read. My pupils will learn how to write and read, but they will never be German slaves.'

She accompanied Andrzej to his country wagon and stayed with him until his departure.

XI

IT WAS IMPOSSIBLE TO CONCEAL THE NEWS ABOUT JULIUSZ from Karolina. Andrzej and Karolina were like one person, together with all their thoughts, all their fears, and all their love. He had to tell her all the truth for her own safety. They had to move very soon, and she had to know what might happen in their village. It was not the right time to distort the terrible reality, even to spare pain. Their fight would be real and they had to know what they were up against.

He did not tell her of Juliusz's feelings about declining the bishop's proposal. It would be too cruel, especially because Karolina was sure that this problem would emerge as a most painful one for Juliusz. She knew that sooner or later Juliusz would feel his mistake and his responsibility for its consequences, for the fate, or even for the life, of Dorota and Zosia. She feared that her parents and Zosia might be transferred to a local ghetto and might not survive the suffering.

She told Andrzej one day: 'My love, this is the worst decision in my parents' life. They were in an exceptional situation for Jewish people. They could be relatively safe and survive this war. Some decisions are irreversible; they can cost your life.' She looked at Andrzej for a long while and said: 'Andrzej, you also made an important decision and you have taken on your shoulders a burden invented by Hitler for Jews only. Therefore my situation is different from that of other Jewish Poles. I was thinking about all that, and I know now something that, at the beginning, was not well understood by me: Love is not a decision, love is not in our brain, it is in our heart. And I admire you and I always will admire you, not only for your decision to marry me immediately after the Nazi occupation, not only because you have given me an exceptional safety. No,

Andrzej, I admire you not for your decision, but for your love for me, and I know well that my love for you is equal. And I admire your parents because they knew that true love is something you cannot change, you cannot abandon.

'We are all now in our "voyage au bout de la nuit." We do not know today if we will see the dawn tomorrow. I will always know why I have lived on this earth. I am sure that one day we will find a better place where nobody will be able to separate us. Therefore I am not crying, I am not afraid. God rewarded me on this earth with the highest prize. He has given me the opportunity to know what true love is.'

She approached Andrzej, hugged him in her arms and kissed him. In this moment her eyes were no longer dry. The tension was too great. She looked at him through her tears. 'Our situation is such as it is, because we wanted to go together through the times of contempt and survive together or perish together. But my unhappy father is in an irreversible situation that he could have avoided,' she said. After a while she added 'My love, trust me, I will be brave. We will move to the village and I will be a good companion.'

One evening, at the end of February 1942, they went to Karolina's uncle, the ophthalmologist, his wife, and their son, the psychiatrist. They had to make this visit in the evening because, during the day, the German police frequently raided the apartments occupied by Jewish families. The police knew the exact addresses of such families and were preparing to move them to the ghetto. The health of the old uncle was failing more and more. He was now on very high dosages of morphine. They knew that their situation was hopeless, because the living conditions in the ghetto were much, much worse than those in which they were living now. Andrzej promised, that after his departure with Karolina, his parents would visit them as often as possible. Such visits were dangerous, but he knew that neither of his parents would leave these people without outside contact. This visit was so heart-breaking that, returning home, they could not even talk about it.

They went to see Father Alojzy before their departure. He was in a very depressed state, having been seriously affected by stories of Nazi atrocities. They discussed with him many problems, and they saw how open-minded this priest was. They discussed with him the problem of informers, those who betrayed because of their profound anti-Semitism. Father Alojzy blamed that situation not only on the

Germans. 'We have to admit,' he said, 'that we have bred our own kind of anti-Semitism in Poland a long time before the war. It was advocated by our own pre-war government – taught by some teachers in the schools and universities, by some physicians in the hospitals, by some lawyers in the courts, by some industrialists in factories, merchants in shops, and, we have to confess, by some of our priests in offering public or private advice, even in the church. This was not what Jesus taught us to do. We need a better society after the war. We have to recognize what mistakes we made and never repeat them again. Our true Polish patriotism has nothing in common with hatred of other nations. Our Catholic religion has nothing to do with the hatred of other religions. The free will given by God means a good will, full of love for other human beings, whatever their religion, whatever their race, colour of skin or social class. Our God does not want false patriots whose principal program is to hate people of other religions or other nations. For the actions of some informers, we have to take partial responsibility. It is our sin that we have not fought hard enough against the hatred in human hearts.' He appeared to them to be inspired by God. He blessed them and promised to be in contact: 'Do not forget to notify me if you feel in danger. Remember that I am praying for you and I will act for you in any capacity that could be helpful.'

Three days before their departure, they saw for the last time Sister Filomena. She had been visiting them regularly, at least weekly since their wedding. When she took Karolina on short walks in the street she always wore her nun's habit. She frequently brought gifts from her convent, such as vegetables or fruit. She could not forget that the Nazis had shot her associate professor, whom she admired. She promised to keep in contact with Andrzej and Karolina by mail and to visit them in the village.

The last days before departure, they were very busy packing their clothes, bedding, some kitchenware, and medical instruments. They filled two big trunks, and Ludwik advised them to register all this luggage directly to Sanok. The night train leaving Lwów at 9:00 p.m. was not direct to Sanok. They had to change trains three times to arrive in Sanok the next day at 7:00 a.m. The train changes were the main reason to register the luggage directly to Sanok.

On the morning of the day of departure, Andrzej, accompanied by Ludwik, went by cab to the station to register the two trunks directly to Sanok. They returned home with the copy of the registration ticket and with two passenger tickets bought in advance to avoid having to stand in line in the evening before departure.

In the evening, Andrzej and Karolina, accompanied by Andrzej's parents, arrived at 8:00 p.m. to the railway station. Karolina was carrying only a handbag, Andrzej a briefcase. They did not know how long they might travel, and therefore they wanted to be free of hand luggage.

In the lobby of the station, they kissed Andrzej's parents and took their leave as fast as possible. They headed towards a long tunnel leading to the platform of their train. The entrance to the tunnel was guarded by Polish and German police and was visible from the lobby. Andrzej's parents waited in the lobby to see them off. Approaching the entrance, Andrzej and Karolina turned to the parents and waved goodbye to them. They were extremely fearful, but had to behave normally and naturally, appearing to be a couple of young people taking leave of their parents. Only a few passengers were in line ahead of them, and, in a couple of minutes, Andrzej approached a Polish policeman standing at the entrance. As instructed by the 'Ärztekammer,' he showed him the official permit for moving and the two tickets. The permit was written in German. The policeman looked at the permit and at the tickets, and asked Andrzej where Sanok was. Andrzej briefly explained to him the location of Sanok. Close to the policeman was an SS officer. He was looking at Karolina, who stayed with Andrzej and tried to maintain a great calm. She was, with confidence, looking sometimes at Andrzej, sometimes at the Polish policeman. She felt that she was observed all the time by the German officer. Only Andrzej knew how full of fear she was, and his anxiety seemed to reach the highest point. At this moment, a Polish railway employee, who had seen Andrzej's name on the permit, showed the policeman a piece of paper.

Their hearts were beating faster and faster, and now they were sure that somebody had informed on them. Looking at this piece of paper, the Polish policeman asked Andrzej if he had, on this day, registered two trunks directly from Lwów to Sanok. Andrzej confirmed this, and added that the police had checked the trunks in his presence. 'We know that, and we wanted only to see if the owner of the luggage is really moving to Sanok,' he said, and passed the permit and the tickets to the German officer. The piece of paper was only the ticket of registration for the trunks. The officer stopped looking at Karolina and asked Andrzej if he spoke German. When Andrzej confirmed this, he asked why, being in a big city like Lwów, Andrzej was moving to a small village. Andrzej explained in his best German, very succinctly, that Lwów had many physicians, but the village where he had some family was short of physicians. The officer looked again at Karolina and said: 'You have a beautiful wife, doctor.' He handed over the permit and the tickets to Andrzej, and pointed to indicate that they had now to enter the tunnel.

Andrzej took Karolina's arm and, still half-conscious from fear, they slowly entered the dark tunnel. All along, they felt that they could be observed from behind and that some passengers were walking close to them. To instil some confidence in Karolina, Andrzej told her: 'The results of the observations of the officer were excellent. They are very important for "das Deutsche Reich."' She smiled.

The train was already on the platform. Without difficulty, they found two seats, close to each other. There was a two-hour delay in the train's schedule. All that time, it was dark and cold; nobody was talking. One hour into the journey, the SS and the Ukrainian police started to make their rounds. They were flooding with light the faces of the passengers, trying to find disguised Jews or wanted people from the Polish resistance. Young men were especially suspect and subject to personal inspection. Young girls were suspected to be liaison members of the resistance groups. In the compartment in which Andrzej and Karolina were travelling were old people only, mostly peasants of no interest to the policemen.

Karolina was following Andrzej's instructions; her head was resting on his arm, her eyes were closed, and she was pretending to sleep. Andrzej answered the Ukrainian policeman's questions in German. He showed him the permit to move with his wife from Lwów to the village where he had work as a physician. He informed him that his wife was sleeping because she was very tired; she was pregnant and did not feel well. If necessary, he could wake her up. Andrzej's arm was close to Karolina's heart, and he could feel its rapid beating. The German policeman looked at Karolina and did not answer; then he opened the door and left the compartment.

Until the first connection station, they did not speak at all. The only contact they had was between Andrzej's arm and the beating of Karolina's heart. He knew that, when the policemen departed, she was much more calm; her heart beat slowed, but she did not sleep, even for a minute.

At about 3:00 a.m., they changed trains and went once more through the German and Ukrainian checkpoints. The connecting train was late and moving very slowly. It stopped at each small station. It was already close to dawn when they arrived at a bigger connecting station. Here they had to change trains for the second time. They were already approaching the region at the foot of the mountains, and it grew colder and colder.

They waited for the next train for about three hours in the waiting room in a dark corner. It was not crowded, and the waiting passengers were mostly peasants. The Polish policemen were drowsing on a bench, not much interested in security in the territories occupied by the Nazis.

At about 8:00 a.m., the train arrived at the platform. It was relatively easy to find two places, and after one hour the train left the station. Each second of this journey by day was agonizing for them. Anybody looking at Karolina was, to Andrzej, a threat. He was afraid that her features might appear not very similar to those of the travelling peasant population and provoke some comment regarding her origin.

Feeling the danger, Karolina was making an all-out effort not to appear afraid. She was speaking with her neighbours, two older women who were mostly interested in the health problems of their grandchildren. Karolina told them that she was a registered nurse and gave them some professional advice, thus gaining their respect. From time to time, she spoke with Andrzej about unimportant matters. Sometimes she pretended to take a nap and closed her eyes. The police went through the car twice without approaching anybody. At noon they arrived at the last connecting station, where they had to take a train to Sanok, which was only 8 kilometres from the station.

Andrzej looked through the window and, seeing the name of the station, said with relief to Karolina: 'We are arriving at the last connecting station.' However, as soon as the train stopped, he whispered to her: 'Don't say a word. Just follow me. We will walk to Sanok.' He had seen through the window that the station was full of Gestapo. They were standing beside another train on the neighbouring track with long whips and police dogs. Before boarding this train, everyone had to undergo a check of personal documents and luggage, and sometimes a personal search outside in the bitter cold. Andrzej had seen through the window a group of about ten persons who were not allowed to board the train, being under surveillance by the state secret police. Some of these passengers were semi-dressed, in their underwear, and had been beaten bloody. Their personal things were thrown on the ground, and they were not being allowed to dress to protect themselves from the cold. They were under arrest and were being brutalized.

Andrzej and Karolina walked directly to the exit, where Andrzej handed over their tickets to the employees of the station. They found themselves outside, in front of the station. Although nobody was present, Andrzej knew from his former journeys that, in a while, the Gestapo would appear. During the so-called Actions, the area was always surrounded by Gestapo. They watched people rushing out of the station and running to the roads leading from the station, thinking that they could avoid the danger of being checked by the Gestapo. Therefore Andrzej and Karolina moved slowly forward. As they approached the roads from the station they saw two soldiers from the Gestapo who had guns trained on them. The Gestapo man shouted 'Halt,' and approached them. Andrzej had in his hands the permit from the Ärztekammer to leave Lwów. The two Gestapo men were very rude, not speaking but shouting at them all the time: 'Polish physician with a Polish wife, travelling to treat Polish peasants? Right? We are not interested in the health of such a subhuman, underdeveloped people as the Poles.' He vaguely threatened them with his gun, but did not really point it at them. They knew that they had to stay calm, and show no fear. After a while, the Gestapo man asked Andrzej when he had left Lwów. 'Yesterday,' Andrzej answered, 'and also yesterday I registered in Lwów our trunks,' and he showed him the certificate of registration for the luggage.

'You mean that yesterday you were in Lwów and not in this region?' was the next question. 'Yes, we left Lwów yesterday at 9:00 in the evening, and we arrived here now, because the train was late and we missed our connections.' The Gestapo man stopped his interrogation, walked around Andrzej, and suddenly asked him: 'Are you circumcised?' 'No, I am not,' Andrzej answered. 'Come with me,' he ordered, and Andrzej followed him behind a tree. After a while, while the other Gestapo man watched Karolina, they returned and, in a very rude way, the Gestapo man told Karolina: 'Your husband is not circumcised. Do you know at least this?' 'Yes,' Karolina answered with great calm. The policeman smiled in a leering way and said: 'I have such a disgust for both of you, I would like to kill you. But we have more important things to do and we have to save our ammunition for more important persons than you, Polish doctor and you Polish strumpet. Do not stay here, move. Continue your miserable lives.' he was shouting now. 'Weg verfluchte Polen.' Both policemen turned around and returned to watching the people approaching from the station.

Andrzej and Karolina began to walk on the highway leading towards Sanok, happy that this encounter with the Gestapo had ended in only verbal humiliation. Now they had to concentrate on their behaviour when walking through the villages by the highway. They were again under terrible stress because in wartime it was unusual to see people walking on the highways and not dressed like peasants but like the inhabitants of a city. They walked in a slow, dignified way. 'We should appear to be ordinary pedestrians going on a visit to our family, and not people rushing to hide somewhere,' said Andrzej.

After nearly two hours of walking, they arrived in Sanok and entered the house of Albina. When Ludwik had lived there many years ago, Albina had been a child. Now, she was already about forty years old. She had never married, and had dedicated her life to teaching. Before the war, she had been very active in scouting.

Andrzej had seen her not long ago on the way to Karolcia's village when he stopped in Sanok. She had told him at that time in great confidence that she was involved in the Polish resistance movement and was a liaison officer between this region and the headquarters of the part of Polish resistance called 'Peasant Battalions' (Bataliony Chłopskie). In this mountain region, this underground organization was very strong. She had asked Andrzej if it would be possible to occasionally have his medical assistance for the members of the resistance in this region. He had instantly agreed and felt happy that, in such a way, he would be able to contribute to this movement.

She had been waiting for him and Karolina since morning because the arrival of their train to Sanok had been scheduled for 7:00 a.m. She greeted them with great warmth. Władek, Andrzej's cousin, had also waited in vain to meet the train that had never arrived. He had decided to return to Albina's and, from time to time, to drive around the station, to see why the train was so late.

Albina immediately prepared a hot meal, and then they started to tell the story of what they had seen in the connecting railway station

8 kilometres from Sanok and why they had decided to walk instead of boarding the train, which was under strict watch of the Gestapo. Władek, since his first encounter with Karolina, became her admirer. He was very chivalrous towards her, especially now, when she looked so tired after travelling and enduring their run-in with the Gestapo.

It was incredibly relaxing to sit now in an atmosphere of warmth with this friendly family. Władek, who was one year older than Andrzej, had in the region the reputation of being a great swash-buckler. Andrzej was happy to see how courteous he was to Karolina. She was as natural and charming with Władek and Albina, as if they were her own cousins and friends.

After an hour's rest following lunch, Andrzej drove with Władek to the railway station to pick up the two trunks registered in Lwów. An employee of the railway station explained to them why there were such large numbers of Gestapo in the region of the station close to Sanok. The previous night a great number of members of the Polish resistance had emerged from the forest, and there had been a battle between them and the German army.

When Andrzej returned with Władek and their luggage to take Karolina to the village, it was already dark. Although still tired, they went immediately in the country wagon driven by Władek to the village. There was no curfew in the countryside, and darkness was the best time for travelling. Karolina was seated on the front seat with Władek, who was showing her how to drive, and Andrzej was on the same seat but turned backwards to watch the trunks. The night was cold and, Władek, with great care, had covered Karolina with a big sheepskin throw and had given Andrzej two warm rugs.

Andrzej was so exhausted that he drowsed the whole journey. From time to time only, he heard Karolina speaking with Władek. They were laughing, and the atmosphere was extremely friendly and warm. He could hardly believe that Karolina could speak as if she were a simple country girl from the village. He admired her ability for the rapidity with which she could adapt.

After three hours, they arrived at the house of Andrzej's aunt, Karolcia. Karolcia waited for them with all her family: two daugh-ters, four sons, one granddaughter and one son-in-law. She greeted Karolina very warmly, hugging and kissing her many times. Then she presented all the members of the family, one after another. Each of them approached to hug and kiss Andrzej and Karolina. They were very interested in the news, how it had been on the 'other side' over the last two years because the family had been divided during that time by a frontier on the river San.

There was a great hatred for the Nazis, and all the family members were very interested in the Polish resistance. They spoke with great pride of the heroism of the 'Peasant Battalions.' Before the war, the son-in-law of Karolcia had worked as an oil worker in Borysław, the biggest oil-drilling centre in Poland. He was active in the Polish Socialist Party and had a very good knowledge of all political events.

Karolina spoke with all of them with the same natural simplicity that had pleased Władek so much. She was so natural in her language and reactions to them that nobody from the outside would recognize her to be an educated girl from the big city. Polish peasants have a strong feeling of the unity of family, and Karolina was accepted as a family member by Karolcia and her family from the first day. They liked her manner interspersed with some good and very kind jokes, and felt very much at ease with her.

After supper, Władek and his elder sister, Stefka, accompanied Andrzej and Karolina to the house rented by Andrzej on his former trip. It was in a distance of 2 kilometres from Karolcia's house, and prepared for their arrival. The oven was warm, and they had prepared a loaf of freshly baked bread, a pint of fresh butter, eggs, and cheese for breakfast next day. The beds were made for the night. Since the Nazi occupation, they never enjoyed such comfort in life.

They were at the beginning of a new chapter in their lives.

XII

THE NEXT DAY, KAROLCIA ARRIVED WITH WŁADEK AND Stefka to help them unpack and to show Karolina how to operate the kitchen oven and the location of the water well. She gave her many practical instructions. Władek had prepared enough wood for the stoves in the office and in their bedroom. They felt relaxed, seeing all the care and love Ludwik's family was showing them.

Andrzej hired a country wagon to drive the next day to the district physician to deliver the permit from the 'Ärztekammer' in Lwów to establish himself in this district. The district physician asked him to accept also the duties of health-insurance doctor for all insured by their professional unions or by regional or governmental authorities. The teachers, community employees, the post office and forest employees had had such health insurance before the war and, all these policies remained in force during the German occupation. There was a shortage of doctors in the country regions, and the insured had to travel to a town to find a doctor covered by insurance. Now, with Andrzej settled in the countryside, the insured could have very close an insurance doctor. This proposal was accepted instantly by Andrzej. His father, as a teacher, had had such insurance, and Andrzej was happy to be now in the situation where he could provide health care to teachers and other insured persons in the district. The salary for this kind of service was modest, but it was a salary for a kind of social work. It would provide Andrzej some cash, which he could not get from the peasants, the majority of whom would pay him in food.

In a couple of days, his office was open for patients. There was such demand that he hardly could handle it. He also was asked to visit peasants' houses to tend to the seriously ill, or to deliver babies when the midwives were not available. Sometimes, there were two or three country wagons waiting outside his house to take him for such cases. He was always available, day and night, because there was no other doctor close to the region. Karolina was very helpful in his work in the office, but he never took her with him when he had to travel to bed-ridden patients. To deal with all this work and maintain the office in a clean state, they hired a young girl from the neighbourhood as their maid.

From the point of view of food and lodging, even with the inconveniences of going outside to the water well, life was much easier than in Lwów. They did not suffer from hunger or cold.

They had now to start a social life to be accepted not only by the family but also by the important persons in the village. They visited and asked for reciprocal visits from the parson and two vicars, the head of the village, the head of the hamlet, the teachers, and the administrators of the former landlord's farm and manor. They felt well accepted by the families of patients, and by their social contacts. They were feeling more secure, but there was always the fear that sometime they might meet somebody who had known Karolina before the war. There were no Germans around, and all the administrative formalities Andrzej handled with the head of the village, or of the hamlet, or with the parson. All these people were Poles, and they hated the Nazis.

On Sundays, Andrzej and Karolina always went to High Mass and took Holy Communion. Karolina went sometimes to confession. In this very Catholic countryside, Sunday was always solemnly observed, and the non-attendance of a doctor with his wife would be interpreted unfavourably. Events in the future would prove how very important it was to be a practising Catholic. It was vital.

The news from Ludwik and Estelle was sad. They did not write freely because of German censorship, but it was evident that the situation in Lwów was difficult. Food and heating materials were scarce and expensive. They had sold nearly all the furniture and were making preparations to move to the village in May.

The news from Juliusz through the intermediary of Stanisław was also very sad. The German police stationed in the nearest town again warned the population that any social contact with Jewish families was forbidden. Juliusz and his family were now not allowed to walk beyond a diameter of 200 metres from their house. The neighbours with whom they had had a friendly relationship ceased to visit them, and in the shops sometimes the shopkeepers were afraid to sell them food. The young teacher, however, continued to visit them, secretly in the evenings, under the cover of darkness. She was the main supplier of food to Juliusz and his family.

At the end of March, Andrzej felt that Karolina was already well rooted in the village, and could be left alone for one day. He decided to go and visit Juliusz, Dorota, and Zosia. As much as Karolina wanted to have direct news from them, she was extremely afraid of the danger faced by Andrzej on such a visit. She begged him to use extreme caution and to choose hours when it was least probable that he would encounter the police. Andrzej had planned the visit for the late afternoon and promised to make a stop at the teacher's place. His further plan depended on the instructions from the teacher.

It was the last day of March 1942, when at about 5:00 p.m. Andrzej knocked on the window of her room in the school in Orelec. Orelec was a small village, and she was the only teacher at the school. She was sitting at the table and writing. She recognized him at once, opened the door, and showed him into her room.

The situation in the village was tragic, she told him. The Nazis were preparing an 'Action' against the Jews in this village and in other neighbouring villages. Nobody knew what kind of 'Action' it would be. 'What we *do* know,' she told him, 'is that neither in the nearest town nor in other more distant towns of this region, are the Nazis preparing a ghetto. We think, therefore, that they intend either to deport them to concentration camps or to murder them in the surrounding woods. It is a helpless situation. If we could help them and rescue them, we would be strong enough to conquer the Nazis and have an independent Poland.' She was speaking like a soldier, reporting some military news. Andrzej understood with whom he was talking. In the summer of 1944, when the Soviet army liberated this region, Albina told him that this brave girl, one of many anonymous heroines of the Polish resistance, was killed by Nazis during one of her missions at the beginning of 1944. She was known by the name 'Janka.' Albina did not know her true name.

Before she switched on the light, she covered the window with a rug. 'At nine o'clock,' she told him, 'I will go with you to Juliusz. It would be dangerous to go earlier. Take a rest on the sofa, but first eat something.' She prepared hot tea, bread, and scrambled eggs for him. Then she returned to her work.

At 9:00 p.m. she was ready to go with Andrzej. It was very dark, and she warned him that visits in daytime might be dangerous for him, because the police frequently checked Jewish houses. He should be ready to return before 5:00 a.m. next morning. She would come at that time to pick him up at the house of Juliusz and lead him in the direction of the railway station. 'Once outside, we will not talk. You will follow me in complete silence.' She led him through very complicated pathways, and after fifteen minutes, they reached the small roadside chapel with a sculpted figure of Christ in Sorrow. The girl stopped for a while, crossed herself and whispered to Andrzej: 'This is the only Jew that the Nazis are unable to kill.'

They continued on their way in darkness, and after a signal knock at the window they entered Juliusz's house. The teacher stayed only for a short while, giving Dorota food that she bought for them, then returned to school.

Juliusz, Dorota, and Zosia were very upset. Juliusz told Andrzej that, a few days earlier, the German police had arrived in the village and visited the houses where Jewish families are living. The Germans behaved in a very rude way. They counted the number of people in each house, registered their names, and reminded then that none of them was allowed to leave the village. Disobedience would be punished by death. Any social contact with the non-Jewish population was forbidden.

Juliusz was afraid that the Nazis were organizing a ghetto in the nearest town, where they intended to transfer all the Jewish population from adjacent villages. There was no way to change the present situation; they had to be prepared for the worst – the ghetto. He asked Andrzej not to visit them any more. If the German police arrived during the visit of Andrzej, he could be killed as somebody helping the Jews. He advised him strongly not to do anything without first consulting with the teacher. He felt relieved that she would be coming to pick him up early in the morning to accompany him to the railway station. It was dangerous enough for Andrzej to stay at night in a Jewish house, and Juliusz wanted Andrzej out as soon as possible, although he was extremely touched by this unannounced visit.

They tried to organize a new, safer way of mail contact in the case of their transfer to the ghetto. Advised by the teacher, Andrzej suggested that the best way would be to maintain contact between the teacher and Stanisław in Lwów. Andrzej promised to organize personally this system as soon as possible.

'I feel that we have much suffering ahead of us. I have to prepare my wife and my daughter' – and he smiled sadly, turning to Dorota and Zosia – 'to be strong enough to go through this awful time. We will suffer, but we will survive. I do not think that the Germans will exterminate millions of Jewish people in Poland. This is impossible; this is unthinkable. We will survive, but we will be brutalized, humiliated, and dishonoured. I am a strong man, and I will give my strength to Dorota and Zosia. If they impose work on our family, I can work for the three of us. Yes, tell Karolina, that we will survive.' Dorota and Zosia listened in silence.

About midnight, Dorota and Zosia went to the kitchen to prepare some food for the late evening meal. Juliusz told Andrzej during their absence all that was in his poor, shattered heart. 'Very often, I think,' he said, 'that we are in a trap without a means of escape and I am afraid that we all will perish. In such moments, God encouraged me. He tells me: "Juliusz, I will not leave you alone. I will be with you and your family. I will rescue you and your family. I will spare your daughter, a young and innocent girl. I am omnipotent and I will defeat Evil. You should have confidence in me." Should I believe my God or should I become a slave to a cruel reality without hope.' He looked at Andrzej with tears in his eyes. He was not sure that God was telling him the truth.

After a while, he said: 'I am allowed to go out of this house only within 200 metres distance. In this perimeter is a roadside chapel with a Christ in Sorrow. I sometimes stay before this chapel for a long time, looking at Christ. It is a historical fact that Christ was a Jew. According to the Catholic religion He was also a God. He certainly was a good, very good human being, who suffered terribly and went through all possible humiliations of this world. I look at Him and telling Him about Jewish misery, which now exists in this world. He is still in sorrow. His sorrow did not terminate with His death. Polish peasants sculpture Him always as Christ in Sorrow (Chrystusik Frasobliwy) sitting and lamenting over sorrows in life. After telling Him the story of our sorrows, I feel a relief.' And after a while he said:

'I deeply regret, that I did not accept the offer of Bishop Baziak. I should have accepted it, especially for Zosia. She would now be safe in a convent and she would easily survive this war, without such sufferings. I wanted to be together with them. It was such a childish idea that in hard times I could always help them, work for them, protect them. Dorota and I, we have had already a taste of life. There were moments of great happiness in our past, but Zosia is at the beginning of life and she should not, she *cannot* perish. My greatest fear is what might happen to Zosia. My terrible anxiety, my personal bitter regret is that I did not accept the offer of the bishop. I am responsible for this irreversible situation, for the fate of Dorota and Zosia.' He lowered his head and cried bitterly.

Andrzej hugged and kissed him: 'Juliusz, 'you are exaggerating now. I was always pessimistic; you were always optimistic. Nobody is trying to kill you or your family. You are persecuted like millions of Jews. I believe that, very soon, there will be a dramatic turning-point in the situation on the military fronts. The Germans will suffer several defeats and will be preoccupied with the worsening military situation. They have to face an international responsibility for all the cruelties and crimes committed during this war, and the hour of this responsibility is closer and closer with each defeat. You just told me that you are strong, and I know that you are. You are an example of strength to Dorota and Zosia, and this is a great comfort and reassurance for them. I know that you are not telling them things you just told me. Even from the physical, medical point of view, you have to spare your health, to sleep more and to eat more. Stanisław gave me money for you. I will leave with the teacher a greater sum, in addition to what I am giving to you now. It will be much safer, because I have heard already of scenes of extortion of money from Jewish families.'

Andrzej felt that what he was saying did not convince Juliusz. It could not because Andrzej himself was feeling that this situation might end with a tragedy. He tried, however, to console Juliusz, to strengthen the remnants of his optimism. Regrettably he was unsuccessful. Andrzej was also very much concerned about Juliusz's health. During the last month Juliusz had grown much older. He had lost weight, and Andrzej knew from Dorota that he did not sleep at night.

'Listen, Andrzej,' he said after a while, 'tell Karolina that I miss her very much, that we are not in bad shape. That we are prepared for sufferings, but that we will survive with God's help. Tell her that I love her very much and that I am happy, yes extremely happy, that you are her husband. For God's sake don't tell her that I have a feeling that I will never see her again. You both have enough troubles. I am not quite sure that she will believe you, because my beloved daughter is too intelligent to be deceived.

'If I really will never see her again, one day after the war, many years after the war, tell her that my sufferings were incredible, enormous, like sufferings in the hell might be. Tell Karolina, one day, that I really was too optimistic in my life, that she was right: my optimism was distorting my decisions. I had too much confidence in the decency of human beings. I was wrong, and she, Karolina, was right. But, as you know, it is too late; nothing can be changed now. The Germans will not spare us; only God could spare us. But that would be a miracle.' He was crying again. He lowered his head, and there was silence in the room.

Dorota and Zosia returned from the kitchen with the late-evening meal. It was already one o'clock in the morning. Juliusz tried to create a more relaxed atmosphere, asking Andrzej about details of their life in the village. He made efforts not to show his anxiety and sadness.

At two o'clock in the morning, they went to bed. Andrzej was in one bed with Juliusz, Dorota was with Zosia in the other. They talked as they could not sleep. Juliusz was talking about Cracow, the life of the family in Cracow, recollections of Karolina's childhood, her brilliant studies, her intelligence and honesty. He had always been very proud of her.

He once more warned Andrzej how dangerous it was for him to come to Orelec and asked him to make no decision without consulting the teacher. He sounded calmer and stronger. He was speaking about the transfer to the ghetto and was convinced that that would be the end of persecutions. They would be forced to work for the German army, for instance, repairing roads, and they would survive.

'And if it will be impossible, so let it be the will of God. Perhaps we have to suffer more and more; perhaps we have to perish because our fate is necessary to immunize the future generations against the victory of Evil in human souls. This would be a horrifying example of the depravity of human beings. Future generations will remember for ever this war, the Nazi cruelties, the terrible sufferings of all mankind. This will be a memento: Never again.'

At 5:00 a.m., the teacher knocked at the window. Andrzej was ready to leave. She entered, and they repeated once more the new scheme for sending mail and transferring money. Andrzej hugged and kissed Dorota, Zosia, and Juliusz. Juliusz told him at the end: 'Tell Karolina that she will be always in my heart. Tell her to be careful and kiss her for me many times.'

Juliusz switched off the light so that Andrzej and the teacher could leave in darkness. After one minute they stopped again before the chapel. The teacher crossed herself and whispered to Andrzej: 'One day He will judge all of us. This will be a just judgment. God's mill grinds slow but sure. And all of us, Juliusz, his family, you, I, and many, many honest people will stay on one side, and all Nazis and other criminalists on the other. We will enjoy happiness for ever. Those on the other side will be punished for ever, and will suffer for ever, because such is the fate of Evil.'

They continued walking in silence, again through complicated pathways and, after half an hour, they were on the road far from the village. It was very dark. She whispered again: 'Now, you go straight ahead and in one hour you will reach the railway station. You will go through two villages, and if somebody meets you, tell him that you are on the way to the railway station because you have to take the train to visit a sick member of your family. At eight o'clock you will have the train in the direction you need.

'Never go to Juliusz without seeing me before. Come to the school when it is dark, not before 8:00 p.m. It is dangerous for you and it could be tragic for you and for many, many people. I don't know who you are, and I don't want to know during these terrible times. I know only that Juliusz loves you. If you will see one day Karolina, tell her that you met a girl, a simple Polish country girl, a teacher who told you that Karolina's father was an extraordinary man and that this girl had the greatest respect for him. Tell her also that this girl tried everything to help him, all that was within the limits of her abilities. Now: take care and God bless you.'

Andrzej thanked her warmly. She shook hands with him and disappeared very fast on the way to Orelec. Andrzej was now walking in the darkness alone. He was crying bitterly in his solitude all the way.

Before dawn he reached the railway station at Uherce.

XIII

WHEN KAROLINA SAW ANDRZEJ AFTER HE RETURNED from the visit to Juliusz, she knew at once the news was bad. He told her everything that happened in Orelec with the exception of the conversation he had with Juliusz in the absence of Dorota and Zosia. Following the wish of Juliusz, he could tell her this only after the war. He did not tell her all about the conversation with the teacher, namely, he did not tell her about the terrible alternative of mass murders in the forests. The news of preparation to transfer them to a concentration camp was already terrible enough for her. Thinking about their fate, she had to consider a ghetto or concentration camp in Lwów, but now, when it would surely become a cruel reality in the nearest future, she felt terrible fear, especially for Zosia, who was very sensitive.

Although Andrzej told Karolina that there were no preparations made for a ghetto in one of the nearest towns, and presented her only the alternative of concentration camp, she must have had in her mind something still more tragic. She looked at him and said: 'Thank you, my love, for all that you are doing. What is going to happen to them could have been avoided. Now nothing can be done. I have the feeling that I am losing for ever my parents and Zosia. For me the worst thing is that my father knows that, accepting the offer of the bishop, he, Dorota, and Zosia could be in a safe situation. This feeling of responsibility for the future, perhaps for the life of his wife and his daughter, must be something terrible for my father. I know him well, his honesty and his tenderness, and I can imagine his sufferings, which are perhaps worse than death.'

She had tears in her eyes, but she made an effort not to cry: 'I cannot cry, because my eyes will be swollen and that could be suspicious. I can only speak with you about my fears, my pains, my sufferings, with you and God. But I do not know if God is listening to me.'

Andrzej could not sleep that night, although he pretended to sleep so as not to worry Karolina. He had seen through half-closed eyes that Karolina was kneeling close to her bed and praying for a long time. He strongly wished that the prayers of Karolina reached God but he knew that there was now no possibility of help without a miracle. He waited until Karolina returned to bed. He felt that she could not sleep. He did not talk to her because there was really no consolation to offer, and he did not want to lie if she asked the question that she certainly had in mind. He could only hug her, kiss her, and encourage sleep. Eventually he said: 'I saw you praying to God. I asked Him to answer your and my prayer. Let us hope that He listens to us.' Karolina was so tired that, after a while, she fell asleep.

Next morning he saw the first patient before 8:00 a.m. Karolina tried her best to help him and to handle the patients, to comfort them in their sorrows. She was looking brave and strong as always.

The next weeks were more or less quiet. Karolina and Andrzej received, through the intermediary of the teacher from Orelec and Stanisław from Lwów, two letters from Juliusz. He described the situation as no better, but it was no worse. It had stabilized at a certain point. The German police did not arrive during last weeks at the village, and no new orders were given. Nobody was speaking of a ghetto in the nearest town. The local Polish police from the nearest village did not appear in the houses of Jewish families.

The news from Andrzej's parents in Lwów was arriving in a regular way, although the mail service was functioning very slowly. The weather was not so cold. They could go out for a walk and, in the apartment, it was warmer. Food was still very scarce. They were exchanging some of their furniture for food on the black market. Sometimes it could be dangerous because some of the vendors on the black market were linked up with informers. The sale of furniture was providing money for which the parents of Andrzej could rent a truck to transport the rest of their furniture to the village.

Estelle was visiting quite often Father Alojzy to bring him news from Andrzej and Karolina. He was interested especially in how Karolina was accepted in the village and how Andrzej was coping with his work there. He was deeply touched by the situation of Juliusz and his family.

Andrzej has decided to visit Juliusz again in April. The date was set for 24 April. Andrzej missed Juliusz very much and wanted to speak with him to give him contact with the outside world, bring him news from Karolina, and in such a way diminish a little his terrible anxiety and show him that they were always with him, with Dorota and Zosia. He wanted to walk in the evening from the railway station to the school and then, under the guidance of the teacher, in darkness walk to Juliusz's place. Karolina was extremely afraid of the dangers of such travel and discussed with him all the details and also all the contingency plans in case he had to change the primary scheme. Andrzej promised solemnly to Karolina that under no circumstances would he visit Juliusz without consulting in advance the teacher. If he could not find her in school, he promised to return immediately to the railway station, then to Sanok, and to return home without seeing Juliusz and his family. He consented eventually to Karolina's wish to accompany him to Sanok.

They decided to rent a country wagon from a neighbour who had two good horses, and Karolina had a very friendly relationship with his wife, who was Andrzej's patient. The neighbour was very grateful because Andrzej had treated his wife, enabling her to eat anything without having problems with her bowels. For Andrzej, it was an easy case to diagnose. The woman simply suffered from great anxiety. Sometimes she was in a panic anxiety, and all she needed was good and adequate psychotherapy and no pills.

Karolina convinced Andrzej that it is better for her own safety to travel a little bit outside the village, like wives of peasants did. They intended to visit Albina in Sanok, because they knew that, on this day, she would be at home after 1:00 p.m. Afterwards, they would go to a beautiful park on a hill, with a view of the river San. Returning from there, they would go for a while to the church, and at about 3:00 p.m., Karolina would meet at the cabstand the neighbours with whom she would return to the village. Andrzej would go to the railway station in Sanok, buy a ticket to the station at Uherce, close to Orelec. They would tell the neighbours, that he had a meeting at the office of the district doctor and would be back next morning, or at the latest in the afternoon next day. They had worked out in detail their behaviour, even where each of them should be seated in the country wagon when travelling. Karolina would sit in front with the driver, who would teach her how to drive a pair of horses, because she knew only how to drive one horse, and Andrzej would sit with the neighbour's wife in the back seat. This was a custom they had observed among pairs of peasants travelling from the 'upper' village to the 'lower' village on Sundays. The neighbour had already taught Karolina how to feed the horses, how to hitch them to the carriage, when and how much water to give them.

Karolina liked the horses very much, and sometimes in the evening, when they had spare time to rest after work, she and Andrzej dreamed about their future. In these dreams was a small house in suburbs of Cracow, a carriage with one or perhaps two horses. On Sundays they would drive to visit their parents at their houses or bring them to this small house of their own. Everybody would live without fear and without the terrible uncertainty about whether you would survive to see the next sunrise. Such dreams were for them like a child's fairy-tale.

In their plans to go to Sanok to accompany Andrzej on the way to visit Juliusz, it was also determined that, after Karolina's return to the village, Stefka would come for the night to keep Karolina company. During the German occupation, even in this village, which was so far relatively quiet, nobody wanted to stay alone at night. Next day, Karolina would ask another neighbour to drive to Sanok and wait for Andrzej in the country wagon at the cabstand in Sanok.

Karolina had to tell everybody that Andrzej was absent at night in the village, because he had to attend an evening meeting at the district doctor's office in Krosno. She expected him to return in the late afternoon. This story was known to Karolcia and, on her advice, Stefka would stay constantly with Karolina. Stefka with pleasure accepted Karolcia's request that she stay with Karolina during Andrzej's absence. It was for her a sign of great confidence from Andrzej.

With impatience and fear, they waited for the day of Andrzej's visit to Juliusz. Andrzej missed Juliusz, Dorota, and Zosia very much. He still nourished some hope that the situation in Orelec was stabilized for a while; under such conditions even a month of such stability was important. At the same time, he was full of anxiety and fear for his journey and was aware of how Karolina experienced the same feelings. But they could not ignore the voice of their conscience.

They did not know that only a small part of their plan would be realized, that the project would be tragically changed, that even the most difficult contingency plans would never be realized.

They were facing the greatest personal tragedy in their lives, the tragedy that would be just one drop more in the ocean of the Holocaust, one more tear in the valley of tears. But even this one drop in the history of humanity could be a flood, a deluge, for one person or one family.

This deluge marked Karolina and Andrzej for the rest of their lives.

XIV

THE EARLY MORNING OF 22 APRIL 1942 IN ORELEC WAS similar to the mornings of the previous days. Juliusz slept restless and awakened early in the morning. It was dark; only in the eastern part of the sky some light was visible. Juliusz liked to observe nature. He got up and went to the kitchen. From here he could better see the sunrise without disturbing Dorota and Zosia, who were still asleep. He opened the door and went out to the backyard. The night was chilly. The day slowly broke in. Juliusz could see how the stars were turning pale as the light zone in the east became stronger and stronger. It was very quiet. The contours of the mountains became more and more marked. Juliusz was looking at all the magnificent changes of colours during the sunrise. When the first sunbeam brightened from the horizon, he returned to the house. A new day was beginning, full of unknown dangers.

Until nine o'clock, it was a day like other days. One hour later, the head of the hamlet made the rounds of all houses with Jewish inhabitants and told them that the Gestapo will come very soon to the village. He came also to Juliusz's house and told him that he had received this information from the Polish police in the next village.

The Polish policemen knew nothing more. They had received an order from the German police in the nearest town that all the Jews had to stay at home and prepare their belongings. The head of the hamlet was afraid that the Germans might organize a ghetto in the nearest town and the Jewish families would be transported to this ghetto. This old Ukrainian peasant was sad to be bringing such news.

Juliusz tried to console Dorota and Zosia, but it was difficult to find words that could diminish their fear and despair. A new chapter was opening in their lives and nobody knew how long it would last and how it would end. Juliusz packed the clothes and all the family's personal belongings in two pieces of luggage and made a parcel of kitchen utensils and food. Dorota and Zosia were unable to do anything but cry.

Juliusz had to be strong: 'Now the Nazis will organize a ghetto in the nearest town, and we will be in this ghetto. But it is sure that they will not kill us. They asked us to prepare our belongings, and this is the best evidence that we will be alive. Do not cry, Dorota; do not cry, Zosia. We have to go through the bottom of human sufferings but we will survive. In this very difficult moment of our life, God is with us and He will not abandon us. Be quiet, be strong.'

They were waiting for the arrival of the Gestapo for more than two hours. About noon, the truck carrying about ten policemen from the Gestapo arrived, accompanied by the local German police from the nearest town. They formed groups of two, and each group approached one of the houses occupied by Jewish families. They did not knock at the door of Juliusz's house; they opened it by kicking with their boots. They stepped inside, and one of them, looking at the paper that he had in his hands, shouted: 'This family consists of three Jews, one man and two females. A couple and their daughter.' He pushed Juliusz and said: 'You are well here, damned Jews, in this beautiful village. But we are preparing for you a surprise. You are leaving immediately this house, taking out your belongings.'

He approached Juliusz, slapped him in the face: 'Fast, move, get out,' he shouted. Juliusz took two pieces of luggage and went out, accompanied by one of the policemen. The other one did not allow Dorota and Zosia to take the parcel with kitchen utensils and food and shouted: 'Get out immediately. You will not need these things. We will provide you with everything' and he knocked Dorota with the butt of his machine-gun.

Outside, they saw some other Jewish families going in the direction of the square before the church. They were ordered to go in the same direction. Juliusz wanted to take with him the two pieces of luggage that they allowed him to take from the house, but a Nazi shouted to him: 'Leave your belongings here, outside the house. We will provide you with everything.'

On the square before the church were now about twenty-five Jewish people – men, women, children. They were surrounded by about ten Nazis, some of them from the Gestapo, some from the German police. One of them shouted: 'Jews, we are beginning now transportation of Jews from this region. We will begin this transportation with an excursion to a beautiful forest. In the forest we will give you further orders what to do. You will never return to this village. You will no more have influence on the non-Jewish population of the village. Now you have to walk. Form a detachment, four Jews in a row. Move.'

The miserable people formed the rows of four persons, and the march began. An empty truck followed the marching column.

The policemen were on both sides of the column, pushing the Jews with the butts of their machine-guns. Juliusz was on the right side of his row, Dorota was on his left-hand side, and on the left-hand side of Dorota was Zosia. The last in this row was an old man, trying to do his best to keep up with the trudging column. After a few hundred metres he was unable to keep the row. He stayed behind, and the distance between him and the marching column grew bigger and bigger. One of the policemen knocked him down with the butt of his machine-gun and shot him. The body was immediately thrown into the empty truck at the rear of the column.

Juliusz had now no doubts that the end was very close. The fact that the Gestapo did not allow them to take their personal belongings and the fact that they told them that they would be walking to a forest, were bad signs. But even now he had some moments of illusion that the Gestapo perhaps wanted only to frighten the Jewish families, that the belongings would be transported afterward, that they were all walking to the ghetto in the nearest town. He was not allowed to talk to Dorota or Zosia, but he tried sometimes to turn his head to them and smile to give them in such a way a signal of hope. Dorota and Zosia were crying, as were the majority of the other marching people. Some of the small children were crying loud and shouting. A small boy who was very afraid and loud was taken from the row by the Gestapo and shot instantly. The body of the child was thrown in the truck following the column.

After more than an hour's march, they arrived at the crossroads. They were ordered to stop. Columns of Jewish people from other villages were coming and also ordered to stop at the crossroads. Now the Gestapo was counting people in each group. In the group in which Juliusz was with his family a policeman, after counting the amount, added: 'Twenty-three, and two in the truck. Alles in Ordnung (all in order), together twenty-five.'

Over one hundred Jewish people were now standing at the crossroads, waiting for further orders from the Gestapo. Many of them were thinking: now we are going to take the road to the nearest town and we will be located in the ghetto. They clung to this last straw of hope, hoping against hope. It is difficult to get used to the idea that you will be killed very soon, being completely innocent. In the minds of many people, among them of Juliusz, the ghetto was now a desired place, one in which it was possible to rest, to eat, to drink, to have the opportunity to continue this miserable life.

After a while, the Gestapo ordered them to continue the march. But they did not push them in the direction of the road leading to the town. They were directed towards a narrow, steep road to the forest seen on the top of the hill. The trucks did not follow them and remained at the crossroads, together with the drivers. The bodies of the killed were pulled out by legs from the trucks by the Gestapo.

The march towards the top was very difficult. Some of the older people and children were unable to climb the steep road. Before the forest was reached, the Gestapo shot two children and another old man. One of the officers of the Gestapo shouted: 'Don't shoot here. Our fellows will be tired pulling the Jewish bodies up the hill.'

Juliusz knew now that they would be killed, that this was to be part of the extermination of the Jews. He knew that his confidence in human beings was false. He knew now that these Germans of the Hitler regime had nothing in common with the culture, science, and art of the past of Germany. These Germans in the uniforms of the Gestapo, pushing him, Dorota, Zosia, and other Jewish people, were simple beasts. He knew that he was witnessing now not only the murder of innocent people, but the deepest degradation of the human being in the history of mankind. The men from the Gestapo were only physically human beings; psychologically, morally, they were worse than wild animals. Such a degradation, unthinkable for

Juliusz, even this morning, was worse for him than the fact that he and his family had to die. He did not want to exist in the world together with beasts in human bodies. He preferred to die.

His only preoccupation was now the degree of sufferings of his wife and of his daughter. He looked at them, at the tired face of his wife, at the fearful face of his daughter, and he asked God to give them a fast death, without long waiting, without torture. He asked God to inflict on him all the sufferings and to spare Zosia and Dorota. And at the bottom of his shattered heart was the constant deep despair and painful regret that he had not accepted the proposal of the bishop to hide all of them in a convent and monastery. Now his decision would bring the tragic end of his daughter's and his wife's lives.

This was the day of Evil and God did not hear any prayers.

After reaching the forest and entering deeper into it, the Gestapo ordered the families to stay in small groups, each family separately. They brought from the trucks shovels and gave to each of the adult Jewish men a shovel. One of them shouted: 'Now you will dig ditches in the ground. They will be the graves for your parents, wives, and children and also for you. Nobody will escape from here. The last moment of your life is already close. If you will disobey, we will punish your mothers, wives, and children. They will be tortured before their death. You will look at these tortures, and their pains will be caused by your disobedience. So dig the ditches. Work hard and efficiently and you will be rewarded. Your families will die without torture. Work hard and efficiently, we would like to finish this work before sunset and rest a little bit in the evening.' The officer who was shouting this was at the same time laughing, and his speech was accepted with loud laughter by other officers of the Gestapo.

Juliusz started to dig the grave for Dorota, Zosia, and himself. The Gestapo were watching the work of the Jews. Sometimes they made loud remarks; they brutalized some Jews, who were unable to work fast enough. They shot two older men, who were so weak and tired that they could not keep the shovels in their hands. The work was advancing slowly. The soil was very hard, full of roots.

One of the officers of the Gestapo ordered all the Jews to undress. The Gestapo wanted to see if, in the clothes or underwear, were hidden jewels or gold. They were checking all the clothes and underwear in a systematic way. Each piece of clothing was cut into small pieces and scrupulously examined. They had prepared a big trunk in which they threw whatever precious they found: jewellery, gold, money. They shouted with joy when they found something precious.

Dorota and Zosia were, like all other Jewish people, naked and shivering from cold and fear. They were staying close to the ditch in which Juliusz was working. He also was naked now. All these people were quiet. They were prepared to die. They wanted to avoid torture. Dorota was looking at her husband preparing the grave for her and their daughter, who stood close to her. They were no longer crying. One idea, one thought, was in their heads: to die as soon as possible and not to be tortured. Looking at the work of Juliusz, their only fear was that he might not be strong enough to finish his work. Juliusz knew that he has in his hands only one task on this earth: to dig the grave for his wife and his daughter, and to assure for them a death without torture. This was the ultimate way that they could have a quiet death – a single shot in the head of his daughter, a single shot in the head of his wife. To obtain for them those two single shots, he was working very hard.

The ditch was, in the opinion of the Gestapo, deep, long, and large enough. They ordered Juliusz to get out and stand aside. They ordered Zosia to stay on the border on the ditch. Juliusz and Dorota were looking now at the execution of their daughter. One shot, and the body of Zosia slipped into the grave. Now Juliusz was to witness the execution of his wife. Dorota was ordered to stand where two minutes before her daughter had stood. Again one shot and the body of Dorota slipped to the grave, onto the body of her daughter.

Now the end was very close, the end of the day, the end of human sufferings, the end of Juliusz's life.

A burning red sky could be seen between the trees. One of the officers of the Gestapo stopped shouting at the Jews, looked at the setting sun, and said: 'It is wonderful in these woods. The colours are superb. I love it. It is so poetic.' But, being a disciplined Nazi, he returned immediately to his job.

Juliusz was until now biologically alive, but he did not see the forest or the dead bodies, and he did not hear the screaming of some who, like him, were still alive. He had now only one desire, to leave as soon as possible this hell on the earth. He was like a person leaving a horrible place for another location and interested only in the nice place he would be very soon. Being a believer, even with many doubts, he was full of trust that God would give him a quiet place where he could stay with his daughter and his wife. It was a relief for Juliusz to feel the cold metal of the gun on his neck and have the feeling that, at last, he would be free, no longer trapped in this hell.

Juliusz was one of the last shot this evening by the troops of the Gestapo. The sun was at the horizon. The officers of the Gestapo, after such a laborious day, had now time to look at the beauty of nature. They were no more disturbed by the Jews.

XV

THE PLAN ELABORATED IN DETAIL BY ANDRZEJ AND Karolina functioned well at the beginning. They left the village on 24 April 1942, in the morning, and arrived in Sanok at noon. The neighbour who was driving them went shopping with his wife. Andrzej and Karolina went to visit Albina. She received them with her usual hospitality and prepared a nice lunch for them. At 1:00 p.m. she expected somebody. They left just before 1:00 and walked in the direction of park. After a couple of minutes Andrzej saw a girl waving her hand to him from across the street. He recognized her immediately. It was the teacher from Orelec. He whispered to Karolina: 'The teacher from Orelec is crossing the street. I am going to meet her and you will follow us, at a distance of about ten metres. My love, if you feel that some trouble might happen, call me by name.' He left Karolina and advanced to meet the girl. He knew the minute he saw her that something bad had happened. During the day, at this hour, she should be at her school in Orelec. The fear that was always inside him at once increased considerably.

The teacher told Andrzej about the tragic events in Orelec on 22 April 1942. Juliusz, Dorota, and Zosia had been shot in the woods on a hill close to Orelec with about one hundred other Jewish people from neighbouring villages. She had seen the terrible march of these miserable people, surrounded by the Gestapo and police. They arrived at the crossroads, where they met with other groups from neighbouring villages.

'We observed from a distance the terrible march of about one hundred Jewish people up the hill, to the forest. On the road, the

Gestapo shot some old people who were unable to climb and some children. All the groups of Jewish people surrounded by the Gestapo disappeared in the woods. After a certain time we heard numerous, very numerous shots. During the sunset, the Gestapo emerged from the woods, entered the trucks, and left the crossroads in the eastern direction.

'After the departure of Jewish families, a German truck arrived at the village and took all the personal belongings left by the Jewish families in front of their houses.'

The teacher looked at Andrzej and said: 'You must immediately cut all contact by mail between Lwów and Orelec because it might be very dangerous for the senders of letters from Lwów and for the recipient, for me. I hope that Juliusz has destroyed all the letters he received and did not keep any addresses at home. I told him many times about the dangers for the addressees.' She was in such emotional state that she hardly could talk.

After a while, she continued: 'Do not show any emotional reaction. We are on the street and people might be looking at us. Everything can today make them suspicious. It was a miraculous chance that I met you here in Sanok today, a chance for you and me. I think that you were on your way to Orelec. If so, you would be entering a tragic situation, and coming to the school you could also involuntarily bring a tragic fate to me. The Ukrainian police until now are in Orelec. They are patrolling the village and searching the houses of Jewish families. I am full of despair and sorrow that I must bring you such cruel and tragic news. Juliusz was a noble human being; his family and many other innocent people were killed by Hitler's murderers. I am full of pain and very angry that nobody helped them. It is certain that, at the end, the Hitlerian beast will be killed, but when?'

She looked at Andrzej and asked: 'I hope that the girl following us and with whom I have seen you, is a honest person?' 'Yes, Andrzej answered. She is the most honest human being that I know. She is —' She interrupted him quickly: 'No, don't tell me who she is. I don't want to know. I never ask names. I know only what I should know to fulfil my duties. One day I may be taken by the Gestapo, tortured. I might not be strong enough or conscious enough, and say too much. Therefore I don't want to know the names.'

She looked at him, her face was full of pain and sorrow. She shook his hand and said, 'Take care, and God bless you.' Then she crossed the street and entered the house of Albina. Andrzej never met this brave girl again. Before the end of the war she was killed by the Hitlerian machine of death.

He turned around and he saw Karolina approaching him. She looked at him, and he knew that she knew. She took his arm and whispered: 'Do not say anything. I am not sure if I am strong enough. I feel that something very bad happened. Let us go to the church and there we will talk. I have seen on this street the tower of a church.' She held him close and very soon they entered a small church. It was nearly empty. They sat down in an empty chapel. On the altar was a painting with Christ on the cross and the Madonna kneeling below the cross.

Karolina looked at the altar, then straight into Andrzej's eyes and whispered with a certain hesitation: 'Andrzej, you have always told me the truth. Tell me now all the truth, even if it is a worse tragedy than I might expect. I don't want a grain of hope, if there is no hope. I don't want you to have pity for me. That would make me a martyr. There are situations in which nobody on this earth can comfort another. Tell me, Andrzej, the truth, tell me if they were transported to a ghetto or to a concentration camp, or were they shot and do not exist in this world?' All the time she spoke, she looked straight into the eyes of her husband.

Andrzej took her hand and, looking into her eyes, whispered: 'They are no more on this earth. On 22 April they were shot in the woods close to Orelec by the Gestapo.'

There was a long silence. She was kneeling and looking at the altar. After a while she said: 'Tell me all what the teacher told you. I will not cry. My despair must be hidden in my heart and can be known only to you, my love. I will be quiet, like this Madonna under the cross.'

Andrzej told Karolina what the girl told him. After a while she said: 'Andrzej, if you had left for Orelec two days earlier or if we had not met the girl today, you would also not exist on this earth. Oh God, you did not listen to all my prayers, but you still had mercy on me. In this most tragic moment of my life, you, my love, are here, close to me and alive.' She had tears in her eyes, but she quickly wiped them away. For a while she could not speak. She was so pale that Andrzej was afraid that she might faint.

He took again her hand in his hands and said: 'Karolina, you have been always very courageous and strong. In this moment of our lives, perhaps the most cruel moment of our lives, we have to be as hard as steel. We have to save not only our lives, but also the life of my parents, the life of Stanisław, of the faithful friend of Juliusz and other people with whom Juliusz had contact by mail. You understand that I have to cut immediately all the postal contact between Orelec and Lwów, and between Lwów and our village. The teacher was right, telling me this. The safety of her life is also at stake. You understand, my love, that the only person who can do this is me. This is a message that cannot be sent by somebody. Do you understand me well, do you understand what I mean?'

'Yes,' she said, and looked at Andrzej with eyes full of fear and despair, 'it is a terrible necessity. Yes, I understand this. This is our duty towards your parents and other people in Lwów and towards the teacher. Even if we will be in terrible fear, separated for a certain time, even if you will be full of anxiety for my safety, even with all the dangers of a trip by train to Lwów, even if I will be in this tragic situation alone, I know that you have to travel to Lwów. We have to remain honest in these times of contempt.'

For nearly one hour they discussed all the details of their decision. In Lwów, Andrzej had to see immediately his parents, Stanisław, Father Alojzy, Filomena, and other people who had contact by mail with Juliusz.

Andrzej had always with him the time-table of trains and now, looking at it, he saw in despair that, on this day, there was no direct connection to Lwów from Sanok. The only way to reach Lwów this evening was to take the train from the junction station 8 kilometres from Sanok. It was the same junction station where he and Karolina had witnessed the terrible encounter with the Gestapo when they arrived from Lwów to settle down in the village.

They decided to tell the neighbours that Andrzej had received from his relatives in Sanok news that his father was very sick, and he felt that it was necessary to go immediately to Lwów. They would ask the neighbours who had driven them to Sanok to give Andrzej a lift to the junction station, so that he could catch the train arriving on the same evening to Lwów.

Karolina would accompany him, with the neighbours, to the junction station, sitting with the driver on the front seat. They would stop for a short while in front of the station, Andrzej would step out, and they would immediately return through Sanok to the village. Karolina would dispatch, after tomorrow, another country wagon from their village, and the driver would wait for Andrzej from noon at the cabstand. Andrzej would stay in Lwów only one day and, with the help of his parents, he would arrange what he had to do in Lwów. He would be back in Sanok, taking the evening train from Lwów and arriving in the morning at the junction station.

At the end of this tragic discussion, Karolina said: 'My love, please don't refuse me if I ask you to do something with the money that my father left with Stanisław in Lwów. This is a reserve of money that he wanted to be sent to him in instalments to Orelec. Three times you were the messenger carrying this money to Orelec. I know how much my father was preoccupied with the safety of your parents. He was aware of the courage and honesty of your parents. He knew that they were risking their lives accepting me as their daughter-in-law and asking me to stay at their home. Now, the rest of this money, which is still with Stanisław, must be given to your parents. They must immediately as soon as possible move from Lwów to our village. They have to rent a truck and arrive with what remains of their furniture and settle down here in the room that we already reserved for them, close to our house in the village. This is the only thing that I can do now, in this terrible world, for people that I love. My love, promise me that you will do that.' 'Yes,' he answered, 'I certainly will.'

During the last fifteen minutes spent in the church they did not talk. Karolina knelt before the altar and prayed. Andrzej was trying to mobilize all his strength to arrange all that he had to do and to overcome the sadness caused by the tragedy of Orelec and to diminish the terrible anxiety that was vibrating in him. The principal cause of this anxiety was that, in such a moment, he had to leave Karolina alone in a situation that could become dangerous. Before leaving the church, he hugged Karolina and kissed her many times. This was their good-bye.

They went to meet the neighbours, waiting for them at the cabstand. They agreed at once to give Andrzej a lift to the junction station and to return afterwards immediately to the village.

Karolina sat in the front seat with the driver, and Andrzej with his wife in the rear seat. The neighbour's wife asked Andrzej about details of his father's health, if his heart condition was dangerous. She advised him to bring his parents as soon as possible to the village, where they could rest and have better conditions of life. She said she had heard that life was very difficult in the cities. Then she told him how very happy the people of the village were to have a physician who has his family, his aunt in the village. They trust much more 'their' doctor, than other doctors who are unfamiliar with their life, their needs.

Afterwards she said something that quite astonished Andrzej and Karolina. His aunt Karolcia apparently had told her that Karolina was from the same family. The aunt had told her that her deceased husband, Antoni, was the brother of Karolina's father. The big eyes of Karolina reminded her of the eyes of her deceased husband, and of her oldest son, Cesiek. Andrzej was so full of fear and despair over the tragedy in Orelec, and so tired, that he thought that he misunderstood the story. But at once he understood how clever Karolcia was, and he said: 'Yes, that is correct. My cousins are at the same time the cousins of my wife. But, you understand, there does not exist a proximity of blood between me and my wife. The church in Lwów where we were married before the war, knowing all the details of relationship between my family and that of my wife, did not see any obstacle to our marriage.' Andrzej saw that Karolina was now also quite aware of the importance of Karolcia's invention and she added some very kind remarks on the population of the village and her 'relations' with the family of Andrzej's father.

One day, this invention of Andrzej's aunt saved the life of Karolina during the Nazi occupation.

In about half an hour they were close to the junction station. They were still on the main road from Sanok to the east, and very soon they had to turn to the left, entering a narrow, straight road, about a half-kilometre long, at the end of which was the building of the junction station.

Fear was affecting Andrzej's breathing, and he was unable to speak. Karolina was in the same condition. Nobody spoke in the country wagon. The driver's wife, sitting close to Andrzej, was saying the rosary, as is the habit of the majority of Polish peasants; the driver was smoking a cigarette. The silence was broken when the driver said: 'Now we are turning to the left.'

Andrzej noted that the place before the junction station was empty. He regained his voice and told the driver: 'Make a stop in the place for just one moment so that I can get out. Then immediately return to our village with your and my wife. This station is usually full of Gestapo. They could come out of the station, and you know well that even a conversation with the Gestapo is dangerous.' He kissed Karolina once more before they stopped and said good-bye to the neighbours, and, at the stop, he stepped from the wagon as fast as possible and went in the direction of the entrance. As he opened the door, he turned his head to see the wagon driving away towards the main road. Karolina was looking at him, waving her hand. He waved in return and entered the lobby of the station.

It was nearly empty, only four peasants sitting on the benches. His train was scheduled to leave at 5:00 p.m. He had more than one hour of waiting. He approached the window and could see that the wagon was already at the end of the narrow road and close to the main road. At this very moment Karolina turned back and looked once more at the station. He did not get out immediately because he was worried that she might think that something was wrong in the station. He saw only that the wagon turned to the right and took the main road to Sanok. In a second, it was out of sight.

Then he went out in front of the station and lingered there. He was not afraid of the dangerous journey to Lwów, or of all that he had to do there. He was more afraid for the safety of Karolina. He was terrified that he might never see her again.

XVI

THE FEAR ABOUT KAROLINA'S SAFETY WAS INCREASING IN Andrzej with each hour. He knew that Karolina's route back to the village was through Sanok, and there was always a high probability of the Gestapo checking travellers. The fear became an obsession. He could not think of the problems that he had to manage in Lwów. He went with no emotions through the Gestapo check-point before entering the train. After a short delay, the train departed.

On this day he was travelling an alternative route to that he had taken with Karolina from Lwów to their village. This time, he had to go through a big junction station, at Przemyśl, 100 kilometres west of Lwów. Przemyśl was on the main railway line from Germany through Cracow, Lwów, to Kiev and Kharkov. All German military transports to the southern part of the eastern front were sent by this route. It was also the return way for all medical transports carrying wounded German soldiers. On his former travels, he had avoided

this route because all the bigger stations were full of Gestapo and
BDM (Bund der Deutschen Mädel). Now, every hour was important,
and it was the shortest route.

He had some moments of doubt, wondering if he was travelling
in the right direction and if he should not return to Karolina
immediately. He had to force himself to continue his journey to
Lwów. He was thinking that, in Orelec, in the house of Juliusz, the
police has found addresses, letters, and he was afraid that the cruel
hand of the Gestapo was close to reaching Karolina, his parents, and
the friends of Juliusz in Lwów. He was afraid that the Gestapo might
already be in the house of his parents and would kill him immediately after his arrival. He wanted to return to Karolina immediately.
He wanted to die together with her.

He tried to calm and persuade himself that, even in the worst
situation, a human being is obliged to fight to rescue those dearest
to him or her.

The train was approaching Przemyśl. It was already nearly 10:00
p.m. An old man in the same compartment as Andrzej told him that,
at night, the Gestapo did not allow civilian travellers to stay in the
waiting rooms of the station. It was dangerous to go to the hotels
because they were under surveillance of the Gestapo and informers.
Knowing that Andrzej had to wait a couple of hours for his connection, he gave him the address of a decent couple who rented rooms
in their apartment.

After arriving in Przemyśl, Andrzej immediately went to this
apartment. In the room they were renting were six beds, each
separated from the next by sheets hanging on wires. In each draped
compartment was one bed and one chair.

His neighbours on the right were whispering only. After a while,
he realized they were a Jewish couple, travelling to some friends
who had promised to hide them. They were very afraid that they
might be recognized as Jews because of their Semitic features. They
were afraid of the Gestapo, of Polish and Ukrainian police, and of
informers.

The owner of the apartment was a kindly woman. She had a very
sick husband, and she worked very hard, turning one of their rooms
into a rental apartment and keeping it relatively clean. This work
gave her some money for her husband's treatment. She entered the
compartment of the Jewish couple to give them some information on
circumcision performed for medical reasons. The woman asked

some additional questions, but her husband did not ask anything, and Andrzej could hear his tearful, tuned-down crying. His wife was trying to console him.

After a while, the owner came to Andrzej's compartment and asked him to keep secret all that he could hear from the compartment occupied by the Jewish couple. At the same time, she warned him that the people to whom she was sometimes obliged to rent a compartment might be dirty speculators, the scum of the society, informers of Jews, collaborating with the Gestapo. The couple occupying the compartment on the left seemed to be this kind of dangerous persons. She told him to be very cautious; if they became provocative, he should not react at all.

Very soon Andrzej heard that, in the compartment on his left, they started to eat and drink vodka and to talk loud about their program for the next day. They planned to visit the waiting rooms in the railway station, to find people whom they could blackmail because of their Semitic appearance. Then they planned to travel to the neighbouring village to buy meat from cattle clandestinely killed by peasants. They would also buy there some butter and lard, which they intended to sell in Lwów. They were loudly discussing how to cheat the peasant sellers by making the cheapest deal, and how to cheat the buyers in the city by selling for the highest possible price.

After they reached some mutual agreements, the woman asked to have sex. During a long time, Andrzej heard all the obscenities shouted during their sexual play. When they finished there was a moment of silence when he could rest. Unfortunately, after a while, they returned to food and drink. They were singing and shouting and, after a certain time, they began to fight. She wanted to continue their sexual activities; he was tired and wanted to sleep. After a wild scene, he went to sleep, and Andrzej could hear his snoring. She asked at once, through the draperies, if she could come to Andrzej's compartment. He was laying silent, not moving at all and pretending to sleep. For a long time, she shouted that he was a Jewish eunuch, but after a while she stopped, and Andrzej heard that both were now snoring.

The Jewish couple continued to whisper, the husband still crying in a subdued way.

Andrzej was still struggling against the fear that thoughts about the consequences of the tragedy in Orelec raised in him. He thought continually about the safety of Karolina. He felt extremely weak and tired, uncertain whether he would be able to surmount the devastating effects of the tragic and dangerous situation. He was afraid that he might fall sick. During his medical studies, he had caught from a patient a tuberculotic infection and had had tuberculous pleurisy. He was treated for nearly one year in a sanatorium, and since that time his health had not been excellent.

At half-past three in the morning, the owner of the apartment came to Andrzej to open for him the front porch of the house and to show him the shortest way to the station. Outside it was very dark and raining heavily. The streets were empty and wet.

In the waiting room, all the civilian passengers travelling to Lwów were ordered by the Gestapo to get out and wait on a platform far away and nowhere near the roofed portion of the station, which offered protection from the rain; that was where military trains were stopping.

After four in the morning, an empty train arrived and the Gestapo, beating with whips the waiting people, herded the passengers into the train within five minutes. After three hours of standing in the overcrowded corridor, Andrzej arrived at Lwów. It was eight in the morning when he reached the apartment of his parents, soaking wet from his wait in the rain.

His parents knew nothing about the tragedy of Orelec. For the previous couple of weeks, all letters had been sent by Stanisław to the teacher in Orelec. They had had no direct contact by mail with Juliusz for over a month.

The tragedy of Orelec was a terrible shock to Andrzej's parents. Estelle could not stop crying. Andrzej's father realized at once that all of them were now in a dangerous situation. He appreciated very much the teacher's advice to cut immediately all mail contact. Andrzej's mother went to the neighbours' to telephone Stanisław to say that she could not come to him, and asked him to come over as soon as possible.

Before Stanisław's arrival, Andrzej's parents told him how bad the situation in Lwów was. Estelle could only for a short time keep up contact with the uncle and aunt of Karolina and their son. Three weeks earlier the son was taken in the streets of Lwów by the Gestapo and was never seen again. The uncle of Karolina, the old, distinguished ophthalmologist, bedridden for many months because of terminal cancer, was thrown out by the Gestapo, with his bed, from his apartment on the first floor to the backyard. His wife was forbidden to approach him to diminish his sufferings. He suffered many physical injuries from the fall and died within one hour, shot by the Gestapo. His wife and all other family members were on the same day transported to the ghetto in Lwów. Estelle was consulting with Stanisław on how to locate them and help, but up to now there had been no possibility of contact.

During the first hour after his arrival to Lwów, Andrzej heard so many tragic stories that, after his recent shock over the tragedy of Orelec, and thinking all the time about the safety of Karolina, he could simply not absorb the full nightmare that reality had become.

Estelle told him that two of his close friends, colleagues from medical school, had been denounced as Jews by Ukrainian informers. To avoid going to the ghetto in Lwów, they were living in an apartment in the same quarter of the city as Andrzej's parents. Both of those friends were married to girls who were also his colleagues from the University of Lwów. He knew them very well and held them in high esteem. One of them was of Jewish religion, the other Catholic. Both were shot by the Gestapo, together with their husbands, one because she was Jewish and the other one because she was hiding a Jew.

Andrzej's emotional reaction to this tragic news was paradoxical. He had a feeling that it would be quite natural and simple if, in the near future, the Gestapo shot him and Karolina. He was not afraid any longer; he wanted only to die together with her. He did not see any aim in prolonging their life in this world, if so many friends, so many decent and honest people, were gone for ever. What would they do together in such a world?

Stanisław, always optimistic, helpful, and faithful, arrived immediately. He was a Polish gentleman, a very decent and honest man, about 60 years old, and a devout Catholic, practising his religion with great faith and fervour. He had known Karolina from childhood, and he had been friends with Juliusz for many, many years. He had always lived in Lwów and, since the beginning of the war, was very helpful to Juliusz.

When Andrzej told him about the tragedy of Orelec, he could not believe it. Andrzej repeated the story for him three or four times. He explained to him that the teacher in Orelec had told him all the details of the crimes committed by the Gestapo against Juliusz, Dorota, Zosia, and over a hundred Jewish people who were shot in the woods on the hill near Orelec. Stanisław simply could not understand why and how such crimes could be committed.

Andrzej was now afraid that Stanisław, who was very courageous and optimistic, might think that there still existed a possibility of help, of verification of the news. It was not easy to convince him that, for the sake of his own and his family's safety, for the survival of Andrzej's parents and of Karolina, not only could he not risk going to Orelec, but he should immediately stop all contact with the teacher and cut all connections leading to Juliusz and his family. After a long talk, in which Andrzej's father also participated, a man whom Stanisław respected very much, Stanisław was convinced of the tragic reality and understood the preventive safety measures that should be taken at once.

Now he was interested only in one problem: What he could do for Karolina, to help the only surviving member of Juliusz's family. Juliusz had left with him some money for the 'black hour' and he wanted as soon as possible to give this money to Karolina. But what could he do for Karolina to protect her from the dangers to which she might be exposed at any time? Andrzej told him that it was the wish of Karolina that his parents move from Lwów to the same village in which Andrzej and Karolina were living. Therefore, she wanted Stanisław to give the money left by Juliusz to Andrzej's parents so they could rent a truck to transport them with the yet unsold furniture to the village. Stanisław promised not only to bring the money immediately but also to help Andrzej's parents to find and rent, as soon as possible, a truck for transportation.

Now all of them discussed the most important question: how to cut all contact that people who were friends of Juliusz had had with him. Karolina had given Andrzej some names and addresses. Stanisław would have to find out if it was possible to contact them. Some were Jewish, but disguised or hidden by their friends; some were Catholic. Stanisław knew all these people and, understanding already how important it was to cut such contact, decided to start immediately that very day to let them know. He promised also Andrzej that he would not mention to anybody where Karolina and Andrzej were now or where Andrzej's parents were moving to. He would simply say that he did not know what had happened to them. He promised also to come to Andrzej's parents next evening to report the details of his actions and to help to rent a truck.

It was early afternoon when they finished their conversation. They had a modest lunch prepared by Estelle. Andrzej was so tired that, towards the end of conversation, he had to lay down, and most of the talking was done by his father.

After one hour of rest, Andrzej was in better physical shape; however, he was unable to sleep, even for a moment. The anxiety about Karolina, who was now without him in the village, was so strong that he felt that he had to return as soon as possible, even though he needed a longer rest.

After resting a bit longer, Andrzej went to see Father Alojzy in the monastery. The terrible story of Karolina's family was an awful shock for him. He could not conceal his tears. He knelt and prayed for a long while. Then he told Andrzej about the terrible events that were taking place in the ghetto of Lwów. It was, in his opinion, the best thing to get away from the city, and he considered the moving of Andrzej's parents to the village as very clever.

He asked in detail about Karolina and her psychological state, and how she was coping with the terrible news of her family. He sent her words of sympathy and obliged Andrzej to promise him to be in constant mail contact with him. If Andrzej was thinking that, for any reason, it would be good if he came to pay a visit to them in the village, he was ready to go any time and stay there three or four days. He would meet then the parson and the teachers and would tell them that he was a very close friend of the family of Karolina – a family of devoted Catholics. God would understand the generosity of such action and would forgive him that, in the fight with Evil, he had to say things that were not always true. Andrzej thanked him for his compassion. When he left, Father Alojzy hugged and kissed him many times.

Andrzej then went to the convent of Filomena. She was terribly moved by the story of the tragedy in Orelec. She gave him a medallion of the Virgin Mary for Karolina and told him that she was ready to give them help at any time. They should keep up with her regular mail contact.

Andrzej walked slowly to the apartment of his parents. He went through the Piekarska street, where he had had his first walk with Karolina, the same street where he had told her stories about their travelling to the Côte d'Azur and about future excursions after the war. He was now less and less certain that such a possibility will come in their lifetime. All was tragic and very dark.

He passed by the house where Karolina had lived with her family. All these people had been shot by the Gestapo or incarcerated in the ghetto in Lwów, waiting for extermination. Lwów was for him now a ghost-town, full of the restless spirits of honest, noble, open-minded people. He did not know if or when the war would end, or what their fate would be. He knew only that he could never return to Lwów to live in this city, the city of his birth.

At about 6:00 p.m. he returned to the apartment of his parents. His train would depart at 9:00 p.m.

After a short rest following dinner, Andrzej left with his parents to take a tramway to the station. He bought his ticket and as he did when he left Lwów with Karolina, he hugged and kissed his parents in the lobby and went to the entrance leading to the long tunnel lined with platform exits. Before entering the tunnel, he turned towards his parents and waved his hand. He approached the Gestapo check-point, and very soon boarded the train. He was not afraid of anything for himself now, but only of what he would find on his return to the village.

He changed trains three times at night and, at about eight o'clock in the morning he was in Sanok. He did not sleep at night, having to spend almost the entire journey in an overcrowded corridor. It was too early to go to the wagon stand; the driver could arrive after 9:00 a.m., then would have to rest the horses for at least two hours, and feed them.

Andrzej went to the church he had visited with Karolina before his departure to Lwów. The small church was again nearly empty, as was the chapel where they had sat for a long time. He sat down on the same bench before the altar. He looked at the painting of Jesus on the Cross and the Madonna kneeling at the foot of the cross. Nothing had changed. The tragedy of the painting was the same. Andrzej humbly asked God not to increase the burden of their tragedy and to permit him to see Karolina alive. This was the only desire of his life.

At 9:00 he was at the stand for wagons from the villages. A young peasant, one of their neighbours, was already there with his wagon, unharnessing the horse. Andrzej tried to behave very calmly and asked him what was the news from the village. The young peasant was in good humour and told him that everything was all right. Karolina had come to his house at six o'clock in the morning because she was afraid that he might oversleep. 'Your wife is a very nice person. She cares much about you. She is kind to us. She is a real lady,' he added, and smiled.

Andrzej told him that he would return in two hours, so that the horses could have rest. He returned to the church and knelt before the altar in the chapel. For the first time in many years he prayed and thanked God.

Three hours later, Karolina was in his arms. She had returned with the neighbours without any difficulties, and Stefka had stayed with her day and night.

Now Andrzej regained his strength. No longer did he want to be shot together with Karolina. He knew that he had to fight, although he was not at all sure that he would win.

XVII

VERY DIFFICULT DAYS WERE APPROACHING. ANDRZEJ AND Karolina were in bereavement after the tragic events in Orelec, and at the same time, were aware of their own exposure to danger. Andrzej would not leave Karolina alone even for one moment. When he had to go to visit bed-ridden patients, she now always accompanied him and helped with his medical interventions.

About ten days after Andrzej returned from Lwów, his parents arrived in a truck, bringing with them a small amount of furniture and personal belongings. All of them were extremely happy to be together now. After their arrival, Karolcia came with her sons and daughters, and they helped so efficiently that, within two hours, the room was completely furnished and ready to be occupied. In the evening, they had a family dinner at Karolcia's house. Since his childhood, Ludwik had been the pride of the family, and they were extremely happy that they had him with them now, even if only for war-time.

After returning from dinner, Ludwik and Estelle told Andrzej and Karolina that one of Juliusz's friends, just two days before their departure, had been arrested by the Gestapo. Stanisław brought them this news. Karolina knew the name of the arrested man. He was a very well-known lawyer in Cracow. His mother was a Polish Jew and his father, a Catholic Pole. According to Nuremberg law, he was a 'half-Jew' and therefore had to be treated as a Jew and conform to Hitler's orders for Jews. Stanisław did not know if this arrest had any connection with the tragedy of Orelec or if it had resulted from the action of an informer. The wife of the arrested lawyer did not know the reason for the arrest, since only their closest friends in Cracow had known about his half-Jewish origins.

Karolina was very afraid upon hearing this news because the lawyer had been a frequent visitor of Juliusz, and Juliusz and Dorota had visited him and his wife in Lwów. Andrzej had met this lawyer in the apartment of her parents in Lwów. She was also sure that Juliusz had given him his address, and most probably there existed correspondence between Juliusz and this lawyer. Karolina doubted very much that anybody in Lwów could have known about the Jewish origin of the lawyer's mother; therefore, his arrest might be connected with his contact with Orelec.

The fear increased in them when they realized that it was highly probable that the lawyer was traced because of the mail exchange with Orelec. As he might have known something about Andrzej's marriage with Karolina, and perhaps also of their moving, they had a terrible feeling of insecurity, especially this night.

The nights were always the most fearsome part of the day. Patients with emergencies knocked firmly at their windows or doors at night to wake them up. In the existing situation, such knocking could be the hands of the Gestapo, a signal of the beginning of the end. Therefore, night never gave them a good rest.

The coming days did not bring any news. Life after the arrival of Andrzej's parents became much easier. His parents usually came to visit them at about eleven o'clock in the morning. Ludwik liked very much to work in the small garden in front of their house, and Estelle helped the young maid, the daughter of their neighbours, to prepare lunch. This assistance gave Karolina more and more time to help Andrzej. She wrote up all the case histories of his patients. If necessary, she spoke with the patients or their parents about their health problems and reported to Andrzej before he examined them. She usually sat at a small table in the anteroom outside Andrzej's office. This table was her office. The patients were happy that 'two doctors' were taking care of them. To an outsider, this family seemed to lead a quite peaceful and serene life. However, all of them were constantly troubled by the incredible tragedy in Orelec and were made anxious and fearful by thoughts about their own future.

About ten days after the arrival of his parents, Andrzej received a telegram from a neighbour of Stanisław, informing him that Stanisław had left Lwów on vacation. The message was in code: Stanisław had been arrested by the Gestapo. When the telegram arrived, Andrzej was examining a patient and had two others waiting on the veranda. Andrzej interrupted his work and asked Karolina to write immediately to Father Alojzy. Father Alojzy knew Stanisław from before the war and knew about the relationship that Stanisław had had with Juliusz and his family. He knew also the lawyer. Karolina was to write a short letter – in the agreed-upon code – requesting information about the illness of their dear friends and asking if their health was better. She had also to ask Father Alojzy to send an answer at his earliest convenience to Andrzej. Because of German censorship, the letters were always written in code to make them seem quite innocuous to the censors.

Andrzej sent the maid to ask his parents to come to their house; he wanted Karolina to go with Ludwik to mail the letter immediately at the post office. The patient whose examination he was just finishing had arrived in an empty country wagon and was most willing to give them a lift.

All that was done very quietly, although it was extremely difficult to concentrate on medical problems in light of such alarming information. It was necessary to act immediately. All was done so fast that as Andrzej started to examine his next patient he could see that Ludwik and Karolina were already sitting in the former patient's country wagon, ready to depart with the letter.

After examining all the waiting patients, and after lunch, when the young maid left, they could sit down and talk freely about this frightening news. They could do nothing for the time being but wait for events to unfold.

They waited in great anxiety for the answer from Father Alojzy. It arrived ten days after Karolina mailed her letter. Father Alojzy wrote, using the code they had established before they left Lwów, that: 'the lawyer died because he had grave pneumonia. His wife was hospitalized for a long time. Probably she caught an infection from him. Stanisław had returned from his journey and was at home, in good health. During his vacation he had not met Juliusz. He was very upset by the death of the lawyer and the disease of his wife.

'Life here is as usual.

'My best wishes of good health and peace, and may God bless you, my dearest friends. Yours ever, Alojzy.'

The real content of the letter read: 'The lawyer was killed by the Gestapo. His wife was sent to a concentration camp. All this was bound with the action of an informer who knew about the lawyer's origin.Stanisław was released from prison in good health. His arrest was not connected with the tragedy of Orelec, and Juliusz's name was not mentioned during the interrogation by the Gestapo. They were interested only in Stanisław's relationship with the lawyer. Stanisław told the Gestapo that he had never heard anything about the ancestors of the lawyer and was released after a short time.'

The warm letter of Father Alojzy diminished their anxiety, but at the same time added new sorrows over the death of the lawyer and the arrest of his wife.

Andrzej told his parents immediately after they arrived about Karolcia's ideas concerning the relationship between Karolina and the deceased husband of Karolcia. Karolcia had spoken about this relationship to many people in the village. Andrzej wanted to know exactly what had prompted Karolcia to tell people this completely invented story. He asked Ludwik to find out, but in such a way that Karolcia would not be told the true story of Karolina's origin. Karolcia was a very clever woman, and Andrzej was sure she must have had a serious motivation to invent such a story.

Ludwik was amazed by this story. He was the only person who could have an intimate conversation with Karolcia. He was also a very shrewd person, one experienced in dealing, with diplomatic skill, with any kind of problem, as he had done in his former career in education administration. For a certain time, Ludwik was not only teaching in college, but had a very high position in college administration in the three provinces of southeast Poland. In Karolina's special situation, when two of the nearest friends of Juliusz were arrested by Gestapo, it was important to know and understand the reasons behind Karolcia's story without divulging the truth.

Such an occasion presented itself on the next Sunday. As always on Sunday, they planned to go, together with Andrzej's parents, to church for the High Mass at eleven o'clock in the morning. After that, they were all invited for Sunday brunch at Karolcia's house, which was very close to the church. Ludwik said, with his dry humour: 'She will certainly be sincere with me. However, if we don't go to Mass because we are already in the other dimension, this conversation will be unnecessary.'

After the lunch at Karolcia's house, Ludwik went with his sister to the garden and they sat down on a bench for a longer conversation. Andrzej and Karolina stayed inside with Andrzej's cousins.

When all the family returned home, Ludwik gave them a detailed report of the conversation with Karolcia.

They had spoken as brother and sister, and as parents who want the best for all their children. Ludwik had simply asked Karolcia why she had had this idea, that Antoni, her deceased husband, was the brother of the father of Karolina. She sincerely answered that, after their arrival from Lwów, Karolina had told her that she had never seen such an enormous, thick candle as that which was standing on the commode in Karolcia's house. Nobody was present in the room at that time. Karolcia had told Ludwik that she was a little bit astonished by Karolina's remark. She had explained to Karolina that such candles, which are called 'thunder candles' are consecrated and lighted during a storm to protect the household from the thunder and lightning and when a peasant is dying they are lighted and put into his or her hands. She had liked Karolina very much from the first moment, and afterwards more and more, because this beautiful, educated girl always spoke so kindly with simple people, as if she were one of them. Karolina was always very warm and extremely kind with Karolcia, and she knew how to defend her from Władek, who was not always very kind to Karolcia. 'Władek listens to Karolina. She knows how to talk with him. It is not easy to gain the respect of Władek,' she said. 'All my children love Karolina and admire her, and I love her as if she were one of my own children. She is very close to my heart, and therefore, perhaps, I feel that she is full of sadness and anxiety. And her beautiful eyes remind me of the eyes of some beautiful saints, who followed our Jesus Christ. You remember, Ludwik, I believe, from our Catholic religion, with all your atheism, that all His society, and our Jesus Christ, in his human incarnation, were Jews. Therefore, I tell people of the village that the eyes of Karolina are like the eyes of my husband and of my eldest son, Cesiek. People see what you tell them they should see.'

In answering, Ludwik was a model of diplomacy. The best professional diplomat could not have invented a better answer: 'My dear Karolcia, thank you for all the good you are doing for Karolina. She loves you very much indeed, and she is an excellent girl. The truth is not important when you are surrounded by murderers and bandits like the Nazis. All is good that can make us more secure and is not dangerous for us, and for our friends. Your idea, my dear sister, was excellent and I support it fully. I will also tell people that Karolina has her family in this village. Thank you, dear Karolcia.'

Karolina, hearing all this, approached Ludwik and, crying, kissed him many times. Ludwik took her in his arms and held her for a long time. Estelle kissed Karolina and hugged her maternally, caressing her hair.

In the evening, after Andrzej's parents left, they tried to relax, taking comfort in having heard the news of how well they were accepted by the village population. However, it was still impossible to find a moment of calm because all their thoughts were focused on the tragedy of Orelec.

The next morning, the youngest of Andrzej's cousins, Bolek, brought to him a sealed envelope, which had been handed over to him by one of his chums. Andrzej came with the letter to Karolina and they read it together. It read as follows: 'Dear Sir, As soon as possible I visited the house. In a drawer in which he was always leaving for me a note or money for shopping with a list of needed food, I found a letter that reads: "Dear Janka, my last thoughts are with my beloved daughter who is not with us. Let her know what happened here because I will never see her again on this earth. Let her know that it is my wish that she obeys in everything her husband, whom I love and admire for his character and courage. If I would have followed his advice, I would not be today with my family in this situation. I leave no other letter or address in this house. Dear Janka take care of you. You are one of the most decent and courageous human beings that I met in my life. Thank you." This letter, written on a small piece of especially wrinkled paper, was signed J. I have this letter and I will give it to you after the war. I wish the best to his daughter. With the help that she has, she will certainly survive this tragedy of humanity. I found your address and your name in such a way, which certainly is not dangerous for you. Be quiet and prudent. Hope to see you after the war. Janka.'

Janka was the name under which Andrzej knew the teacher in Orelec. He never received from her the letter of Juliusz and never saw her again. She was shot by the Nazis just before the end of the war.

This letter from Juliusz to Janka, this letter from 'beyond,' was an enormous shock for Andrzej and Karolina. It represented more proof of how terribly Juliusz had suffered while he waited for the Gestapo with his wife and daughter, having full awareness that he had made a mistake that would cost them their lives. They were full of pain knowing how enormous were his sufferings and how mortally hurtful was his feeling of the irreversibility of his decision. They spoke of all that the next evening and night and could not detach themselves from the memories of the cruel last moments of the life of the person whom they both loved so much.

With day-break, they had to start again their daily work: seeing patients, travelling sometimes day and night by country wagon to bed-ridden patients. They had to continue their social duties: invite and visit with the parson, the vicars, the teachers, participate as guests of honour at some peasants' weddings. And they had to do all that with a serene face, showing no signs of concern. It was an uneasy life.

The despair and pain caused by the tragedy of Orelec persisted, unchanged, throughout the lifetime of Andrzej and Karolina. Time does not heal such wounds.

XVIII

IT WAS SUMMER OF 1942, AND HARVEST TIME. ANDRZEJ HAD fewer patients to see than usual, because during the harvest the peasants work from the early morning hours until late evening and come to a physician only in the case of emergency.

At that time, the extermination of the Jews began in the region in which the village of Andrzej and Karolina was located. The method was not the same as in Orelec. The few Jewish families in the neighbouring villages were transported by the Gestapo to the nearest small town, to live in its worst quarter, separated by a barbed-wire fence from the rest of the town. This was the local ghetto for all the Jews of the town and the neighbouring villages.

The Gestapo escorted Jews, who had to transport their furniture and personal belongings on wagons to the ghetto. If a Jewish household had no horse, the house owner had to draw the wagon himself, with the help of his wife, parents, and children. None of the Polish population was allowed to help the Jewish people. It was a very tragic exodus.

Andrzej and Karolina could see through their windows the cruelties of the Gestapo, the beating of the old people and children when they did not move quickly enough. On his way to visit a bed-ridden patient, Andrzej had once seen a Nazi shoot an old Jewish woman who was unable to maintain the walking pace ordered by the Gestapo. The emaciated body of this woman was laid on the wagon by a young Jew, who was drawing the wagon himself, with tears on his face. He was probably her son or son-in-law. A young woman, following the wagon with three children, was crying bitterly.

Similar tragedies during those times of contempt were often seen on the roads of Poland. You could be only a silent witness of such tragedies. For any gesture of protest you would be shot.

The ghetto in the small town existed for a few months. Young men and women alike worked in the forests, cutting the trees under the surveillance of the Gestapo. Children and old people were not allowed outside the ghetto. They worked in special barracks for the German army, sewing big bags for transportation of linen and underwear for soldiers.

The amount of food rationed to the population of ghetto was insufficient. The rate of morbidity and mortality was high and rising constantly.

As a physician of insured patients, such as teachers, foresters, letter-carriers, and their families, Andrzej had to go once monthly to the nearest small town, Brzozów where was located a pharmacy and the residence of the regional doctor. Andrzej had to hand him over monthly reports and to replenish periodically the supply of emergency prescriptions held in his office. On the occasion of such a visit, Andrzej had the opportunity to speak frankly with the regional physician and gathered some information about the tragic situation of the Jews in the ghetto. Knowing that they were obliged to work for the Germans, the regional doctor had some hope that the people in the ghetto would be able to survive the war. However, he was very concerned with the rate of morbidity and mortality. He was not allowed to enter the ghetto. A Jewish physician from the surrounding area was working in the ghetto. The regional doctor was trying to send as much medication as possible, but the opportunities were very limited. Nevertheless, if an occasion arose where Nazi control could be circumvented, he was doing so, taking an enormous personal risk if the nature of his actions was discovered.

For a while Andrzej had some suspicions concerning the behaviour of an eighteen-year-old Polish boy named Kazek. He was the younger son of a very respected widow in the neighbourhood. His older brother was a decent, very hard-working hammersmith in the village. Kazek very often travelled to Sanok and was seen there in the company of people who were suspected of having contact with the Germans. It was unclear if this contact was founded on the compulsory deliveries of grain, meat, and other food to the Germans or on informer collaboration.

One of Andrzej's cousins, Bolek, who was a member of the 'Peasant Battalions,' warned Andrzej to be very cautious with Kazek, who was suspected of being one of the Nazis' informers. The resistance was investigating his activity; if he was found to be a Nazi collaborator, he would be lawfully punished by the court of the resistance.

Kazek very often hung around near Andrzej's house. Just opposite was a shop belonging to the cooperative of a peasant organization called 'Agricultural Circle.' In this shop, peasants could buy necessary agricultural tools such as scythes, sickles, ploughs, etc. The shop was also a centre of social life, like a café. The peasants came there to speak with friends in and in front of the shop. A great deal of gossip was exchanged around this place.

Outside the shop, Kazek treated the neighbours with beer, and sometimes with German cigarettes or German wine, which no Pole could buy. He spoke very seldom, but listened with attention to the conversation of the neighbours.

He also observed what was going on in Andrzej's house: who was coming as a patient and why. He spoke with peasants who were waiting in their country wagons for their visit in Andrzej's office or to take Andrzej to a bed-ridden patient in another village. Kazek tried to establish closer contact with the young cleaning maid in Andrzej's household. He also tried to approach Karolina, when she was speaking on the veranda with the peasants or going outside. She was, however, too busy to waste time gossiping with Kazek.

After the harvest, two young boys from the village were arrested by the Gestapo. They never returned home, and the peasants knew that they belonged to the underground resistance. It was evident that they had been betrayed by somebody from the village. Kazek was the prime suspect. The investigation of his activity by the command of the resistance for the Sanok region proceeded quickly.

One evening, Bolek came to Andrzej and told him that the military court of the resistance had pronounced a sentence of death upon Kazek, and that Kazek would no more travel to Sanok. 'Don't be afraid of him,' he said, when leaving.

Two days later, Kazek was, in the evening, alone in his house. His older brother was working in his hammersmith's work place; his mother had been invited for dinner at neighbours. Four members of the resistance arrived in a country wagon, which they stationed in the backyard of his house. They called Kazek out of his house. In the backyard, they read him the verdict that led to the death sentence by the martial court of the resistance. They presented him with several proofs of his treacherous activity and being a Nazi informer. Kazek pleaded guilty and was shot by two members of the resistance: one bullet in the heart, one in the brain. The corpse was immediately thrown into a bag, put on the wagon, and buried on the same evening in a distant forest.

The mother and the brother of Kazek never spoke of him. Nobody in the village mentioned his name. When, two weeks after the execution, the Polish police asked Kazek's mother what had happened to her son, she answered that Kazek had left the village forever.

This was the only case of collaboration with the Germans known to Andrzej in this region. The Polish peasants had organized a united front against the Nazi occupants of Poland.

The confidence in such a front, combined with the ingenuity of the Polish peasants, led, under some incredible circumstances, to out-witting the Germans.

A young peasant, Wojtek, was taken to Germany for forced labour. When his mother died in Sanok of cancer, he was given a short leave to go to her funeral.

Andrzej did not know Wojtek, who had been taken to Germany before Andrzej's arrival at the village. However, he did know his mother, whom he had been treating for a terminal cancer, and also Wojtek's fiancée, a young, very pretty girl named Anna. Before Wojtek was taken to Germany, Anna became pregnant by her fiancé. She delivered a healthy, beautiful son with the assistance of Andrzej just one month before Wojtek arrived at the village on his short leave.

At that time, a child born out of wedlock was very badly accepted by the religious Polish peasants. For its lifetime, it was called 'bastard,' and its chances of a good family life were poor. An illegitimate child was always considered as evident proof of a sin. Anna and her mother were very unhappy during the last months of her pregnancy. But now Wojtek, the father of the child, was here and it was possible to change the situation.

To Anna and her mother was born an ingenious idea. There were many clever women in the village; not only Karolcia had wonderfully imaginative ideas.

One evening, a couple of days after Wojtek's arrival at the village, Anna and her mother came to Andrzej with a bizarre idea. They wanted to have a medical death certificate for Wojtek from Andrzej, and they wanted to ask also the parson for such a death certificate from the church. Wojtek, healthy and happy, would at once marry Anna and not return to Germany. Instead a death certificate would be sent. The child would be baptized as a legitimate son, in the church. Wojtek could not be forced to return to Germany because he was certified as dead. 'A dead person cannot travel and return to Germany for forced labour,' argued Anna's mother.

Andrzej liked this woman. She was not like other mothers, blaming for ever their daughters for the mortal sin of illegitimate pregnancy. All her anger was concentrated on the Germans. Because of the German occupation, Wojtek had been taken for forced labour to Germany. Because of the German occupation, he had been nervous and unable to take the normal precautions to avoid making his fiancée pregnant. All this mess, all the sufferings of Anna, were caused by the German occupation. 'Yes,' she told Andrzej, 'I agree it was a sin to have sexual relations and to become pregnant before marriage but, for God's sake, not every sin is a crime. Nobody, even in these conditions, would think of abortion. Without the German occupation, Wojtek would have married Anna immediately after knowing that she was pregnant. The child would have been born seven months after the wedding. That would not be an exceptional case, even in our village.'

Andrzej liked very much this historical, political, broad approach to the problem of Anna's pregnancy. He also liked Anna, who accepted with humility the result of her 'sin,' never thought of abortion, and endured for many months the atmosphere of contempt for being pregnant and unmarried.

Andrzej listened with attention to Anna's mother's arguments and promised her that he would do his best to help them and that he would also talk to the parson. However, he wanted them to seek cooperation among the population of the village in this endeavour and to garner a guarantee that the story would be kept confidential within the village.

Karolina liked very much the idea and encouraged him to help Anna and her mother. Karolina knew Anna and had had with her a couple of sessions of rational psychotherapy during her pregnancy.

In the evening Karolina told Andrzej: 'I am sure that Jesus Christ in His human incarnation would like these young people and would bless them and their son, despite the sin. Anna's mother was right, this sin was very far from being a crime.' With a smile Andrzej asked Karolina: 'I am sure that you are right. But what about Jesus Christ as God? Are you sure that He would do the same as God?' 'Why have you no confidence in our God when, at the same time, you are attached to the philosophy of goodness of Jesus Christ?' asked Karolina. 'Are you really not astonished, looking at all that is going on around us in this world?' answered Andrzej. That was the end of their conversation for the day. It was late and they were tired.

Andrzej went to the parson, but not alone. He asked for the assistance of a young, very pretty teacher, who was known to have great influence on the parson. Andrzej did not want to analyse the reasons behind this influence. He felt only that her presence during the conversation with the parson was quite essential to the outcome of the discussion.

At the beginning of the conversation, the parson was a little resistant, but, knowing very well the life in the villages, the sins of the parishioners, and that Andrzej probably knew some of the parson's own sins, and, above all, seeing that during this conversation the teacher looked at him with expectation, he surrendered very soon. He decided to create a new Catholic family, and thus to diminish the number of Poles in Germany for forced labour. He promised to baptize the baby immediately after the marriage as born legitimately, to date the certificate of marriage one year back, to create circumstances that would not cause any complications for the child. On the basis of Andrzej's certificate, he would officially confirm the death of Wojtek.

After working out small details, Andrzej returned home and immediately opened Wojtek's file and made an entry dated ten days before the planned 'death' of Wojtek. He noted that Wojtek had come to him in a serious state and was diagnosed as having viral pneumonia. Although he had received the best possible treatment, the illness had proved fatal, and an official death certificate was issued by Andrzej. The date of death was one week after the baptism of his son. The parson could now write an official death certificate. Both certificates, one from Andrzej and the other from the parsonage, were sent to the head of the village. After duly entering them in the village's books, the head of the village sent them to the German authorities in Sanok.

For the Germans, Wojtek's case was terminated. They simply could not imagine how ingenious the Polish peasants were.

Since that time, Wojtek was called in the village 'the man who died.' He and Anna and his son lived in the house of his parents-in-law. 'The man who died' worked outside, ploughing the soil for his wife and his parents-in-law.

On Sundays, he regularly went to church, not to High Mass but to one of the Lower Masses, early in the morning. After Mass, they went to the cemetery, where Anna put the wreath on the grave of her mother-in-law.

XIX

ANDRZEJ WAS WORKING VERY HARD, FROM MORNING until late evening. He was the doctor of poor people, and his professional activities gave him great satisfaction. He had excellent relations with the peasants of the village and the neighbourhood. Karolina was liked very much by the women of the village. She listened attentively to their worries and gave them practical advice. She was many times asked to be a godmother, and she knew perfectly well how to perform those functions. Both of them and Andrzej's parents were often invited to weddings as guests of honour. Andrzej had real peasant roots, authentic peasant descent. Karolina had the same roots, thanks to the invention and wisdom of Karolcia.

One day, in fall 1942, the Gestapo arrived in the village looking for young people to send to Germany for forced labour. They entered the house of Andrzej because they had seen the young maid cleaning and cooking there. One of the two men from the Gestapo spoke fluent German, and it was evident that German was his mother tongue. The other one also spoke German, but with an Ukrainian accent. Both were very rude. Andrzej tried to ensure that the young maid would be spared from forced labour, explaining that her mother was a very poor widow and that the departure of the oldest child, then sixteen years old, would create a very difficult situation for all the family. He did not mention that the presence of the maid in his household was for him also important, because he knew that such an argument would not be well accepted by the Gestapo. He did not want to speak about his office, his profession, his household. He wanted, above all, to avoid any discussion of Karolina.

But such was impossible. The Gestapo man who spoke fluent German asked him what the young girl was doing in his house, if he was a physician. If she was cleaning his office and resi- dence and cooking for him, his wife, and his family, he could only be shocked: 'You, Polish doctor, you know that, in such a way, you are diminishing the strength of "our Vaterland." The Germans could win this war earlier and rule the world if, instead of cleaning your office and living quarters, this young Polish girl could work for German industry in Germany. I swear to you' – he was shouting – 'that she will do this in the nearest future. Today she is working the last day in your house. In two days she will be sent to Germany to help the Germans win the war. And you, Polish doctor, you will clean with your wife and your family your place. You will begin a day earlier and do all the work yourself. Your wife, the Polish "lady," will have no servant. Our German women, wives of better doctors than you, are working very hard in Germany, and they have no maids. Do you understand, doctor, what I am telling you, or shall I teach you in another way?' 'Yes,' Andrzej answered, 'I understand, and we will do all the work ourselves.' He was thinking only of how to end the presence of Gestapo in his house.

The conversation would have ended there if the Ukrainian Gestapo man had not said that he wanted to see the Polish 'lady' and to know exactly what the young girl was doing in the doctor's residence.

Karolina was terribly frightened when Andrzej entered their living quarters with the Gestapo man. She knew that he had tried to do all to avoid her encountering the Gestapo and that he had failed.

The Ukrainian Gestapo man was very rude with Karolina: 'I wanted to see the Polish "lady" who is dawdling in bed and doing nothing, whereas our heroic nation is fighting for the future of the world. But we are coming here to put an end to such a situation. Your maid will leave this village and will be sent to Germany to do something more effective than cleaning the apartment of the Polish "lady."' He looked for a long time into the eyes of Karolina with evident disgust and asked after a while: 'Are you really Polish, you, the wife of this country doctor?' Karolina did not blink. She tried to stay cool-headed and answered very kindly and with dignity: 'Yes, of course I am Polish, and my husband is a Pole. Yes, we will clean our house ourselves, we will cook for us. We are not afraid to work. I am not thinking now of me. We are able to cope with our household problems, but the young girl is only sixteen years old and is very frail. Please be so kind, if you are sending her to Germany, as to find her work that would not be too hard for her.' 'Mind your business, Polish lady. In Germany she will be much better off than in this dirty Polish village.'

This conversation was interrupted by the other Gestapo man: 'John, it is time to leave. We still have a lot of work to do in this village.' And both of them departed, leaving the door open.

One hour after their departure, one of Andrzej's neighbours came to his house and told him that one of the Gestapo men who spoke Polish had asked her if the wife of the doctor was Jewish. The neighbour had told him that Karolina was Catholic, that she was a very religious woman, and that her family were peasants of the same village. The Gestapo man had told her that he accepted this answer; however, if it was a lie, the neighbour would be shot for helping the Jews and that the doctor and his wife would also be killed. Andrzej accepted this information, trying to be very quiet, and told the neighbour: 'All this is a pure nonsense. I see that the Nazis are not only criminals, but they are completely crazy.' He was trying to minimize the story.

This was the beginning of an extremely difficult period in the lives of Andrzej and Karolina. They did not even tell Andrzej's parents this story because Andrzej's father had very high blood pressure and he badly needed rest and calm. They were afraid that the Gestapo might come any minute. They were afraid that their neighbour would speak about this incident with other peasants and that such gossip might be very dangerous. Fortunately, the neighbour was clever enough not to talk about the incident with anybody.

The Gestapo stayed in the village, and in the region, for several days. For Andrzej and Karolina, it was a time of fear, of sleepless nights, of enormous tension. During this time Andrzej was constantly with Karolina. She travelled with him to visit the bed-ridden patients in the neighbouring villages. The nights, which always had been a time of greatest fear, became now a period of martyrdom. Every knock at the window or door was perceived by them as a signal that the last hour of their lives had struck.

Several days after the Gestapo had entered their house, Andrzej had to travel to Brzozów the nearest town in the region to bring the monthly report on insured patients to the regional doctor and to refurbish his supply of emergency drugs. He decided to take Karolina with him because the Gestapo was still in the region, hunting for young people to send for forced labour. Karolina had already once visited this small town and been invited, with Andrzej, to take lunch with the regional physician. Now, in a poor part of this small town, was a ghetto for the regional Jewish population.

Andrzej has asked one of the neighbours, who had a good horse and a sufficiently comfortable country wagon, to drive them down. It was a beautiful, but already chilly day of the golden Polish autumn. After two hours' drive, they entered the town. It was quiet. They dropped in for a short visit at the office of the regional physician. From there, they went to the pharmacy to refurbish Andrzej's supply of emergency drugs. When they were in the pharmacy, several trucks with Gestapo entered the town. This was a special kind of Gestapo, for special functions, mostly to exterminate the Jews. It was called 'das rollende Gestapo' (the rolling Gestapo), which meant that it was a mobile unit, driving from one place to another to perform its 'special' functions.

Andrzej and Karolina made an all-out effort not to show their state of mind. They continued their work with the pharmacist, and their professional conversation. A Ukrainian policeman entered the pharmacy and asked the pharmacist if all the people in the pharmacy were there for medical reasons. When the pharmacist confirmed that, the policeman ordered that all of them should stay in the pharmacy for a certain time because the Gestapo had ordered a stop of all the traffic in the town and the streets were closed. 'We are,' the policeman said, 'performing now the final solution of the Jewish question in this town. We wanted to give the Jews a certain opportunity, a chance to work in this town for us. But, as you know, the Jews are lazy, dirty, and sick. A lot of them died. A lot are sick and cannot work. So, all the business that was supposed to work in this ghetto does not work. We have to finish that. In one or two hours, the ghetto will be empty, and you will be allowed to go out. I advise you people not to talk.' He asked the pharmacist for the keys to the door of pharmacy and, going out, locked the door, so that nobody could get in or out.

When he left, complete silence set in. In the pharmacy were present about thirty people, some of them residents of the town, some of them peasants from the neighbouring villages. Nobody was sure who was who. Nobody was certain that, among them, was not a German informer.

Andrzej and Karolina silently continued their work with the pharmacist: Andrzej gave him the report on used drugs, Karolina noted what drugs and in what amount they had to take with them. This purely professional activity protected them from slipping into reality. They did not know if they would be alive when people were allowed to leave the pharmacy. From time to time, shots were heard, coming from the far west where the ghetto was situated. After a while, shots were heard nearly constantly, and from the far north. The people did not speak because the policeman had told them not to. The first shots had probably been the Gestapo killing the old and sick Jewish people in the ghetto and the later ones, the extermination of all the Jews from the ghetto in the neighbouring forest.

It was already dark when the Ukrainian policeman returned. He told the people in the pharmacy that now they could return home and that now they were free of Jews.

Andrzej and Karolina returned to their country wagon. The driver told them that the Nazis had killed all the Jews from the ghetto in the nearby forest. 'How does God allow such atrocities to happen on this earth?' he asked. He had been outside through it all, staying with the wagon and the horses, and had heard the shooting from the ghetto and from the forest.

Andrzej and Karolina left town with him. At the exit from the town, two Gestapo men stopped the wagon and asked Andrzej for his identity card, which he showed them. They asked who the woman with him was. He answered that she was his wife. They accepted that without further formalities. One of them said: 'You, doctor, you will have now fewer patients. The Jews were always infecting the region. They were dirty and carriers of diseases.'

Andrzej and Karolina did not talk on their way back home. One is speechless at the bottom of hell. When they returned home, Karolina could not restrain herself from crying in the evening. At night, they talked many hours about Juliusz, Dorota, and Zosia. They did not sleep that night.

Two days after travelling to the town, Andrzej and Karolina had a visit from the teacher who had accompanied Andrzej to the parson to make arrangements for Wojtek and Anna. She told Andrzej that, earlier, a Ukrainian policeman had come to school and had asked her if the wife of the doctor was Jewish. She had answered that such an idea was a pure nonsense, that Karolina was a member of family of peasants of the village known 'for ages' as very religious Catholics. 'We know now,' she added, 'the name of this Ukrainian Gestapo man. Sooner or later a day will come when he will pay for all the crimes that he has committed. I wanted also to tell you, doctor, that all the Gestapo together with this policeman left the region yesterday.'

Andrzej and Karolina felt a certain relief. They were extremely exhausted by the general situation, by the cruelties of the Nazis that they had witnessed, by the disasters and calamities taking place around them, and by their own feeling of insecurity each day, each hour, each minute. The relief they felt when the Gestapo left the region was only like a short moment to draw a deep breath during a dangerous climb. They were not sure they would have the strength to climb higher until they reached a safe haven on this forced excursion to the hell.

XX

ANDRZEJ AND KAROLINA WERE INDEED VERY FAR FROM A safe haven, although news from the fronts was better. In October 1942, Montgomery routed Rommel at Alamein in North Africa. In November 1942, French and British forces invaded Algeria. The Germans suffered enormous losses on the eastern front during the winter. The German 'Blitzkrieg' was finished.

It was before Christmas 1942, and snow was already everywhere in the village. As always, the worst moments were night time knocks at their windows or doors. The high level of anxiety that plagued them mounted to intolerable levels during such situations. They had always the feeling that the end of their lives was close, that the Gestapo was coming for them.

That night the man who knocked at their door was a peasant from their village; his connection to the resistance was known to Andrzej. He arrived with three other men from the resistance. Two stayed outside; one followed the man who knocked at the door. A man was wounded, and it was an emergency situation in which Andrzej had to amputate his right thumb, contain the bleeding, and dress three more superficial wounds. The man was very weak because of loss of blood. Karolina helped Andrzej during this intervention. Andrzej gave him some injections and, after two hours, he left in better shape. His wounds were from a military action of the resistance against the Germans.

The next day the Gestapo has found the man. He was asleep in one of the remote houses in the neighbouring village. After taking him, the Gestapo burned the house, killing four adults who lived in the house, and, using hay-forks, threw six children into the fire. The wounded man was arrested by the Gestapo and tortured. The Nazis wanted to know about the organization of resistance, the number of fighters, and the relations between the organization and the local population.

Andrzej and Karolina heard this news from the peasants, and they were prepared for the worst. In the afternoon, a German military car stopped before their house and its driver asked Andrzej to enter the car and took him away. Andrzej was prepared for all possibilities and left the house as quickly as he could, not wanting the Gestapo to enter and have any contact with Karolina. Sitting on the front seat, close to the military driver, he was brought very soon to a building that belonged, before the war, to the former landlord. In front of the building were parked about five German military cars and one military truck.

The driver showed him into a room where an officer from the Gestapo was sitting at a table. He was drinking coffee and smoking a cigarette. He was about thirty, elegantly dressed. He addressed Andrzej in a very polite way, inviting him to sit down at the table opposite and offering him a cup of coffee and a cigarette. He asked Andrzej very kindly about his work as physician in the village, the conditions of his work, when and where he had taken his medical studies. But Andrzej did not let himself be confused by such a polite approach. He knew that he was speaking with a cruel enemy and that his presence here was linked to the medical intervention of the previous night. One idea only was in his mind: would they kill Karolina after killing him, or would they not kill her. If they did not kill her, what would happen to her after his death?

The officer offered a second cup of coffee to Andrzej and another cigarette and continued to talk in a polite manner. Suddenly he interrupted, and with a kind smile and in a hard tone, he said: 'Drink, Herr Doktor. Drink this second cup of coffee, drink it slowly, because afterwards I am perhaps going to shoot you. Yes, if you are helping the Polish terrorists, who call themselves the resistance, I will shoot you personally today. The amputation of the thumb of the terrorist was done by a professional, by a doctor. And you are the only doctor in this region.' He did not shout. He spoke in the same low, although hard, voice. He smiled all the time.

He called one of the Gestapo men and, after a while, the man from the Polish resistance was pushed into the room. He was so changed that Andrzej hardly recognized him. His face was covered with blood; his clothes were torn. The man from the Gestapo asked him in Polish: 'Do you know this gentleman? He is the doctor in the village. Have you seen him ever before in your life? Have you been in his office?' The man looked for a long while at Andrzej, and Andrzej looked at him. The man was holding Andrzej's life in his hands. He answered in a very low, tired voice: 'I have never seen him before in my life. I do not know him.'

This conversation was translated to the officer. He said in his hard voice: 'Now we will shoot' and paused. After a while, he added: 'We will shoot the Polish terrorist in the prison. Take him out.'

After a long while he turned again to Andrzej and said, still smiling: 'And you, Herr Doktor, you are free. You can drink one more cup of coffee with me or you can at once return home to your wife. She is, I think, waiting for you with certain impatience. My driver will give you a lift.' Andrzej told him that he wanted to return home and left the room. He was full of admiration for the heroism of the man from the Polish resistance.

The car stopped before Andrzej's house. In seconds, he had Karolina in his arms and they were together again. Andrzej felt that her suffering while waiting for him to return was perhaps greater than his during the conversation with the Gestapo officer. For the first and the last time in his life, Andrzej had a long conversation with an officer from the Gestapo. He would remember for a long time his apparent politeness, his cynical cruelty, his horrific sadism. The recollection of his smiling face would haunt Andrzej.

The Gestapo left not long afterwards the house of the previous landlord. After one week, Andrzej's cousin, Bolek, told him that the man from the resistance had been executed in prison by the Gestapo. After the war, in his native village, a simple cross was installed close to the cemetery. The circumstances of his death were described on a plaque hung on the cross, together with a military decoration that was awarded to him.

XXI

AT THE BEGINNING OF 1943, ANDRZEJ, KAROLINA, AND Andrzej's parents received new identity cards (Kennkarten) distributed among the population of occupied Polish territories by the occupying authorities. To obtain such a document you had to present the originals of your birth and baptism certificates and of your marriage certificate to the German authorities in Sanok, where they were thoroughly examined. Andrzej and Karolina presented the certificates given them by Father Alojzy. It was again a very difficult waiting period for them, this one lasting several weeks, until they received the identity cards issued by German authorities for all the population. Karolina had now an official German document testifying that she was Polish and Catholic. They would never forget with what anxiety and fear they awaited these identity cards.

The news from the fronts was encouraging. In February 1943, the Soviet counter-offensive resulted in the surrender of the German 6th army at Stalingrad. The hopes for the victory of the Allies became more realistic, although it was still very difficult to predict how long the war would last, which was making the life of Andrzej and Karolina incredibly hard.

The cruel extermination of the Jewish people was going on in the Polish cities; the ghettos were destroyed and Jews were killed.

The history of the biggest ghetto in Poland, the Warsaw ghetto, is excruciatingly tragic. In 1940, the Germans isolated the Jews in the Warsaw ghetto. It contained, at the beginning of 1942, half a million people. The conditions of life in this ghetto were so terrible that, in 1942, its population was already decimated by hunger and illness. During 1942 alone, nearly four hundred thousand Jews from the ghetto were sent to their death in the gas chambers of extermination and concentration camps. A heroic uprising started in spring 1943. It was crushed by the Nazis who killed over sixty thousand survivors desperately fighting the overwhelming force of the occupying army. The struggle lasted over one month. From the beginning the uprising had no hope of succeeding. It was an act of ultimate heroism of the Jewish people, led by Anielewicz, who chose rather to perish in battle than to be exterminated without an act of protest.

Although the news from the fronts was bad for the Germans, the cruelty did not diminish. The Nazi crimes were countless, and the organization of their cruel acts was incredible. Mattresses were made from the hair of victims in concentration camps. Lamp shades were produced, under Ilse Koch's direction, from the skin of Jewish women.

The defeat of the Nazi regime was approaching slowly, too slowly for many to survive. The resistance in Europe, although heroic, had not the means to attack with stronger blows, efficient enough to kill the still powerful Evil.

In July 1943, the Allies conquered Sicily and, soon afterwards, started the invasion of mainland Italy. The air warfare has turned in favour of the Allies. The destruction of many German industrial and communication centres and of the German cities began. On the eastern front, the Soviet Army continued an uninterrupted offensive.

The common day-to-day life of Andrzej and Karolina was full of hope, of expectation, of impatient calculation whether their chances of survival were realistic. Andrzej was working hard from early morning until late at night, and Karolina was helping him. They spent hours in country wagons, driving to bed-ridden patients. Andrzej's parents helped them a lot in their household. Apparently life was the same as before. There was, however, a certain change in its quality. Even the smallest hope that the nightmare would be over, that they would see a new sunrise and the return of human dignity and freedom, gave them more strength for survival.

Late in the evenings, when they were resting after a day's work, they dreamed of a future, when peace had come. The strength of human beings is sometimes superhuman.

Reality very often brought them down to earth from their dreamland. They learned that, if you live believing too much in your dreams, they might never become true.

One day Karolina rented a wagon to pick up flour at the mill. For safety reasons, Ludwik accompanied her when Andrzej was busy with his patients. She was an excellent driver, and the peasants rented her their horses with pleasure. Since the delivery of the identity cards to the population, it was compulsory to have them always with you. Karolina had them always at hand, but on this occasion she forgot her card at home. Returning from the mill, the wagon was stopped by a patrol of Gestapo. They asked Andrzej's father to show them his identity card, then they asked the identity of the woman driving him. Ludwik, knowing that Karolina had forgotten her card at home, answered: 'This is my daughter.' The answer was pronounced so matter-of-factly that the patrol did not even ask Karolina to show her card. Such an incident could become the beginning of a tragedy because a traveller without an identity card could be arrested. Once in the hands of Gestapo, you could never predict how the situation would end.

All of 1943 was full of their best hopes for the Allied victory. But the question was always open: who would survive, who would see the day of victory, would they be among these happy people? Even with these unanswered questions, the hearts of people in the occupied territories grew more and more trusting.

New Year, 1944, arrived, and Andrzej and Karolina were still alive. Their hopes were nourished by the news coming from the fronts. In January 1944, the Soviet Army advanced westward across the pre-war Polish frontier. Very soon it was close to Tarnopol; Lwów was recaptured in July 1944.

The retreat of the German army was visible to everybody. This was not a military parade, as it had been in 1941 in Lwów, when the Germany army crossed this city in its victorious offensive against the Soviet army in disarray. Now, on the roads of the village, Andrzej and Karolina saw dirty trucks filled with tired German soldiers. No more songs, no more arrogant officers. None of them wore a monocle. Without monocles, they could see that total defeat was approaching. 'Hitler kaput,' people were saying, reading newspapers or listening to the German army headquarters communiqués that informed of 'planmässiges' regroupment. However, the cruelty of the Nazi administration persisted until the last day of their occupation. The Gestapo killed in concentration camps thousands and thousands of people during this retreat.

On 6 June 1944, the Western Allies landed on the beaches of Normandy, and the long-awaited invasion of France began.

In July 1944, Andrzej and Karolina heard at night for the first time the resonant noise of the approaching front. Only a few days later, they saw on the road the first Soviet tank. But the Nazis were not yet on total retreat. Two hours afterward, they saw on the same road three German tanks. The situation was unclear and evidently dangerous. Their house was near to one of the main roads. In the afternoon they decided, with Andrzej's parents, to leave their houses, and they went to a neighbouring small village beyond the hill and remote from the main roads. They were accepted with great hospitality, and they spent the night in the house of one of the peasants.

Early in the morning, they had news from their village that the occupants were gone and that this region of Poland was free, thanks to the offensive of the Soviet army. The village in which they spent the night had been, since that very morning, full of Soviet jeeps, horse-drawn wagons, and Soviet soldiers. They came on small roads and trails where no one had even seen a German soldier. They were welcomed very warmly by the Polish peasants. For Andrzej and Karolina, they represented saviours bringing strength, demolishing and destroying the Nazi regime.

Andrzej and Karolina returned, with Andrzej's parents, to their house. Their village was full of Soviet tanks, jeeps, and soldiers. On the crossroads leading to other villages, young girls in military uniforms were regulating the enormous traffic of Soviet troops. On trees, fences, and houses, you could see pieces of cardboard or paper, put up by Soviet soldiers, on which was written: 'Our cause is right, we have won,' 'I went to Berlin to kill the German beast in its hiding,' 'Glory to the invincible Soviet Army.' All along the way, women were offering flowers to Soviet soldiers and welcoming them joyfully.

After returning to their house, Andrzej and Karolina cried with joy.

XXII

THE SOVIET ARMY ENTERED THE VILLAGE IN JULY 1944. BUT that was not the end of the war, nor was it the end of the suffering of Polish people or of those of other nations. The Polish uprising, which began in Warsaw in August 1944, was a heroic act in which more than two hundred thousand Polish people lost their lives.

Polish soldiers were fighting on the eastern and western fronts. Polish blood was shed in the battle of Monte Cassino and of Lenino. Polish pilots were fighting in the Royal Air Force, and Polish soldiers were fighting in the Kościuszko army, formed in the Soviet Union.

In the concentration camps in Poland, the cruel machinery of extermination was in full swing and would continue until the first hour of liberation. During the war, the Nazis killed in extermination camps and in concentration camps three million Polish Jews and three million Jews from other countries; three million of Polish Catholics perished. At the moment of liberation of Warsaw in January 1945, only about two hundred Jews remained alive in the ruins of the Warsaw ghetto.

The Soviet offensive has stopped about 40 or 50 kilometres west of the village where Andrzej and Karolina were living with Andrzej's parents. There were small battles around, but the mainstream offensive had stopped a couple of weeks earlier. The population of the liberated regions was living now under the constant fear that the Nazis might return, even for a short while, and take revenge for the enthusiastic welcome of the Soviet army. People from the village heard that, for political reasons, weighed, on the one hand, by the Soviet Union, and, on the other, by the Western European nations and the United States, the offensive had stopped before the Vistula line. For how long, nobody knew.

After about two or three weeks of such uncertainty, Andrzej's parents had a long talk with Andrzej and Karolina. Ludwik told Andrzej and Karolina that it was good luck or God's will that all had gone well during the Nazi occupation concerning Karolina's new identity. Who could guarantee that, when the front, for strategic or political reasons, moved eastward again, and the Nazis came back, even for a couple of days, the same luck would be with them. It was, in Ludwik's opinion, much safer to return, for instance, to Lwów, which was much farther away from the front lines and where certainly better information about the future would be available, than to stay so close to the front lines and risk another encounter with the Nazis. Ludwik's suggestion was that Andrzej and Karolina should return to Lwów, and he and Estelle would move to Andrzej's house temporarily. As soon as the front lines moved westwards, or as soon as it was known why it will not move but stabilize, Andrzej and Karolina could return home.

Andrzej was convinced that Ludwik was right. However, he and Karolina had very serious reservations about this plan and rejected it. Ludwik had high blood pressure. He was being treated by Andrzej, who sometimes consulted with the regional doctor for the best options of treatment. If Andrzej and Karolina went to Lwów for a couple of weeks, they would, of course, leave Ludwik under the care of the regional doctor. However, no doctor in the world could protect Ludwik from the fear caused by a long absence of his only son in a time in which no communication was available for private citizens. Knowing Andrzej's reasons for rejecting his proposal, Ludwik convinced Andrzej to accept this plan in a very simple, matter-of-fact way: 'My dear son, of course I will be full of anxiety until you both return here safe. But my anxiety will be much less intense than what I might feel at the slightest sign that the Nazis could return. I do not see real danger in both of you travelling to Lwów although, I know that it will not be a comfortable journey. So, let us prepare for that in the nearest days. Of course, if the front moves at once westwards, you will stay here. Don't worry about my health. You and I have full confidence in the regional doctor.'

During the short time when the front was going through the village and its nearest region, Andrzej helped in treating the Soviet soldiers who were wounded during the action. They had in the village only a nursing staff and no doctor, and were extremely grateful for professional medical care brought to them by Andrzej. To express his gratitude, their commandant wrote for Andrzej a certificate saying that, thanks to his medical work, the lives of many Soviet soldiers had been saved and that the Soviet authorities should take these facts into consideration and be of assistance to him. Ludwik reminded Andrzej about this certificate and advised him to ask for help in transportation from the village to Lwów.

The first military truck moving in an eastward direction was halted by Andrzej, who showed the driver this certificate. After having read it, the driver was more than happy to give Andrzej and Karolina a lift to Lwów.

It took four hours of uninterrupted driving for Andrzej and Karolina to get to Lwów. The driver was a seventeen-year-old Russian boy; the passengers were soldiers returning eastward to various places for a short leave. They were all in an excellent mood, happy and proud of the victorious offensive. They were extremely kind to Andrzej and Karolina and shared with them their military food. Andrzej and Karolina participated in their joy and ate their food, but could not participate in their consumption of vodka. It was quite amazing to see the amount of vodka they drank directly from the bottles and difficult to understand how they could still drive the car at such a great speed and in almost a bravura way.

The soldiers told them stories of the crimes of Nazis in the Soviet Union that were not different from stories in Poland. Many members of the families of those soldiers who were from the western part of the Soviet Union were murdered by the Nazis in the most vicious ways. Villages were burnt down, and everything was left in ruins after the backward march of the defeated German army.

They arrived at Lwów at midnight and had to spend the first night in a rented room. Next day, they went to Stanisław, who offered them a room in his apartment for the time of their stay in Lwów. The meeting with Stanisław was very emotional. He hugged Karolina for a long while and thanked God that she had survived the Nazi occupation. They spoke for a long time about Juliusz, Dorota, and Zosia. Their bodies were in a mass grave in the forests at the foot of the Carpathian mountains, but their memories were always alive in Andrzej's and Karolina's and Stanisław's minds.

Andrzej and Karolina went twice to see Father Alojzy. His joy when he saw both of them alive, both of them survivors of the 'time of Evil,' was enormous. He knew from former visits of Andrzej about the terrible fate of Juliusz, Dorota, and Zosia and felt extremely unhappy that Juliusz had not accepted the proposal of Bishop Baziak. 'Maybe all the family would be alive today,' he said, with tears in his eyes.

During their second visit, Father Alojzy returned to the question of Polish anti-Semitism. He had heard from the monastery in Warsaw that some Poles were behaving in a heroic way, risking their own lives to help the Jews in the Warsaw ghetto, smuggling in food and medical supplies, especially vaccine against typhoid fever. Some were hiding in their apartments Jewish people, whom they had helped to sneak out of the ghetto. However, there were still cases of hatred towards Jews. Unfortunately this hatred had been – as Father Alojzy had told them before – fuelled in Poland over many centuries, and not enough effort was being made to eradicate it. In this sense, all of the nation should have a feeling of guilt, especially as this was a profoundly Catholic nation. He was glad to see that the attitudes of many Poles who were anti-Semitic before the war had changed when they saw to what crimes racism and anti-Semitism could lead. 'The problem of hatred is still not yet fully eradicated and after this tragic historical lesson given by the Nazi occupation, we should fight against it with all our strength and Catholic faith.'

Father Alojzy understood also very well the present political situation of Poland and was seriously concerned with the probability that Lwów might not return to Poland and might be taken by the Soviets. It was difficult to predict how this loss will be compensated to Poland. If Poland would lose Lwów, then there should be a possibility of option for the population of this region: either to stay in a non-Polish Lwów or to leave and settle down somewhere in the new Poland. In this case, the Bernardine Monastery would be transferred to Cracow.

Unfortunately Andrzej and Karolina could not see Filomena. She was absent from Lwów, working in one of the provincial hospitals.

It was possible in Lwów at that time to have exact political information. There was news about the formation of the Polish Committee of National Liberation (PKWN – Polski Komitet Wyzwolenia Narodowego) in Lublin, already recognized by the Soviet Union as representing officially the provisional new Polish government. At the same time, there was news about the disagreements between this provisional government and the Polish government, residing during the war in London, with Prime Minister Mikołajczyk.

The loudspeakers in the squares and in the streets of Lwów announced what the situation was on the fronts. The news dispatched from the Pacific front told of the heroic struggles of the United States. Since the treacherous attack of Japan on Pearl Harbor, counter-attacks against the Japanese were undertaken and great steps had been made towards future victory. Many milestones of the war, for instance, the Casablanca Conference and the Teheran Conference, became known and better understood.

The Polish population of Lwów was politically divided and disoriented. The Soviet army had liberated Lwów and ended the Nazi occupation, but the Soviet army was, at the same time, changing the pre-war situation. A great part of the Polish population of Lwów was so patriotically attached to this beautiful city that they did not want to think of Lwów becoming a part of another state.

Andrzej and Karolina walked through this city where their love was born and where so much unhappiness had been visited upon Karolina's family. They walked down the Piekarska Street, where, at the corner of Sakramentek Street, during the first two years of war, Juliusz had lived with Dorota, Karolina, and Zosia, self-exiled from Cracow. In the same house lived, also self-exiled from Cracow, the family of the uncle of Karolina. They walked up Piekarska Street towards the beautiful villa with a small turret where, on the first floor, was the apartment of Andrzej's parents and where Karolina had come to visit Andrzej for the first time when he was sick. They went to see the garden in which was situated the building of pharmacology, where Karolina had worked under the guidance of the Soviet professor and where Andrzej used to pick her up every late afternoon after work. They went to see the coffee and pastry shop of Welz where Andrzej and Karolina had sometimes gone. It was a nostalgic and painful tour, darkened with the tragic memories of those who were martyrs of the war and illuminated, at the same time, with romantic memories of their love.

After nearly ten days in Lwów, Andrzej felt an increasing anxiety about the health of his father. He told Karolina that he had a kind of premonition that his father needed him. They decided to return at once. The Soviet offensive was still halted about 50 kilometres west of their village, and the front seemed stabilized. The German army had a second front in France, and the armies of Allies were in Italy.

Andrzej and Karolina took leave from Stanisław and his wife. They did not know that this would be the last encounter. Before the end of the war, Stanisław would die of a heart attack.

Next day, Andrzej and Karolina were in the suburbs of Lwów, trying to stop a military car on the road leading to the west. When they showed the certificate signed by the Soviet officer to the driver of the first military truck that halted at their signal, he was more than happy to give them the lift to the west. However, they did not know that, during their ten-day stay in Lwów, the political situation had changed and there was no more possibility of travelling from Lwów to their village without crossing a new frontier established between the Soviet Union and the newly formed Poland. This frontier was east of Przemyśl, on the road leading from Lwów to Sanok.

After driving about 80 kilometres in the military truck, they were stopped by a young Soviet soldier who was guarding the new frontier. Andrzej and Karolina had to get out of the truck and give some explanation to the frontier military guard. They were told that, without a Soviet or a Polish passport and corresponding visas, they had no right to pass the newly established frontier. The certificate written by the Soviet officer did not help. The argument that they were returning to their house and that Andrzej's father might be sick did not convince the frontier guard. To their complete amazement, the guard told them: 'The Polish people want to have in Poland the London-backed Polish government. This means that you want to have a Polish kingdom with King Mikołajczyk, who is coming from London. Thus, you have now this frontier, which separates the Soviet Union from the Kingdom of Poland. Without pertinent documents you will never pass the frontier.'

The air was hot; they had not eaten or drunk anything since morning. As well as being hungry and thirsty, they were in pro-found despair. They tried several times to convince the guard, who soon became hostile to them and repeated in Russian: 'Eto gosudarstwennyj kordon. Nielzia' 'This is the state frontier. It is forbidden.' It was so exhausting that they could not stand any longer in the heat. They sat down under a tree and discussed what to do.

At once Andrzej had an excellent idea: 'Let us wait for the change of the guard. Maybe somebody less zealous and more understanding will come and replace this one. We should disappear from his sight so that he can forget us and not influence the judgment of the guard who will come to replace him. Let us go and lay down somewhere in the bushes, not far from the road. Maybe the change of guards will come in one hour or two, or we might wait several hours more. We are exhausted, hungry, and thirsty but we must cross this frontier and only patience can bring us some hope. We have never heard of Mikołajczyk as Polish king, although we have heard of him as the prime minister of the Polish government based in London. Maybe the next frontier guard has never heard such stupid news, and maybe he will respect the certificate of a Soviet officer.'

They moved to the bushes, where they waited until sunset. They were unable to understand that the Soviets who, in such a heroic way had defeated the Nazis and liberated their own country, could not liberate the brains of their citizens from rigidity and bureaucracy. This was not a favourable sign for the future.

After five hours of waiting, just after the sunset, there was a change of guard on the frontier. They did not move until the former guard had disappeared in the shadow of the coming night. Then Andrzej and Karolina approached the new frontier guard and showed him the certificate of the Soviet officer. He read it with attention and was delighted to have the opportunity to help a Polish doctor who had given medical assistance to Soviet soldiers. His only concern was that the first truck that he halted to pick them up was transporting tar and was very dirty. However, they hailed it with enthusiasm and instantly boarded it. In the tar truck, they crossed the new frontier and stepped out in Przemyśl. There they picked up another truck that drove them straight into their village.

Here they heard that Andrzej's father had had a heart attack and was still in bed, recovering slowly under the care of the regional doctor.

XXIII

WHEN ANDRZEJ AND KAROLINA RETURNED TO THE village, Ludwik was resting in bed after his heart attack. There was enormous joy in his big blue eyes when he saw his only son back safe from his journey, which was conceived by Ludwik himself to protect Karolina from another encounter with the Nazis. Karolina was moved to tears, seeing him sick in bed. She had had a feeling of guilt towards Andrzej's parents from the very moment at which she had understood the mortal danger they had subjected themselves to in accepting and protecting her from Nazi persecution. She had never shared the optimism of Juliusz and, since the terrible scene when she had been threatened with being shot by the officer of the Gestapo, she had understood what it meant in reality to be at the mercy of a beast.

Under the tender, loving care of Estelle, Andrzej, and Karolina, Ludwik's health improved and, after six weeks of absolute bed rest, he could get up and walk and returned slowly to a normal life.

In autumn 1944, Andrzej bought a horse and a country wagon. This made their life much easier, and the patients were happy to see that their doctor could visit on call bed-ridden patients. Karolina drove this horse as coachman, and she also took care of its feeding and cleaning. She liked this work very much. Andrzej's medical practice was growing. He was very much respected by the peasants, who had an enormous confidence in his medical skills and appreciated very much his direct and simple approach.

The Western Allies advanced fast. In October 1944, the first city on the territory of Germany was captured. It was the historical city of Aachen. On the Pacific front, the U.S. army was clearing the way for the U.S. occupation of the Philippines.

Christmas 1944 was the first Christmas without Nazi occupation in their village. It was a time of great hope. The joy of this moment was in their family darkened by memories of the tragic death of Karolina's family.

In January 1945 the Soviet army started its offensive. The front, which had been for such a long time only 50 kilometres west of their village, moved far west in one week, and Cracow was liberated. Very soon, the Soviet army crossed the river Oder. Warsaw was liberated, and the time was approaching for great changes in all the nations persecuted by Nazi occupation. Great changes in the lives of Andrzej and Karolina were on the horizon.

The time to leave the village was approaching: Karolina had to resume her studies; Andrzej had to continue his specialization. They had heard that Cracow University had reopened, as had Warsaw University. Cracow survived the war nearly untouched, and the University was able to return to its buildings, Warsaw was 95 per cent destroyed by the Nazis, and the Medical Faculty functioned on the right bank of the Vistula, in a Warsaw suburb called Praga.

Andrzej and Karolina had many very warm feelings for the inhabitants of their village and the neighbouring villages. They had made many friends and had found a relatively quiet haven during the dangerous days of the Nazi occupation. They were for ever indebted to all the members of Ludwik's family, and especially to his sister, Karolcia.

After the war, Karolcia told Ludwik that, from the arrival of Andrzej and Karolina at the village, she had had suspicions that Karolina was of Jewish origin. This suspicion was awakened by the fact that Karolina had never seen the thunder-candle. Although she knew everything about the catechism, although she could say the Mass in Latin, although she knew how to behave as a godmother, this small void in her Catholic education was conspicuous. They never discussed this among themselves during the Nazi occupation. Karolina was for them Andrzej's wife, a member of their family. Their moral principles were to help and protect and save the life of any member of their family. Inspired by the idea of Karolcia, all members of her family informed the other peasants in the village that not only Andrzej, but also Karolina was their relative. Nothing has greater speed than gossip, and this gossip saved Karolina's life and was a decisive factor in her survival.

Since the beginning of January 1944, they had been discussing the possibility of leaving the village, first to look for a suitable place to settle down. They knew already that Lwów was lost to them. They were thinking about Cracow or Warsaw. How would they get there? The answer seemed simple: they had a country wagon and a horse. Travelling about 50 kilometres daily, they would reach Cracow in about four to five days. They would travel only in daytime, and at night ask for the hospitality of parsons in the villages on their way. If it was necessary to go to Warsaw, they would try to go by train. Apparently the trains were already running for the civilian population in liberated Poland.

Their plan was theoretically very good, but very difficult to realize. In the early spring of 1945, Poland was, in fact, the backland of an enormous Soviet front. The war was still on. With great confidence in their ability to get through, they started to prepare to realize their plan. They have even arranged to take with them a young peasant boy as a 'valet' to help them on the journey and who was eager to go and see the world beyond his small village.

One beautiful, sunny morning, at the beginning of March 1945, Karolina herself took the horse from the stable, harnessed it, and attached it to their country wagon. With the help of their newly hired 'valet,' they put a piece of luggage containing a change of clothes on the country wagon. They took leave from Andrzej's parents. Ludwik was already in good shape and encouraging them to go and explore the possibilities of settling down somewhere in the new Poland, in a city with a university.

They had about 200 kilometres to cover to get to Cracow and, according to their plans, they should arrive there in four days. They were fortunate; the weather was beautiful, the sun shining, and there was no snow on the roads. However, some parts of the road were destroyed, and the detours dangerous as some fields were packed with mines. Some bridges were blown up, and they had to wait a long time for a ferry boat.

When, after all these troubles, they reached the main highway from Lwów to Cracow and Silesia, they found themselves in the mainstream of the Soviet army. Among the military tanks and motor trucks, their horse was at first very flustered, but he adapted very soon and even the big, roaring tanks did not disturb his stoicism.

They started out every day early in the morning, immediately after sunrise, and finished before sunset. During the day they made three or four stops to feed and give water and rest to the horse and to take rest themselves. They spent the nights in the parsonages, always received with great hospitality. They told the parsons the goal of their journey and that they would be back again in about ten days or two weeks to pick up Andrzej's parents. The parsons understood very well that the people from Lwów were now homeless and moving around to find a convenient place to live. They always invited them to share dinners and breakfasts, and blessed them for the next part of their journey. There was always some room to accommodate their valet, and a place in the parsonage stable for their horse.

On the fifth day of their journey, they crossed the bridge on the river Vistula and entered the streets of Cracow. They stopped at the apartment of one of Juliusz's ex-employees, who, for many years, had worked at the graphic factory. He arranged for them to stay in Cracow with one of his friends, who owned a house with a nearby garage, where they could keep the horse and the country wagon. The employee and his wife were themselves preparing to leave Cracow for Wrocław (Breslau), which had not yet been captured by the Soviet army but was to be conquered very soon and become the capital of Polish Lower Silesia.

After a short rest, they started to tour Cracow. From the beginning, they understood that it would never be possible for Karolina to live again in Cracow. Each street of this beautiful city, which was one of the few not destroyed by the war, each place, each park, evoked painful reminiscences for her.

The painful memories of Juliusz, Dorota, and Zosia were with Karolina everywhere in Cracow. She showed Andrzej, with eyes full of tears, the house where she lived with her parents and Zosia, the school and the gymnasium where she went with Zosia, and where they both passed the Matura. She showed him Jagiellonian University, where she was graduated with her doctor of laws in 1937; the Faculty of Medicine, where she finished her first two years of medical studies in 1937–39. She showed him the graphic establishment, Akropol, created by Juliusz, and the house of her grandparents in the most beautiful street of Cracow, Floriańska Street. Her grandparents' apartment in this house contained, before the war, the administrative office of Akropol and of Salon Malarzy Polskich, and there had been space enough to have there an apartment for them and Andrzej's parents.

They visited the Department of Psychiatry, where the department chairman offered Andrzej excellent possibilities of work and continuation of his specialization, together with didactic and scientific work. They visited the office of the dean of the Medical Faculty, where Karolina was told that she could without any difficulties resume the studies she had begun in Cracow and continued through the first two years of the war in Lwów.

Everything seemed easy for their stay and work in Cracow. It was, however, emotionally impossible for Karolina. The shadows of

Juliusz, Dorota, and Zosia and of almost all the family of Karolina, murdered by the Nazis, made Cracow a cemetery in her eyes. It was impossible to begin a new life in a cemetery of beloved ones who had perished in such a tragic way. The tragedy of Orelec that both of them carried in their hearts for all their lives was already a heavy burden. It would have been unbearable to add to this burden constant recollections of the past. Andrzej understood this very well and suggested they go to Warsaw and examine the possibilities of settling down there.

Travelling to Warsaw was exhausting because only a freight train was available, and it was overcrowded with people. The cars were open, and it was very cold. In the morning, they arrived in Warsaw, or rather at the ruins of the city that had been the capital of Poland before the war. They had heard that Warsaw was the most destroyed city in Europe during the Second World War. What they saw was unbelievable. The city did not exist at all; 95 per cent of it was completely demolished. They made their way through streets buried under the rubble of destroyed houses. No traffic existed in this city. The people were forced to jump slowly from one stone to another among the ruined houses.

On the right bank of the Vistula river in the intact suburb of Praga were the offices of the newly formed Polish government, the Polish Committee of National Liberation. This government had to negotiate a common language with the Polish government in exile in London. History has shown that it was not simple. It was full of deceptions from both sides, full of tragic consequences for those who, with confidence, returned from self-exile in London.

In Praga was also the temporary seat of the Faculty of Medicine. The Department of Psychiatry, which before the war was located in the hospital of Saint John the Divine, was burned by the Nazis with patients in situ, along with some doctors who had made the heroic decision to stay with their patients until the end. Andrzej could not continue his specialization in psychiatry in Warsaw. He has found in Praga some physicians he had known in Lwów and he accepted the invitation of the Chairman of Neurosurgery to join his department. Karolina was accepted on the basis of her four years of medical studies as the student of the fifth year of medical studies at the University of Warsaw.

Having made these arrangements, they returned by train to Cracow, where they had left their valet and the horse with the country wagon. They returned from Cracow in the horse-drawn wagon, directly to their village. The return trip lasted only four days, as there was less military traffic and the horse, on the fourth day of travelling, showed amazing strength spurred on by the proximity of a rest in his own stable.

Now they made, together with Andrzej's parents, a plan to move from the village, and the framework of further plans for settlement.

Andrzej went to the regional physician to discuss with him in detail how to engage a replacement doctor who would succeed Andrzej in the treatment of the peasant population and of the insured patients. At that time, it was not yet known that the peasants would also have the right to health insurance and therefore Andrzej's greatest preoccupation was with finding a doctor who would be interested in treating the peasant population. Fortunately enough, the regional physician had an excellent candidate in mind. Karolina prepared for him the medical files.

The most difficult emotional problem was with leaving the family of Ludwik, especially Karolcia. All of them understood very well the need of Ludwik and his family to stay in a university city and, although it was for them heart-breaking to know that they might not soon again see them, they wished them a happy future in the new Poland. They understood also how hard it was to lose the possibility of returning to Lwów and to make new friends in the unknown surroundings.

Andrzej sold the horse and country wagon. They rented a truck, and left with Andrzej's parents for Cracow. The ex-employee of Juliusz offered them one room in his apartment in Cracow. With leaving the village, one chapter in the life of this family was finished, and another one in unknown surroundings was opened.

One of the contingency plans for the future entailed Andrzej's parents waiting in Cracow until Andrzej and Karolina settled down for good in Warsaw. It was impossible to move them to the ruins of Warsaw, and the conditions of life in the overcrowded suburb of Praga were very hard. Andrzej had also in his head a plan that involved moving where the remaining population of Lwów would move if they chose to leave.

The ex-employee of Juliusz and his wife were very busy organizing a Polish team to administer Wrocław after its capture from Germany. Wrocław was still German, but was already surrounded by the Soviet Army, which captured it in May 1945.

At the end of March 1945, Andrzej and Karolina began their new life in Warsaw. It was extremely hard. They rented a room in Praga. The roof of the building was damaged and on rainy days they had plenty of water inside. It was not easy to get proper food. Andrzej was working in the neurosurgical department; Karolina was busy attending lectures and practical lessons as a medical student. Andrzej also had some didactic tasks to perform with students. The conditions of work in the hospitals, or in buildings converted to hospitals, like the school in which the Department of Neurosurgery operated, were very hard, but the patients were given the best possible care.

This was a time of great enthusiasm in the emerging new, free Poland. One could feel in the air the approaching end of the war, the defeat of the Nazis. It was an atmosphere of hope, trust, and optimism that the future would bring a more humane face for the liberated nations. Not everyone was satisfied with the indication that Poland might be greatly dependent on the Soviet Union, although some changes in the social system made by the provisional Polish government were positively accepted. The PKWN government had decided to reconstruct Warsaw and keep it as the capital of Poland. A special office for the reconstruction of Warsaw was organized.

After the Yalta Conference, the possibilities of a collaboration between the provisional Polish government (PKWN) and the Polish government based in London became very slim. The Western Allies agreed during this conference that the PKWN recognized by the Soviet Union as the provisional Polish government should become the nucleus of the Poland's Government of National Unity. Such a government of national unity never was realized.

The Soviet army was in Berlin; the Western and Soviet armies met in Saxony. The unconditional surrender of Germany was the question of coming days.

The day so much wanted and expected by Juliusz was close. Andrzej and Karolina survived to see this day. Juliusz, Dorota, and Zosia remained for ever in the forest of the Carpathian mountains.

On 30 April 1945 Hitler committed suicide.

The unconditional surrender of Germany was signed in Rheims on 7 May 1945 and ratified in Berlin on 8 May 1945.

On 9 May 1945, Warsaw celebrated the end of war in Europe. The tyranny and crimes of the Nazis had ended. The possibilities for a better humanity were emerging. Were the times of contempt really over?

PART THREE

—

TIMES OF EXPECTATIONS AND DECEPTIONS

But he who hates his brother is in
the darkness and walks in the darkness,
and does not know where he is going,
because the darkness has blinded his eyes.

The First Letter of John
2:11

I

THE LIFE OF ANDRZEJ AND KAROLINA IN WARSAW WAS
very hard not only because of difficult conditions in their apartment
and shortage of food, but because they felt lonely and missed
terribly Andrzej's parents. They had been uprooted from Lwów and
uprooted from the village, and, in the city, devastated to the degree
that it practically did not exist, it was not easy to settle down. For the
population of Warsaw who had fled after the uprising, Warsaw,
although destroyed, was still home, and they firmly wanted to
rebuild it.

In June 1945, Andrzej and Karolina had received a letter from the
former employee of Juliusz. He was working with the team preparing the Polish administration in Wrocław, which was to become the
capital of Polish Lower Silesia. The University of Lwów had been
reorganized in Wrocław and would form a single administrative
unit with the Polish Technical School from Lwów. Many Polish
people were moving from Lwów to Wrocław. He encouraged them
very much to leave the difficult life in Warsaw and move with
Andrzej's parents to Wrocław.

Andrzej and Karolina decided to go to Cracow and consult with
Andrzej's parents. The idea seemed attractive; Andrzej could
continue his specialization in psychiatry, and Karolina could finish
her medical studies. They could be with Andrzej's parents and feel
much less socially uprooted, living with the Polish population from
Lwów who had chosen to settle down in Wrocław. They would find
their friends from Lwów and have a social life in an environment
known to them for many years. There were also good possibilities of
finding an apartment for Andrzej and Karolina, and for Andrzej's
parents. Ludwik could probably lecture in Latin at the University of
Wrocław.

In June 1945, when Karolina finished her academic semester at the
University of Warsaw, they left Warsaw and moved to Wrocław.

Karolina continued her medical studies in the Faculty of
Medicine at Wrocław university, which consisted of the members
of the former Faculty of Medicine in Lwów. Andrzej was working
with a team of psychiatrists whose task was the organization of
the psychiatric department of the university. The chairman of the
department from Lwów was there, and Andrzej found many
psychiatrists that he knew from Lwów. In general, the team of the

Medical Faculty of the University of Lwów had moved to Wrocław.

They worked very hard. The life in Wrocław was not easy, because this beautiful city was 50 per cent destroyed. It was impossible for them to find an apartment immediately and therefore they stayed, as did many other physicians, in a former private clinic turned into a hotel. Food was scarce and modest, but they felt at ease in the company of many physicians already known to them and they understood very well that they – like other Poles from the territory taken by the Soviet Union – would have to rebuild this city and make it their home. They hoped that this new Poland would be a righteous one, that it would fulfill dreams they had had during the Nazi occupation. Each day of hard work separated them from the nightmarish time, of war and fear of danger. But anxiety and sadness and recollections of the times of contempt would not fade away that easily. They still had restless nights, with constantly interrupted sleep, and the feeling of insecurity. Nevertheless, trust in the future was there.

In autumn 1945, they joined the Polish Socialist Party, which had a long tradition of strong social democratic programs (education, health, insurance, etc.).

After the work day they spent the evenings at the hotel. The city was still dark at night, making it dangerous to go out. During dinners with other members of the team, they participated in the lively discussions on the future of life in Poland after the war. Opinion was divided. Some people, especially the older ones, were convinced that their stay in Wrocław was only temporary, and for a short time. They hoped that the Allies would very soon restore order in Eastern Europe, and Poland would have its pre-war frontiers. The London government would return from its exile and rule Poland. These people were so much attached to Lwów, or to other cities taken at that time by the Soviets, that they could not imagine that, for the rest of their lives, they might stay in Wrocław. They loved Lwów, its atmosphere; its promenades, parks, and streets; its institutions, where they had worked before the war. It was for them incredibly difficult to begin a new life, in a new city, in new conditions, and under a new social system. One could not call these people conservative. They simply could not adjust their conception of life and of Poland to the existing reality.

Some people were outright conservative. They praised the pre-war government of Poland. For them, the new social system was absolutely unacceptable, and threatening to the Polish identity.

Some people were outspoken Communists, full of enthusiasm. The great bulk of them belonged to the Polish Worker's Party (PPR – Polska Partia Robotnicza). Many of them were, before the war, members of the Polish Communist Party (KPP – Komunistyczna Partia Polski). Among them were also young people who had never been members of a Communist party, but who believed that the Communist system was the best one and that the best ally of Poland was the Soviet Union.

Some people, like Andrzej and Karolina, who had a liberal conception of the social system, believed that the best system was the social-democratic, with government-guaranteed health care for all the population and a reasonably organized education and welfare system. Many of these people belonged to the Polish Socialist Party (PPS – Polska Partia Socialistyerna). These people were very critical towards the pre-war system in Poland, towards the 'Poland of colonels' with its racial and religious prejudices and inadequate social obligations, including no health care for peasants and not enough welfare for the unemployed poor. Such people looked forward to social changes, but, recalling the times of Soviet occupation, were also very critical towards the system imposed in the Soviet Union. They had in memory the Soviet Lwów of the years 1939–41, and their satisfaction with the abolition of the pre-war Polish system was moderated by their critical attitude towards methods applied by Soviets.

At that time in Poland various political parties existed: PPS, the Polish Socialist Party (Polska Partia Socialistyczna), the Democratic Party (SD – Stronnictwo Demokratyczne), the People's Party (SL – Stronnictwo Ludowe) and the Polish People's Party (PSL – Polskie Stronnictwo Ludowe). The Polish People's Party had many ties to the Polish government in exile in London, whose prime minister, Mikołajczyk, had been enthusiastically received in Poland by this part of the population, which was very critical towards the Soviet Union. The Polish Workers Party (PPR) had many ties with the Soviet government and, of course, with the PKWN, which was the Polish provisional government founded in Lublin in 1944 under the protection of the Soviet government.

The discussion between the members of the team residing in the modest hotel was sometimes very animated, but never hostile.

In August 1945, the United States dropped an atomic bomb and devastated Hiroshima; three days later, a second bomb was dropped on Nagasaki. More than two hundred thousand people were killed, injured, or missing. The Allies accepted the Japanese surrender.

The Second World War was over. It had brought death to about fifty million people. The end of the war brought mankind the threat and danger of an atomic era. Despite the creation of the United Nations, the world remained politically unstable. The political consequences of the war meant a diminution of the power of England and France and an increase in the influence of the Soviet Union in Eastern Europe. It also meant a growing discordance between the United States and the emerging superpower of the Soviet Union. The 'cold war' had yet to begin.

The sufferings of millions of people during the war did not seem to influence international relations, in the sense of inhibiting nationalist hatreds. The terrible lesson of what hatred might lead to, the martyrdom of millions of people, the death of fifty million people, did not have any visible influence on world policy. Hatred was again fed by the political situation in the post-war world.

In 1946, anti-Semitic riots erupted in Poland in Kielce. Many Jewish people who survived the Nazi times were killed, many wounded. A shameful shadow was laid on the history of the Polish nation. The hatred against the Jews was still present in some Polish hearts. The blood and martyrdom of millions of innocent Jews murdered by the Nazis during the Holocaust was not enough for those who inspired the 'pogrom' in Kielce. Again the Jews were exterminated only because of their race and religion.

The events in Kielce were a deep, painful shock for Andrzej and Karolina. Their hearts were full of vivid memories of the tragic murder of Juliusz, Dorota, and Zosia, and all the terrible crimes committed by the Nazis against the Jews. They recalled what Juliusz had told them about his strong emotional ties to Poland, about his dreams of a new, righteous Poland after the war, of a Poland free from racial and religious discrimination. What kind of Poland was emerging now before the eyes of Andrzej and Karolina after all the Nazi atrocities? Was it impossible for the new Poland to become a good mother for all its citizens, regardless of race or religion?

II

ANDRZEJ AND KAROLINA WERE ALWAYS HAPPY IN THEIR marriage, in their love and understanding. Each morning awakening was full of happiness deriving from togetherness, from the feeling of confidence in each other.

Life in Wrocław was slowly stabilizing. Towards the end of 1945, they had found an apartment. Apartments were given to people in Wrocław by a commission charged with distributing the means of resettlement to the population that moved from Lwów and other places taken by the Soviet Union.

They could now move Andrzej's parents to Wrocław from Cracow. Ludwik was appointed lecturer of the Latin language at the University of Wrocław. There was a great improvement in the distribution of food, and the people of Lwów were slowly accepting life in Wrocław, although there was always a certain nostalgia for Lwów.

In 1946 Karolina finished her medical studies and received her diploma. Andrzej worked hard to finish his doctor's thesis and in the same year he received the diploma of medical doctor (in Poland, a scientific degree given to physicians after presenting and defending their doctoral thesis). Andrzej was working now as a senior associate professor in the Department of Psychiatry, and Karolina started work as a resident in the Department of Neurology at Wrocław University.

After having obtained these diplomas, they both made applications for foreign fellowships, preferably in France. France, at that time, had excellent scientists at the Sorbonne. It was a great joy for Andrzej and Karolina when they received fellowships for Paris. Such fellowships were given by the French government as one of the ways to help Polish science after the losses of the Second World War.

They were especially interested in clinical electroencephalography. This branch of clinical neurophysiology had been developed primarily by the famous German psychiatrist from Jena, Hans Berger. Hans Berger had committed suicide during the war, pushed to it by despair over Hitler's crimes. This branch of clinical neurophysiology was very well advanced in France, and it was applied as a non-invasive diagnostic and research tool in neurology and psychiatry.

They had in mind to introduce in Poland this method of diagnosis and research on brain-wave activity. Poland has lost, during the war, many of its outstanding scientists. Some of them were killed by the Nazis, like many of the professors of the Medical Faculty of the University of Lwów; some emigrated at the beginning of the war; some died. The new generation had, in many cases, to look for sources of education abroad and then return to Poland to teach students finishing their studies in order to fill the gap between the level of Polish science and that of science abroad. During the war the universities were closed, and the process of education of young people was interrupted. In Paris, Andrzej and Karolina could not only get acquainted with this method of diagnosis and research, but also, under the guidance of excellent masters of psychiatry and neurology, perfect their clinical knowledge in these two specialities.

This year in Paris was not only one of hard and ambitious work, but also a year full of joy of life in this most beautiful of cities. They very rarely used the subway because the journey on foot from the hotel where they stayed to the Jardin des Tuileries, with its perspective to l'Arc de Triomphe de la Place de l'Etoile in one direction, and to the small Arc de Triomphe du Carrousel in another direction, was so beautiful. Then, in the fresh morning spring weather, they walked to the Salpetrière through the streets of the city.

During their stay in France, unexpectedly one of the dream stories told to Karolina by Andrzej, in the early days of their love in Lwów, came true. When the Paris university closed for summer vacation for two months, Andrzej and Karolina, eager not to lose even one day of their fellowship without acquiring new knowledge, decided, on the advice of one of their mentors, to go to the University of Nice in the South of France. On one of the weekends in Nice, they bought bus tickets to tour the Corniche. And Karolina reminded Andrzej of his story from Piekarska Street. 'Don't now look to the right. Listen to me now. We are on the Grande Corniche.' Then she said: 'Andrzej, I am looking to the right. And *it is* the Grande Corniche.' Would their other dreams come true? Especially the dream of a new, righteous Poland?

They made many friends among other physicians from various countries who came during the post-war period to Paris. Those friendships were to last very long, many, many years.

They returned to Poland, very happy that they had accumulated knowledge that could be transferred to new generations of students and doctors, whom they were teaching in the departments of psychiatry (Andrzej) and neurology (Karolina).

The political situation in Poland after their return was still formally unchanged. There still existed various parties within the framework of the multiparty system. However, one could feel the winds of the cold war. The Polish Workers Party came increasingly to dominate the other parties and was under Soviet indoctrination. The Polish Peasant Party, and its leader Mikołajczyk, were losing political prestige from one day to the next on the field of battle for political power, although it was still very well accepted by the population as an expression of the will of Poles. In October 1947, Mikołajczyk fled to England after a fixed election. There was an atmosphere of political suspicion, poisoning the lives of the citizens. All this was masterminded by some very powerful politicians, taking their instructions from the Communist Party in Moscow. The cold war between the Western powers and the Communist bloc of nations was more and more evident. It was also the beginning of a split within the Polish Workers Party itself; some of its members in high positions refused to accept Soviet meddling in Polish affairs.

One afternoon, in the early spring of 1948, something happened to Andrzej and Karolina that took away their confidence in the future, in the possibility of the existence of an independent, righteous Poland, and threatened their own future.

Andrzej's parents lived three houses away from their apartment. Estelle, who was always very helpful to everybody, had made friends with Marysia, a very nice Polish lady, a lawyer who was working at the Law Faculty of Wrocław University. Marysia was living on the ground floor, just opposite Andrzej's parents. As she had to leave early for work in the morning, Estelle took her milk from the milkman and handed it over to her at lunch time. Always after a short rest after lunch, Andrzej's parents came to the apartment of Andrzej and Karolina to prepare, together with them, a dinner in the evening.

One afternoon, in the early spring, when Andrzej and Karolina returned from work, they did not find Andrzej's parents in their apartment. Worried that something had happened to Andrzej's father, they went to Ludwik's apartment. They rang the bell, and knocked at the door several times. Nobody answered. Then they decided to knock at the door opposite to find out if Marysia knew something about Andrzej's parents. After several knocks at the door, nobody responded, but they heard some suspicious murmurs and low voices. That frightened them so much that they immediately returned to their apartment. It was still an unquiet time, even though the war had ended three years earlier. Anything could happen to Poles in this city.

Andrzej and Karolina decided not to call the police, but turned to one of their friends, Maciek, who had been a pupil of Ludwik's, of whom he always spoke with great respect and admiration. At that time, he was the secretary of the Polish Socialist Party in Wrocław, and they asked him what they should do in such a situation. They had not finished their story about the disappearance of Ludwik and Estelle when Maciek interrupted: 'If something has happened to my most respected teacher, I cannot wait for police, or anybody. I will come immediately myself and bring with me a PPS member of the Polish Parliament, who is just here with me. Wait for us in your apartment.' Indeed, in about ten minutes an official limousine from the Wrocław headquarters of the Polish Socialist Party halted before the apartment, all four of them (the Secretary of the Polish Socialist Party, the PPS member of Parliament, Andrzej and Karolina) knocked at the door of Marysia's apartment. When they heard a suspicious murmur from behind the door, the Secretary of the PPS and the member of Parliament took out revolvers from their pockets and pointed them at the door. The door opened at once, and they saw inside three men with guns pointed at them. One of the men said: 'Drop the gun, and all of you enter immediately or I shoot.' They entered immediately. At gun point, the men showed them into the dining room, where, at the table, were sitting Andrzej's parents and the wife of the house's janitor, who was nursing her baby.

It was a scary situation. It was still unsafe after the war. Various illegal groups were active, and sometimes their activities were closer to crime than to politics. The situation was dangerous and absolutely unfathomable.

The Secretary of PPS, who was a very courageous man, decided to gamble, to get to the bottom of this mysterious situation. He told the gunmen who he was, and showed them his identity card and the card of the PPS member of Parliament. If they had been terrorists, acting against any leftist party, they would have shot him at once. But they were not. They explained, in a rather rude tone, that they were members of the Ministry of Public Security, and that they had orders to detain in this apartment anybody who entered. Such an apartment was called by them a 'cauldron,' and anybody who came there was under a suspicion of being connected with a crime committed by the person living in this apartment. None of the persons detained could be released before the end of this covert operation.

The first person who has fallen into this 'cauldron' was Estelle. She was so insistent about being let in because she had something to give to Marysia that they let her in, eager to know what this 'something' that tied Estelle to Marysia was. To their disappointment, it was only a bottle of milk. Nevertheless, Estelle was detained and seemed very suspect to them because, when she showed them her identity card, they saw that she had been born in Paris. Marysia had been arrested and was already being detained in prison because, according to their data, she was a member of a big spy ring. And here was Estelle, a person born in a foreign country; she might also be involved in spying. Estelle was told to sit quietly and not say a word if anyone knocked at the door.

The second person who was detained in this 'cauldron' was Andrzej's father. When Estelle, sitting quietly in the dining room, heard his voice, asking the gunmen if they had seen her, she shouted loudly 'Ludwiczku.' Then, although they had not intended to let Ludwik in, they had to admit him and he had to be detained.

The third detained person was the janitor's wife. She had the keys to Marysia's apartment because she was cleaning it. She had brought her baby with her because she had nobody to leave it with. The gunmen said that the things had started to get interesting now because, in this spy operation, were also involved the Secretary of the PPS and the PPS member of Parliament and two other people, Andrzej and Karolina, whom they knew had spent a year in France and, not long ago, returned from there. The French 'attaché culturel,' who granted them their French visa, had had to leave Poland as *persona non grata*.

Hearing all this, Andrzej and Karolina thought that either they were crazy or the gunmen were paranoid. Who was the spy in this room? Andrzej's parents? the janitor's wife? themselves? the PPS party secretary? the member of Parliament? For whom was this frame established? Even Andrzej's father, who had spent seven years in Siberia and had seen incredible things during the revolution, was astonished. His face expressed his disbelief as the gunmen recounted their story.

Their amazement reached its peak when the gunmen revealed that they would not allow the PPS Secretary and the PPS member of Parliament to leave. The argument that a member of Parliament has constitutionally guaranteed immunity did not impress at all the employees of Public Security.

After long negotiations, they agreed to call their superiors and ask them about the possibility of releasing at least the member of Parliament. The PPS party secretary was, in the meantime, trying to explain to the two employees who were not involved in phone negotiations that an incredible mistake had been made – to no avail. The Ministry of Public Security considered itself above the law, and certainly above the constitutional rights of citizens of the country. Its employees told the PPS Secretary to mind his own business and not interfere in matters involving the security of Poland.

Eventually, after long phone negotiations, the superiors in the Ministry of Public Security permitted the member of Parliament to go, under the condition that he keep in secrecy the location and function of the 'cauldron,' but the PPS Secretary had to stay, awaiting further clarifications. He was released one hour later. All the other people caught in the 'cauldron' had to stay in it, and in one room. They were under the constant observation of the three employees, who did not ask them any questions but, from time to time, took some notes.

It was already late in the evening. They were tired and hungry. After diplomatic negotiations, Estelle was allowed to go to her apartment, accompanied by one of the employees, and bring money to buy food. One of the employees took this money and went out to the nearest shop to bring them eggs, ham, and bread. Estelle, under the supervision of one of the employees, was permitted to go to the kitchen and boil some water for tea for all the 'hostages.'

During their modest dinner, the number of 'hostages' increased. The janitor, who knew that his wife had gone to clean Marysia's apartment knocked at the door; he was let in and not permitted to exit. Andrzej's friend, also a doctor, who wanted to discuss some medical questions with Andrzej, having not found him at home, looked for him at his parents' apartment. As nobody answered, he knocked also at Marysia's apartment. He was let in, and not permitted to exit. After a while, he was followed by his wife, his mother-in-law, and the dog, taken for his evening walk. The 'cauldron' now contained nine adults, one baby, and one dog.

Late in the evening, one of the 'bosses' of the Ministry of Public Security in Wrocław arrived. He started to interrogate the persons caught in the 'cauldron.' He spoke in a very rude, arrogant way. He started with Andrzej and Karolina, asking them about the details of their stay in Paris, what the real aim of their stay in Paris was, what the names of their French friends were. Had they associated with people from other foreign countries? What was their relationship to the lady lawyer?

Afterward, he questioned Estelle. She had been born in Paris, but had left when she was seven years old, together with her parents, brother, and sister. They went to Lwów where, in the nineteenth century, her father was born, and where the rest of his family lived. This had all happened before the First World War, at the time of the Austro-Hungarian Empire. Since that time, Estelle had never returned to Paris, and she had no information about the political situation of contemporary France. No, she had had no friends in France since she left Paris. Estelle's answers caused evident dissatisfaction in the Public Security 'boss.' Ludwik could add nothing of interest to the inquiry. There was no time to interrogate the other people caught in the 'cauldron.'

The 'boss' announced that the lady lawyer, who lived in the apartment where the 'cauldron' was installed, had been put into prison and detained, suspected of spying for a foreign country against Poland. When Andrzej could not restrain himself from expressing his doubts about that, the 'boss' became extremely rude and told him that he had the power to transfer Andrzej to another place that certainly would be less pleasant for him. 'You are underestimating the power and the knowledge of the Public Security organs,' he shouted. 'We are the guardians of the Communist regime in Poland.'

It was midnight when he left, instructing his employees to be watchful and to take notes of conversations among the detained persons or of remarks made by them.

There were only two beds in the bedroom. On one slept Ludwik and Estelle; on the other one, the mother-in-law of Andrzej's colleague and the wife of the janitor with the baby. Other people slept on the carpet in the dining room. The dog slept on a small carpet in the corner.

Andrzej and Karolina had a restless night. They had never thought that something like this might happen.

In the morning, one of the employees of Public Security went to the nearby shop to buy food for all the detained persons and the dog. During the day, the number of detained persons increased. Six new persons knocked at the door, one of them with a dog. By evening, the number of detained persons increased to fifteen adults, and one baby, and there were now two dogs.

In the evening came again the Public Security 'boss.' He examined, one after another, all the detained people. The ordeal lasted five hours. Nobody understood what was going on, and people grew more and more frightened.

The next day started again with breakfast bought by one of the employees of Public Security. Although the detainees were frightened, they could not refrain from remarking that the shop-keeper was probably amazed by the number of eggs bought daily by the Public Security employee.

Nobody knocked at the door in the morning. In the early afternoon, only one person came. It was one of Ludwik's students, who was in a hurry to pass his Latin exam. He had been married early in the morning and wanted to pass his Latin exam scheduled for this day. He could not find Ludwik at the university and somebody gave him Ludwik's home address. As nobody answered his knocking, he came to ask where he could find Ludwik. The nearest neighbour's was the apartment of the lady lawyer, just opposite Ludwik's apartment. He was let in and not allowed to exit. It was a tragic situation for him, because his new bride was waiting for him to go on their honeymoon after his exam, and there was no opportunity to explain to her why he had suddenly disappeared. He begged the employees of the Public Security to let him go. The more he begged, the more suspect he appeared to them. Why did he want so much to go? Where did he intend to go? Why did he want to pass the Latin exam before his honeymoon? All the explanations given by him seemed suspicious.

During the next week, only five persons knocked at the door of the 'cauldron.' When the employee of Public Security kept coming to the shop to buy food for so many people, day after day, the shopowner asked him how many people were now sitting in the 'cauldron.' That meant that everybody knew about the location of the 'cauldron.'

All the detained persons were extremely tired, and in a very nervous state. It was evident also that the employees of Public

Security were tired, bored, and angry. They also wanted to see their families.

But the 'boss' from Public Security came each evening and spoke individually, one after another, with the detained persons. The questions were always the same, directed to finding the spy. The answers always led to a dead-end. The 'boss' was very angry. His anger was especially directed towards Andrzej because, in his opinion, the 'deconspiration' of the 'cauldron' had been caused by Andrzej. It was Andrzej who had brought to the 'cauldron,' the PPS Secretary and the PPS Parliament member. They had arrived in an official car that attracted the attention of everybody in the street. The 'boss' could also not hide his hatred of Estelle. Since her childhood Estelle mixed the Polish and French languages because her own mother never learned Polish. This mixed language was very suspect to the 'boss' who constantly interrupted her, asking what her French words meant.

After three weeks in the 'cauldron,' some people were allowed to go home, some people were detained, and some were transferred to prison. Among those permitted to return home were Andrzej and Karolina, Andrzej's parents, the janitor with his wife and baby, the student who had missed his honeymoon, and some others unknown to Andrzej and Karolina. Among those not released was Andrzej's colleague, who was detained in prison for nearly three months. The lady lawyer in whose apartment the 'cauldron' was installed spent one year in prison. She was released with no trial, physically and emotionally destroyed. She returned to her work in the Law Faculty only after several months of rest and treatment.

Those who were released were obliged to take an oath that they would not reveal anything about their presence in the 'cauldron.' They were told that their behaviour would be watched very carefully after the release from the 'cauldron' and that any 'subversive action' would be severely punished.

Many years after that episode, the PPS Secretary told Andrzej and Karolina that he had to guarantee personally that Ludwik, whom he had known since the time he was his student, was absolutely above any suspicion of spying and so was his entire family. He considered that such a suspicion must have been born in a disturbed mind.

The spy was never found. Simply, he did not exist.

III

ALTHOUGH THE SPY SIMPLY DID NOT EXIST, WHAT DID exist, and what persisted, was an atmosphere of suspicion, of fear, and anxiety. After their experience in the 'cauldron,' life in Poland was never the same for Andrzej and Karolina. This atmosphere of suspicion did not exist only in their imagination. The 'boss' of Public Security told not only them, but everybody who was released, that they would be watched carefully and that any 'subversive action' would be punished. What entitled him to speak of 'subversive action'? They had returned from Paris to Poland with only one thing in mind: to bring to the new Poland all the medical science that was not yet available in Poland, to teach the younger generations about new trends in psychiatry and neurology, and to introduce interest in the new field of clinical electroencephalography. How did the employees of Public Security dare to deprive them of freedom and keep them in a 'cauldron' for three weeks? Why did they threaten that they would be under constant observation? They had treated with the same contempt the PPS Secretary. Was there inside the new Poland a secret superpower above the Parliament, above the parties? Was it like the Soviet presence of the always feared NKVD (Narodnyj Komitet Wnutriennych Dieł)? Could they also deport Polish citizens to Siberia? Were some of their French friends right, telling them not to return to Poland, because it is a Communist country, exactly like the Soviet Union? Andrzej and Karolina were so proud of the fact that, at the time they received the fellowships from the French government, Poles were permitted to travel abroad; that there was a multiparty system in the country; that the parties were fighting between themselves was a common phenomenon in all social democratic countries.

When they were released from the 'cauldron,' the multiparty system still existed, however the general atmosphere in the country had changed. Not only Andrzej and Karolina were under suspicion. Not only Andrzej's colleague, the physician, was taken to prison for nearly three months and, with no trial, released. It happened more and more often that Polish people who returned from exile during the war from other Western countries were considered as suspect, and put into jail, accused of spying for the Western countries. The cold war between the Soviet Union and the Western Allies became more and more ardent.

Inside the country, the fight between the PPS, to which they belonged, like many members of the liberal intelligentsia, and between the PPR, to which belonged the members of the pre-war Polish Communist Party, was more and more fierce. And inside the PPR, there was also internal fighting for power between those members who, like Gomułka, were opposed to the Soviet domination of the party and those who were totally, with their souls and bodies, partisans of the Soviets. These PPR members were called Stalinists because they were uncritically faithful to Stalin. Their leader was Jakub Berman, one of the secretaries of the Central Committee of the PPR, and deputy prime minister. He accumulated enormous political power, and his adherents were placed in the most important posts in the government and in the party. Under his absolute command was also the Ministry of Public Security.

At the end of 1948, the Polish Socialist Party was 'swallowed,' or as the members of the PPR put it, 'united,' with the Polish Workers Party, under the name of the Polish United Workers Party (PZPR). All the members of the PPS, whether they liked it or not, became now the members of PZPR, automatically. In such a way, Andrzej and Karolina, one day members of the PPS, became on the next members of the PZPR. Why did they not leave at once the new party? They were at that time simply afraid that such a gesture would arouse suspicions of spying. They could not forget that they were watched all the time and what had happened to Marysia.

The political situation became intolerable, especially for Poles who, during the war, were in England, mostly as members of the Polish army. They were fighting on the western front against the Nazis. The commanding generals were under the jurisdiction of the Polish government in exile in London. The Poles affiliated with this government in exile were treated worse and worse; they were under constant suspicion of being enemies of post-war Poland. Many of them could not find work; many were unjustly accused and put in the prison.

It was ironic that a similar fate had dogged the first secretary of the PPR, Gomułka. He was stripped of his position, persecuted, and put into prison in 1951. He was replaced as secretary general by President Bolesław Bierut. Many members of the former PPR faced the same fate.

All this was masterminded by the omnipotent Jakub Berman. A new system of life existed now in Poland. The increasing political dependency from the Soviet Union, the isolation from Western Europe and the United States, were more and more evident. The people were afraid of having even formal mail contact with their relatives or friends from 'the West.' The 'iron curtain' had come down, separating the Eastern European countries from the non-Communist Western European countries, and from the United States. People did not talk freely by phone, nor even between themselves in their apartments because they knew that the phones and the apartments were bugged. Old friends ceased to trust one another. Apparently many people were forced to spy and inform the Ministry of Public Security. At the same time, there was a terrible rigidity of indoctrination with the rules of so-called Marxism-Leninism.

This new system brought also some other changes. Poland, which was before the war 70 per cent agricultural, with a large population of poor peasants and a few extremely wealthy landlords, underwent an industrial transfiguration and changed its demographic structure. The government was developing a free education system and a free health-care system, both available to everybody. The children of peasants who were too poor before the war to go to colleges or to universities had free access to higher education. In a certain way, the underprivileged classes from before the war were now given privileged status in the competition for the places available at the universities. Origins in the worker or peasant class garnered additional points on the admission exams.

These changes were positive and very promising for a great part of Polish population. The same was true for the health care. Out-patient and in-patient departments were free of charge for any segment of the population. Medication was free for people of golden age and also for some people at the poverty level. There was no unemployment.

However, the right to strike or walk out practically did not exist. New trade unions were organized, so-called 'vertical,' which meant that blue-collar workers were in the same trade union as white-collar workers if they worked in the same type of industry or education. For instance, the janitor working in one of the university buildings belonged to the same trade union as the principal or any of highly qualified research scientists at the same university. The trade unions were, however, not independent. They were formed under the pressure of the omnipotent party apparatus, and there were no free elections to the unions' leaderships.

Many Jewish Poles who survived the war in the Soviet Union or in Poland did not want to stay in Poland. Such was especially the case for a majority of them who were evacuated by force to Siberia. Seeing how life was in the Soviet Union, they started to emigrate upon invitations from their families abroad in Western Europe or in the United States. The first big exodus of Jews from Poland started after the proclamation of the independent state of Israel in May 1948. However, among the Jewish survivors of the Holocaust were also many with very strong emotional ties to Poland. They were assimilated, and identified themselves as Poles of Judaic religion or without any religion at all. These Poles, very often open-minded liberals, dreamed of a Poland with a social-democratic system, with no racial or religious prejudices, with non-nationalistic patriotism and pride, with an understanding of other people's national traditions or religious faith. They wanted to stay in Poland, and they hoped that their ideals would be realized.

There were also Polish Jews who were Communists. Many of them, like other members of the KPP, had bitter reminiscences of prewar Poland because they had spent many years in prison. Now, together with other members of the former Polish Communist Party (KPP), they were hoping to build a new Poland of social justice.

When Andrzej and Karolina got an apartment in Wrocław where there was space for a guest, the first person they invited was Father Alojzy. His monastery moved, as he predicted, from Lwów to Cracow, to the Bernardine Monastery, located very close to the old royal castle, Wawel.

Father Alojzy, always open-minded, evaluated with great objectivity the situation in Poland. He was satisfied that the Polish peasants had now a better life, with opportunity of education for their children and free health care. But he was not pleased at all with the interpersonal relations that existed in Poland under the new regime. He was aware of the fear, insecurity, envy, and opportunism. He was also unhappy with the anti-religious trend of the Polish government, which was not only contradictory to the human rights of any individual, but also detrimental to the moral standards of society.

Everybody could see that the belief that the new regime would create a better human nature was naïve and clearly divergent with reality. The psychological climate accompanying the new regime was in no way helpful in creating a better human being. On the contrary, the young people were being educated in an atmosphere of hypocrisy, of hatred of other nations, of very primitive indoctrination. They were indeed 'brain-washed,' repeating imposed slogans and deprived of independent thinking. Informers were encouraged to inform Public Security about anybody who was not following the imposed pattern of rigid ideas, even if this somebody was a member of the immediate family or a very close friend.

He ended his remarks with a theocratic reflection: 'God only can save us. But, remember, God has given us a free will and He will help us when our intentions are righteous.' It was a small comfort to Andrzej and Karolina in their situation. They could sense how depressed and disappointed with the post-war Poland Father Alojzy was. He saw a very grim near future.

The news about Filomena brought by Father Alojzy was sad. Andrzej and Karolina had tried for a long time to locate her, but could not find her. Now, at last, they were given the address of her convent transferred from Lwów. He knew also the address of the hospital in which she was being treated.

Two weeks later, Andrzej and Karolina went to the Surgical department of the teaching hospital in Katowice. Filomena had been operated on two years earlier for cancer of the stomach and had undergone irradiation therapy. It had not helped very much, and now she was again hospitalized with metastases and considered terminally ill. The doctors told Andrzej that the months of her life were numbered. She was very weak, and she had also serious cardiac problems.

She was very grateful for their visit. Knowing that her condition was serious, she accepted it with great humility and in a very quiet way. She told them that she was leaving very soon for something much better. 'My prayers will be with you. You know, Andrzej, how very attached I was to you, and you know, Karolina, that I loved you since the first moment we met. Remember our conversation when I accompanied you to the bus stop after your first visit in our Department of Psychiatry in Lwów? I know that God is with both of you and will help you also in these unhappy times, as He helped you to go through the Nazi hell. Let us hope that God will give His goodness to the righteous people.'

This visit has deeply touched both of them. Karolina cried late into the night. She loved Filomena very much, and respected her highly. Karolina suffered painfully from anti-Semitism in pre-war Poland,

and Filomena was the first Polish nun who told her that the fighters for supremacy of any religion are wrong-doers, sinners, because God is universal and He created all human beings, whatever their religion, colour of skin, or nationality might be. During her labourious life, dedicated to alleviating human suffering, Filomena had always been faithful to this idea.

Three months after their visit to Filomena, Andrzej and Karolina received a letter from the Mother Superior of Filomena's convent. Filomena died quietly in the convent. She was fully conscious until the end, waiting with patience to see God.

Andrzej and Karolina worked with dedication in their departments in Wrocław. They were involved in the active treatment of patients and in didactic duties and saw how much their stay in Paris contributed to their perfection in psychiatry and neurology. It was, however, extremely difficult to get an electroencephalograph because Poland was short of foreign currency, and the government could not afford to buy even one such instrument. Therefore, Andrzej had the idea to use an electrocardiograph with special amplification instruments to obtain the registration of human brain potentials. It had only one channel, and it was very often necessary to have an engineer check and repair its functioning. They worked on it late at night and eventually could publish the first clinical electroencephalographic research paper in Poland. They were very proud of it because one of the pioneers of this method of exploration of electrical brain activity was also a Pole, A. Beck, who had published the first experimental work on animal brain potentials in the nineteenth century. Andrzej and Karolina dreamed of doing research work on such an electroencephalograph as the one on which they had worked in France.

At the end of 1949, Andrzej received from the Ministry of Health a letter, asking him if he would be willing to participate in the organization of a psychoneurological institute in Pruszków, one of the suburbs of Warsaw. There was also a possibility of later transfer to Warsaw after the construction of a suitable building. It seemed to them that this might give them better conditions for research and a chance to get, after some time, an electroencephalograph. Andrzej accepted this offer and was appointed scientific director of the institute, and Karolina was appointed the chief of the electroencephalographic laboratory of the institute. However, all the burden of organization and finding the means and ways for it was on their shoulders, especially on Andrzej's. It was a high-risk endeavour, but with their persistance and enthusiastic approach to work, it might work out.

They gave up their rather comfortable apartment in Wrocław and received a very small and modest apartment on the grounds of a big psychiatric hospital in the suburbs of Warsaw. They also found a nice room for their parents in a big apartment belonging to one of the older physicians on the same grounds. One of the pavilions of that hospital would be the future location of the institute.

Nothing existed when they arrived, only an empty pavilion, waiting for reconstruction with central heating, architectural planning for neurological and psychiatric departments, laboratories, library, and a complete clinical and research outfit.

It was winter, and many times they had to use a small iron stove not to freeze, because the central heating was not yet installed. There was no electroencephalograph waiting for them. They had to travel by local train about 20 kilometres to the Ministry of Health in Warsaw to negotiate the means and credits for all this enterprise. Andrzej had to hold meetings with architects to adapt the pavilion to the needs of the future research institute. All this was very time-consuming and left very little time for professional work.

They found a great help in this organizing work by engaging a young newly graduated doctor, Danuta, who had finished her studies with honours and was strongly dedicated to working for the new Poland. She gave all her time to find proper outfits for laboratories and various research tools and equipment.

It took one year of intensive work to have, at the end of 1950, the institute functioning.

The academic, scientific, and teaching activities were now in full swing. Professional satisfaction permitted them, although only partially, to forget the deceptions caused by the miserable quality of human relationships in this new Poland.

The tragedy of Orelec was never out of their minds. In summer 1950, it became possible to visit Orelec. During the first years after the war, this region was full of unrest, with ethnic violence.

At the time they decided to visit Orelec, there was still some sporadic unrest, but, in daytime, it was relatively quiet. They reached Orelec on a Sunday before noon. They went to the head of the hamlet, a new man in this region. In the framework of exchange of population, resulting from right of option between Poland and the Soviet Union, Polish peasants arrived in Orelec from villages close to Lwów, belonging now to the Soviet Union. Immediately after the war, the region went through a turbulent period because the majority of population, which was Ukrainian, had to move to the Soviet Union, and did not accept this with enthusiasm.

Many Polish peasants who lived in Orelec during the war preferred to move to more quiet regions in Poland, even to go far west to the regions in Silesia. Many houses were destroyed during those turbulent times. The house where Juliusz lived with his family from fall 1941 to spring 1942 was not destroyed. It was empty; nobody lived there. Since the Nazi massacre of the Jewish population in Orelec in April 1942, nobody wanted to move to houses formerly occupied by the Jewish families.

The head of the hamlet had heard of the massacre from older peasants living until now in the village. They went to see one of these peasants. The man, in his sixties, repeated the tragic information given to Andrzej in Sanok by the teacher Janka, on 24 April, 1942. Like the heroic teacher and other peasants, this man had seen two days prior the cruel behaviour of the Nazis, the tragic march of the Jews through the village. He had witnessed the shooting by the Gestapo of the old man and Jewish children during their march to the forest. He had heard shooting from the forest on the hills until sunset. He had seen the Gestapo going out of the woods.

When the Gestapo moved out from the region, only then had he dared to go and see the place in the woods. The ditches were slightly covered by earth, and one could see in some places the bodies of the murdered victims. The bushes were covered with blood. After the war, in 1946, the Polish military forces exhumed the remains of the Jewish bodies and buried them in a mass tomb on a glade, just on the edge of the woods.

The peasant described the crimes of these days with strong emotion. He had never forgotten the tragedy of many families that he knew well. He went out to the garden and, before Andrzej and Karolina took their leave, he asked Andrzej: 'Are you a Jew, a survivor or a relative of one of these Jewish martyrs, killed here by the Gestapo?' Andrzej shook his hand and said: 'No, I am not a Jew, but I am a survivor of the Holocaust.'

The village was silent as always on Sundays. They returned to the square in front of the church. All was the same as eight years ago: the same church, the same houses around the square, the same sun, shining in the sky. It had the aspect of a very calm, nearly serene place, and it was difficult to imagine that, in this place, Polish Jews, innocent inhabitants of the village, had waited for their deaths at the hands of Hitler's tormenters and that the only reason for their martyrdom was the fact that they were Jewish.

Andrzej and Karolina went to the house where Juliusz lived with Dorota and Zosia. They were accompanied by the head of the hamlet, who had keys to the house. Inside, Andrzej found the same bedroom, the two beds, a table, a wardrobe, and four chairs. In the kitchen were still some of Juliusz's utensils, dishes, pots. It was like a house that somebody had left for a while. Andrzej looked at Karolina. She was quiet, and very pale. She sat on a chair close to the table and opened the drawer. In it was a photograph of Zosia. She asked the head of the hamlet to be allowed to take the photograph. She kissed it and hugged it to her heart.

They returned to the square in front of the church and, from there, they went towards the forest on the hills, following the route that Juliusz, Dorota, and Zosia had taken eight years earlier. They stopped before the chapel with Jesus in Sorrow. The expression of sorrow was still on His face. It seemed to Andrzej that there was more pain in His face. Or was it simply the aging of the wood? Karolina knelt before the chapel and prayed for a long while. When turning to the cross-roads, near the woods, Karolina told Andrzej: 'I prayed not only for my parents and Zosia, but also for Janka, the heroic teacher who was so good to my family, so helpful to you during your visits to Orelec, and who was sent as God's messenger to stop you in Sanok from going where death could meet you. Janka had a heroic death, fighting against the Nazis.' Karolina knew from Andrzej that Janka stopped always to pray before this roadside chapel for a better future, for victory over the Nazis, and for permanent peace after the war. They stopped at the crossroads for a long time.

The road up the hill was narrow between the bushes. On the glade at the edge of the forest, the head of the hamlet showed them the mass tomb of the victims. It bore a provisional inscription on the wood that here are buried about one hundred Polish Jews, murdered by the Gestapo on 22 April, 1942. They were martyrs of the Nazis' crimes during the Second World War.

They left some flowers before the grave marker. Karolina knelt here again and prayed for a long time. Then they walked around the forest and found the traces of ditches. They took some earth in a handkerchief and stood for a long while in silence, close to the ditches. This was a farewell to Juliusz, Dorota, and Zosia.

The head of the hamlet told them that they were the first visitors to this tomb. He did not ask who they were and what was their connection with the Jewish martyrs. During the war, he himself had been active with the Polish resistance in his native village, close to Lwów. He had moved from there to Orelec because he did not want to stay in the Soviet Union. He was satisfied with the new Poland because, before the war, he had been a poor peasant in a small village and now he had, in Orelec, a much bigger farm. His three children were in high school and college, one had already been accepted as a student at the University of Cracow. All of them had scholarships from the government.

Andrzej and Karolina returned from the forest trail, back to the village, and went to the school to commemorate Janka. She and hundreds and thousands of Poles fighting in the Polish resistance during the war were treated by the German occupiers as bandits and terrorists. For the Poles, they were and are heroes, and they will remain in the future heroes of the humanity. 'They will never be forgotten,' said Andrzej when, together with Karolina, they looked through the window into the room of the teacher.

It was vacation time, and the school was closed. Through the window, they could see the table on which Janka worked, the couch on which Andrzej rested before going with her at night to visit secretly Juliusz and his family. They stood for a long while before this window, thinking of this extraordinary, courageous girl. Karolina did not know her personally; she had seen her only for a moment, from a certain distance, when Janka had warned Andrzej of the danger of going to Orelec just when the Gestapo was exterminating all the Jews there. This unexpected and unplanned meeting had saved Andrzej's life. Anybody helping the Jews was treated by the Gestapo as a Jew.

They returned once more to the centre of the village to look again at the house where Juliusz, Dorota, and Zosia had lived until their tragic death.

It was already close to sunset. They left the village for Warsaw.

IV

IT WAS HARD FOR ANDRZEJ AND KAROLINA TO ADAPT TO the new situation. Life was not easy in the small suburb of Warsaw, in their extremely modest apartment on the grounds of the psychiatric hospital in Pruszków. Nor was it easy for Ludwik and Estelle to exchange their quite comfortable apartment in Wrocław for one rented room in a big apartment of one of the doctors of the hospital. In general, all the doctors working in the hospital had their apartments on the grounds belonging to the hospital. But they had lived there for a long time and were used to the atmosphere of a small community of doctors.

Andrzej and Karolina, coming from Wrocław, where they knew nearly everybody because 'all' of Lwów had moved to Wrocław, found themselves in a place where they knew nobody, with the exception of the director of the hospital and a few officials from the Ministry of Health who had given Andrzej the task of organizing the first Polish laboratory of clinical electroencephalography. They started their work with such enthusiasm that the inconveniences of their private life did not bother them very much.

Very soon after their transfer to Pruszków, they were both many times called by the so-called Department of Science of the Central Committee of the PZPR in Warsaw, where they were submitted to regular 'schooling' related to their attitudes as scientific researchers. They were told that the newly organized Institute of Psychoneurology had to propagate in all medical science the theory of Pavlov. 'Pavlovism' had to be the reigning theory everywhere in medicine. Of course, they knew very well the theory of Pavlov and his teaching, his discovery of the mechanism of conditioned reflexes. This physiologist, of Nobel Laureate fame called *Princeps physiologorum mundi* was an inspiration to many researchers. However, they had never considered that his conceptions had political meaning. They heard, on the contrary, that Pavlov himself was very critical of many things in the Communist system in the Soviet Union.

Now, in the Department of Science of the Central Committee of the PZPR, they were 'schooled' in the belief that the only scientific tool in research has to be materialistic, that 'Pavlovism' was a materialistic approach, and that the facts that a scientist has to discover must be aimed at proving that the materialistic theory is the right one. This view was in strong contrast to their attitude that theories should be constructed on the basis of facts, and not the other way around. Pavlov certainly did not base his discovery of conditional reflexes on any political theory.

Another Nobel laureate, Adrian, told them in Cambridge, where they went on an excursion from Paris in 1947, that preconceived theories might be dangerous in research because they might lead to ignoring or falsifying experiences.

They both remembered very well some very primitive 'schooling' of the theory of Marxism-Leninism in Lwów in 1939–41. But this was a purely political indoctrination and, at that time, nobody interfered in the very special problems of research in biological sciences in such a way. What had happened? Why should this be done in the new post-war Poland? It was not easy to understand. Andrzej told Karolina that she was invited to come to the next 'schooling' with him and that he had a lot to learn, from the 'ideological' point of view. Karolina told him that she would prepare herself for this 'schooling' and that she wanted to ask them some questions that might embarrass them. Eventually they turned all of this into a joke and made fun of it.

They were wrong. There was no joke and no fun. The people in the Science Department of the Central Committee of the PZPR were deadly serious. They did not like at all the attitudes of Andrzej and Karolina, and they decided that further 'schooling' was absolutely necessary, to make out of Andrzej and Karolina serious researchers, 'involved' in ideology and not in the 'soulless' research of facts. They told them that this type of 'schooling' was going on everywhere in the Soviet Union, that there was a great ideological struggle among the most famous neurophysiologists and psychiatrists about the role and influence of the theories of Pavlov in medicine, especially in psychiatry and clinical neurophysiology. The struggle was going on also in the field of genetics, where the Mendel's theory was seen as anti-progressive and, instead, a new theory was proclaimed as 'in line' with the materialistic, dialectic approach. The new theory was named the 'Łysenko theory,' and their mentor in the Department of Science was an ardent propagator of it.

When they tried to discuss problems from another point of view, they were informed that their attitudes were influenced by the false doctrine of the former PPS. 'You never fully recovered from the approach preached by the Polish Socialist Party. We will teach you and watch carefully how you apply in your scientific work the Marxist-Leninist theories of Pavlov.'

The situation became threatening once they heard that they would be 'watched carefully.' They had heard this already in 1948 from the 'boss' who examined them in the 'cauldron,' and they could not forget that some of the people caught in the 'cauldron' had been jailed for a long time. They decided not to say anything, just to listen.

Late into the night they discussed between themselves what to do. They had the feeling that it was naïve and foolish to accept the proposal to become the scientific director of the Psychoneurological Institute.

Karolina felt that they were in a trap from which it was impossible to escape: 'We are completely detached from the Western world. The PPS does not exist any more, and whoever was progressive and revolted against the PZPR, like Gomułka, is in prison now. What are we going to do? They have such a tremendous power that they can annihilate us completely. In addition, if we listen to them too long we might become 'brain-washed.' It was a moral inferno into which they had put themselves, accepting the proposals of transfer to Pruszków. It was now clear that somebody used them to organize the Psychoneurological Institute, not for the sake of the Polish science, but as a fortress of ideological struggle, without any true scientific interest. 'Therefore,' Andrzej told Karolina, and she agreed, 'the only way is to work hard and prove by our work what we mean by real research and that we can show it. Our work will convince them.'

It seemed to be the right attitude. Andrzej had the talent to attract to the Institute young, talented people, teach them how to find interesting problems, show them the methodology of scientific research. He put all his intelligence and soul into the organization and creation of serious research. He also found time to finish his habilitation thesis and to defend it at Warsaw University. He was promoted to docent of psychiatry at Warsaw University by the chairman of the Department of Psychiatry. Karolina found time to write her doctoral thesis and was promoted as doctor of medicine, which was a scientific title, in addition to gaining her diploma of physician.

This hard work and the political climate of lack of confidence were badly influencing Andrzej's health. He had increased blood pressure and frequent attacks of very painful kidney stones. Nevertheless, all his life was dedicated to making the Psychoneurological Institute the best place for patients' treatment, for research, and for the education of young scientists.

Although he was very proud of the prestige gained by the growing of the Institute, inwardly he was less and less happy with the situation. More and more, he realized what a destructive influence was exerted on them by the Department of Science of the Central Committee and the Ministry of Health. He was also worried about the constant remarks that he was not fighting hard enough against the 'idealistic' theories prevailing in the pre-war period. He published some critical essays on this problem, and they were subject to censorship and 'improvements' by the Science department without his consent. One night he told Karolina: 'If they have power to put Gomułka in prison . . .' He did not need to finish the sentence. Karolina understood very well what he meant.

The years 1951 and 1952 were a period when Stalinism was at its peak in the Soviet Union and influencing political life in Eastern European countries. There were strong pressures in each branch of science, especially in philosophy, but also in biology and medicine, to accept theories based on 'dialectic materialism.' It was a very hard time, from the moral point of view, for both of them. They did not feel at ease with their own attitudes.

The second half of 1952 was one of the most difficult years for all the family. Ludwik, who for a long time had suffered from high blood pressure and had had a heart attack during the German occupation, fell seriously ill. He had a brain haemorrhage and was hospitalized for a long time. He never fully recovered. There were many months of suffering and misery for all the family.

In December 1952, Ludwik passed away, leaving Estelle, Andrzej, and Karolina in deep sorrow. This man of greatest integrity, respected by everybody, had had a remarkable effect on the organization of the Polish educational system of high schools and colleges in the pre-war period. During the Nazi occupation, he had been involved in secret teaching, after the occupiers closed many schools.

Ludwik had had the most important role in saving the life of Karolina during the Nazi occupation. He had masterminded all the details of the transfer from Lwów of all the family to his native village. He was the one who brought to Juliusz the proposal of Bishop Baziak and insisted that Juliusz accept it. If Juliusz had listened to his advice and accepted the idea of hiding in a convent and monastery, Juliusz, Dorota, and Zosia probably would have survived the war. Respect nurtured for Ludwik by one of his students saved all the family from the persecutions encountered by other people caught in the 'cauldron.'

And now Ludwik was gone. His fine personality and courageous progressive ideas survived for ever not only in the memory of his family, but in the memories of all people who knew him.

Now all the family had to live without him, and Andrzej and Karolina had to fight in this world without his clever advice. Estelle was in a deep depression, and nothing could console her for a long time. Each and every day, she went to his grave and cried for Ludwik, with whom she was married for nearly fifty years. Her love was always as fresh as on the first day they had met.

V

TWO MONTHS AFTER LUDWIK'S PASSING, THE PEOPLE IN the Department of Science of the Central Committee of the PZPR called Andrzej in to tell him that he had not shown enough strength and dedication to defend Pavlovian theory and not attack 'idealists' during one of the conventions. Andrzej felt that he was lost because in the official PZPR journal, *Trybuna Ludu*, an article was published, criticizing the organization of a convention for Pavlov's teaching, for which he was made responsible.

Several days later, he was called to the Ministry of Health for a discussion. He knew what it meant and had decided to tell them everything from the bottom of his heart. Absolutely everything. And he did it. When he returned from the Ministry of Health, he told Karolina that morally he felt much better now, but that he was terribly afraid of what they might do to him. He had not long to wait.

The next day he was called again to the Ministry of Health, where a young employee, trembling and pale, handed him over, with no comment, two envelopes, one addressed to him and another one to Karolina. They contained two letters with the same content, signed by the Minister of Health. Both of them were discharged from the Institute and officially transferred to a provincial psychiatric hospital to work there as ordinary doctors. The letters were dated for the previous day, on which the discussion with Andrzej had taken place. The hospital to which they were being sent had the reputation as the worst psychiatric hospital in Poland. Such an order meant the complete ruin of their scientific and didactic work, expelling Andrzej from the Institute he had organized and depriving both of them of their didactic and research work. It meant that the Stalinists, who were at that time on the peak of their power, had demolished two people who did not accept any more their commands. It also showed how little the Ministry of Health cared for the patients who, from one day to another, were deprived of Andrzej's medical experience.

'What are we going to do? We are finished. We have immediately to pack our belongings, take Estelle, leave the fresh grave of my father and go into exile.'

Karolina felt that they had to fight, even though it would be a dangerous battle: 'We will not move now from here unless they use force. Over my dead body they will move us to that hospital where nothing more than vegetation and slow death is waiting for us. I am going to-morrow to tell the Minister of Health that we do not accept his decision and that he will have to move us with force. I know that this clique is not well accepted by some still decent members of the Central Committee. We will ask them for help.' Andrzej smiled, with an expression of doubt on his face: 'My dear, nobody can fight with Berman whose henchmen have finished us. People are afraid. Don't you see that terror is everywhere.' 'I will go anyway,' she replied. 'There is nothing to lose and perhaps something to gain.'

Next morning, when she went out, she saw how fast the news had spread and what a terrible impact it had even on honest people. Some people very grateful to Andrzej, who had enabled them to work in the Institute, were crossing the street so as not to greet Karolina as usual with a friendly 'Good morning' and a short chat. They were simply afraid that contact with one 'expelled' by the mighty clique in the Ministry of Health might be dangerous for them.

When Karolina arrived at the Ministry of Health, they made her wait for a long time before she was granted an audience with the minister. She told him that neither she nor Andrzej would accept the letters of dismissal in which no reason for transfer from a scientific

Institute to a provincial psychiatric hospital was mentioned. In addition, from a legal point of view, such orders were not acceptable because they were pre-dated, indicating that both of them were transferred on the preceding day. On the preceding day, they were still working in the Institute and had full rights as Institute employees.

He listened to her with a hostile expression on his face, saying nothing. Then Karolina, in despair, told him that Andrzej had been sick for a long time, with high blood pressure and frequent attacks of kidney stones, and that he could not at once leave his treatments and his nephrologist in Warsaw. He answered: 'I am in command here and this story has a seal of approval from Comrade Berman. And as minister of health, I am telling you that, if your husband is sick, nobody forbids him to be sick in this provincial hospital and be treated there. It is your business and not mine to find for him a specialist there for his kidney stones.'

Karolina could not refrain from saying: 'I heard that, before the war, you were a very open-minded person of great integrity. Therefore, I came to you. But I see who you are now. I am sorry for you.' And she left, but did not give up her fight.

When she returned home, she told Andrzej: 'I was right to be afraid of being brain-washed by the schooling. This man is already completely brain-washed. I don't think that he is terrorized by Berman and his henchmen. He simply believes that whatever they do is honest and in the best interests of Communism. He has complete confidence in them, and he is hostile to everybody who opposes orders with Berman's seal of approval.'

She told him also how the people were afraid to have contact with her because they had heard that they were expelled from the Institute. Andrzej replied that he had just had a visit of Professor Józef Handelsman, the chairman of the Psychiatric department in the Academy of Medicine. He was warned by everybody not to visit them because he might be persecuted for a contact with them. This did not scare this very honest and distinguished psychiatrist, who had always wanted to have Andrzej as his successor. On the contrary, he had come to comfort Andrzej and to tell him that he still had and always would have full confidence in him. It was a great relief for Andrzej.

Karolina was in a fighting mood and wanted to act as fast as possible. Andrzej felt also stronger, encouraged by the visit of the chairman of the Psychiatric department.

Together they made a plan. They knew that the corridors of power that made Berman so dangerous consisted of the fact that, as one of the secretaries of the Central Committee, he had under his absolute jurisdiction certain branches of government and, at the same time, as a deputy prime minister, he had absolute jurisdiction over other branches of the government. He and his henchmen acted so quickly, in one or another capacity, that other secretaries of the Central Committee had no time to change or discuss his decisions. Therefore, Andrzej and Karolina had received pre-dated orders with instant enforcement. Berman acted here as a deputy prime minister, having an absolute jurisdiction over the Ministry of Health.

In this situation the only way was to go to the Secretary of the Central Committee who had jurisdiction over health and could interfere with administrative power. They have heard that this Secretary was a very honest and courageous man. They did not have access to such a highly situated person but Andrzej knew one of his high officials in the Central Committee, who not long ago had congratulated Andrzej for the work at the Institute. Knowing all the difficulties with creating new institutions, he told Andrzej that if there were some problems in organization, Andrzej should call him.

Andrzej called him and asked for an emergency appointment. He was granted this appointment on the same morning. It was the day after the unsuccessful audience Karolina had had with the Minister of Health. They both went to the Central Committee where an entrance permit awaited Andrzej. Karolina had to wait for him in the lobby. The entrance permits to the secretaries and high officials in the Central Committee were given only on their orders. A citizen could not get an entrance permit without an order 'from above.'

The high official listened to the story narrated by Andrzej, and could hardly believe how far the absolute power of Berman to destroy people who dared not to obey them had gone: 'They are treating people as manure to fertilize the revolution. That is how they are treating you and your wife. It was clever of you not to panic and stay. Very few people have such courage.

'As a matter of fact I don't think that Berman himself gave this order to the Minister of Health. You are – with all the due respect to your work – too small a fish to find yourself in Berman's net. Most probably it was a person very close to him, like the Red-Head, as we call him here, or one of his agents in the Ministry of Health who masterminded this story. I will immediately go to consult with people above me, and we will find out. Don't expect too much. Berman always endorses the manipulations of Red-Head, not to compromise him. Red-Head is so cynical that he tells people that nobody can oppose him, because he sees Berman every morning. However, there is one thing that I can tell you now: don't move from Pruszków before I do something. I know that you are deprived of work and that you cannot even enter the Institute. Stay at home and inform everybody you can about your dismissal. The Red-Head and his agents have a rotten reputation everywhere in the party, and their only power resides in the fact that Red-Head has indeed immediate access to Berman. We know also that Red-Head is in absolute command of the Ministry of Health; unfortunately, the Minister of Health, who before the war was a man of great integrity, is now his tool. I am also sorry for the minister because I always liked him. I like the story of Karolina's conversation with him, although I don't think that she was able to impress him very much.

'Please don't call me. I will call you as soon as I have the necessary information. It might take a couple of weeks. But one thing is sure: you will never be transferred to this provincial hospital. What Karolina told you: 'Over my dead "body." I am repeating: over *my* dead body. Although we cannot undo everything, still we can do something.'

Karolina could not sit quietly in the lobby; from time to time, she got up to look at the staircase. This made the janitors suspicious, and they told her that, unless she sat quietly, they would expel her. After about an hour, Andrzej appeared, extremely tired, but his blue eyes were twinkling with joy.

'Did he promise you to do something for us?' 'Yes, he did, but we have to wait perhaps a couple of weeks, because it is not an easy fight. We won't go to the provincial hospital anyway. That is promised already.'

A long and devastating waiting period began. They were not allowed to enter the Institute. Some of their friends did not behave very courageously; some, however, like Dr. Teresa decided to stay openly on their side and even intervene in the Central Committee, risking their own work. One of their friends who worked in the Ministry of Health told them the background behind their dismissal.

Red-Head asked Dr. Jan W., the psychiatrist-in-chief in the Ministry of Health, which psychiatric hospital was the worst in Poland, with the worst medical cases, the poorest library, and the worst staff. Then he ordered to add immediately to the budget of this hospital two positions for two doctors, without indicating their names. Then Red-Head, through his agents, talked with eminent psychiatrists in other cities, asking if they would accept the position of scientific director at the Psychoneurological Institute. Everybody declined. In this situation, Red-Head asked a psychiatrist who had just returned from the Soviet Union, at the end of a three-year scholarship, to accept this position. She accepted with great joy. She had no research capabilities and in general was evaluated by the professional psychiatric community as a person that absolutely should not be employed in such a high scientific position. Her nomination was accepted with a general contempt for the Ministry of Health.

After six weeks, the same high official from the Central Committee called Andrzej and asked him to come for the final decision to the Central Committee. Karolina again waited for him in the lobby. After one hour, Andrzej emerged with a smile, but not very triumphant. He told Karolina that, indeed, it was not a decision of Berman himself, although he endorsed a part of it, *post factum*, of course. All the intrigue was played by Red-Head. But, because he is a villain, he said that he had nothing to do with that.

The official had told Andrzej: 'Red-Head told us that he did not sign such an order; the Minister of Health did it. Thus, the Minister of Health is solely responsible and, if we are dissatisfied with him, we are free to dismiss him at once. But nobody from our secretariat wanted to do that. First, we believe that the minister is not yet completely destroyed morally and he might one day recover from the bad influences; second, we know that Red-Head has already a plot to put in his place one of his most vicious agents.

'We could leave you both in Warsaw only if we dismiss the minister. As we did not want to do that, we negotiated something that will save the minister and give him time to recover. He will write you a letter in which he will appoint you as co-chairman of the Department of Psychiatry at the Academy of Medicine in Łódź. This is the second-largest university in Poland. Karolina will receive a letter appointing her associate professor in the Department of Neurology at the Academy of Medicine in Łódź. They just received an excellent electroencephalograph.'

This was, of course, not a bad solution, but neither Andrzej nor Karolina liked it because the Department of Psychiatry was in one of the suburbs of Łódź and the Department of Neurology in the city. 'For how long should we be in exile?' asked Karolina. 'As long as Berman is alive,' Andrzej answered, 'Red-Head will never forget nor forgive that he has practically lost with us. I was warned that we should proceed with great caution because they are able to make provocative steps. But, my dear Karolina, although it is an exile for life in their decision, we will not stop fighting and will work together, although not in the most favourable conditions.'

They received notice that there was an apartment waiting for them in Łódź. It was, of course, in the poorest quarter of Łódź, so-called Bałuty. It was on the third floor, because they knew that Andrzej had some cardio-vascular problems and that Estelle was already in her seventies. What else were they going to do to harm them?

Transportation was paid for and organized by the Ministry of Health. It was a motor truck to which was attached an old-fashioned furniture truck, used only for horse-driven transportation. What everybody predicted happened: the axle of the furniture truck, after about 80 kilometres drive, caught fire and all their belongings, furniture and personal things, were burned.

They had to return to Warsaw, and then undergo again the agony of moving to Łódź with what remained of their half-burned furniture and belongings. They hired a lawyer to claim an indemnity from the government. The lawyer was a very distinguished lady who had been a member of the PPS before the war and who was a friend of Juliusz. She could not hide her anger against the Ministry of Health and all the harm they were doing to Andrzej and Karolina. 'We are defenceless, but they did not kill us until now. And, I promise you that I will win this law suit. I am not afraid of Berman or his henchmen.' And she won.

They lived with their half-burned furniture, which for one year did not lose its smoky smell, that was affecting their breathing in the Bałuty quarter of Łódź. They worked very hard, and were accepted with great respect by their colleagues and co-workers in Łódź. The people did not speak much, out of terror, but their behaviour showed what they were feeling.

Very soon after their transfer, Andrzej and Karolina heard from the loud-speakers all over Poland that the 'genius of humanity, the most superb human being, Stalin' died. This fact marked in the Soviet Union, and in the countries of Eastern Europe dependent on the Soviet Union, the beginning of a thaw, a very slow one. Power was still in the hands of the Stalinists. 'The emperor died, but the generals remained,' the people were saying. The thaw gained speed only when Nikita Khrushchev, the new Secretary General of the Soviet Communist party, in his famous speech, unveiled Stalin's terror and tyranny, his falsification of history and self-glorification.

In Poland it took a good while before Red-Head was fired from the Ministry of Health, and Berman, the great chief of Stalinism in Poland, was fired from his position in the government and in the politbureau, and eventually from the party.

Gomułka, arrested in 1951, was released in 1954 from prison. He was reinstated in 1956 as First Secretary. Already a couple of months before his return to the position as First Secretary of the party, one could feel in Poland greater personal freedom and some greater social and economic freedom.

During this period, when the 'generals' were still in power, Andrzej and Karolina did not stop fighting for return from exile to Warsaw. This fight was for a long time interrupted when Andrzej became so seriously ill that he had to be operated on for kidney-stone removal.

At the end of 1954, Andrzej was promoted and appointed Professor of Psychiatry at the University of Łódź. Karolina was appointed 'docent' at the beginning of 1955 at the same university.

When more favourable winds started to blow in 1955, one of the new secretaries of the Central Committee, Władysław M., convinced the Minister of Health that Andrzej and Karolina should return to Warsaw. In the second half of this year Karolina was appointed docent in the Psychiatric Department of the Academy of Medicine in Warsaw, and Andrzej received the appointment as scientific vice-director of the Psychoneurological Institute.

Many years later, Andrzej, whose work became respected abroad, and who was a member of the panel of experts on mental health in the World Health Organization, had to participate in a WHO convention in Geneva. The Polish team was led by the same Minister of Health who in 1953 fired Andrzej and Karolina from the Psychoneurological Institute. In Geneva, the minister approached Andrzej very closely and in most sincere words apologized for the harm he did to him and Karolina.

When he returned to Warsaw he called Karolina and offered also her his apologies. Listening to him and trying to keep no rancour in her heart, she could still not refrain of thinking of the words of the

Polish Queen Jadwiga: 'Even when you reimburse those whom you have hurt, who will return them the tears that they have shed?'

VI

THE THAW THAT STARTED IN POLAND IN 1955 DID NOT LAST very long, but still those years were the best in Poland after the war. They brought freedom of expression, of the press, of research, of travelling abroad, of having contacts with foreign countries, of scientific exchanges with Western Europe and United States. Andrzej and Karolina could participate in conventions abroad and obtain for their co-workers research fellowships in France and England.

In 1960 was realized the wish so many times expressed by the recently retired chairman of the Department of Psychiatry in Warsaw. Andrzej was appointed chairman of the Department of Psychiatry in the Warsaw Academy of Medicine. He felt that this position was much more suitable for him because the tasks of the Psychoneurological Institute became more and more administrative and there was no time for scientific research and didactic work, which had a priority in Andrzej's professional life. Karolina was already working in this department, and they could again work in the same institution.

In 1963, Andrzej received a fellowship to deliver lectures in the United States. He and Karolina received also invitations to lecture in Canada. Both went for over two months to Canada and the United States. Estelle was, at that time, in good health, and they could leave her under the care of their friends, and maintain constant phone contact with her. Although there was still a certain thaw, all three of them were never allowed to go abroad together. One person had always to stay in Poland to guarantee that the others would return. Even when Estelle had the possibility to realize her long-nurtured dream of visiting Paris, which she had left as a child of seven years, she could be accompanied only by Karolina; Andrzej had to stay in Poland.

The Psychiatric Department, under Andrzej's guidance, attracted many talented young people. Thanks to the contacts with the

Psychiatric Department at the Sorbonne in Paris, which dated since 1947, and to the contacts with the Institute of Psychiatry in London, and to numerous other scientific contacts abroad, Andrzej could provide to the patients of his department the most up-to-date mental health care. At the same time, he was teaching students and residents in psychiatry and showing young researchers how to master the research methods.

Since the very beginning of his work as chairman of the Department of Psychiatry in the Warsaw Academy of Medicine, Andrzej was thinking how to transfer the department from the suburbs to Warsaw. Before the war, this department was located in Warsaw at the premises of the Hospital of Saint John the Divine. During the war, it was ruined completely by the German bombs. Even before that, the Nazis had exterminated the mentally ill by starvation and shooting. They did the same in other hospitals for the mentally ill.

Andrzej believed that this department should be relocated in Warsaw. There were many common teaching and treatment problems connecting psychiatry to other medical specialities. Also the fact that only the Psychiatric department was outside the city, created a certain stigma for the patients. It certainly was not favourable for convalescence, rehabilitation, or resocialization. In Warsaw it would be possible to organize a day and a night hospital where the patients could stay for only twelve hours daily and spend the other twelve with their families and friends. They could go to the cinema, theatre, or museum; walk in the parks; and be resocialized much sooner than in a suburb, where the only possibility of a walk was on the premises of a big psychiatric hospital – not a joyful experience for a recovering patient.

The plans for rebuilding Warsaw did not foresee in the near future construction of a Department of Psychiatry. He had to look for an old building that could be adapted to the needs of a hospital. When he heard that the Ministry of National Defence was finishing a new military hospital, an idea like lightning passed through his head. He told Karolina: 'When they finish the new hospital, they will leave empty their old one in the centre of the city. A marvellous place, but the building belongs to the Ministry of Defence; they will never give it to us. And they will argue that it is impossible to have mentally ill in the very centre of the city.'

'Yes,' Karolina answered. 'If you go to them and ask them for it, they will think that you are crazy.' 'Never mind, I want the best conditions to treat and rehabilitate my patients. We are now in the era of active psychopharmacological treatment. A psychiatric department is not any more a place where the patient will stay with no treatment until the end of his days. He needs social stimuli in addition to his psychopharmacological treatment. I am going straight to the Minister of National Defence and, to make my claim stronger, I am also going next day to the PZPR Secretary of Warsaw to tell them about the psychiatry of today and what a society is obliged to do for its mentally ill. I will ask them if they know that every third hospital bed is occupied by a psychiatric patient and that the problem has a social dimension.' 'The idea is clever, but do you know the Minister of Defence?' 'No, but he is going to know me and I will convince him.'

One of his friends told Andrzej that he should not go to both because, in the fight for power between the two, he might lose his cause. He was advised to go to a more powerful person in the Department of Social Affairs in the Central Committee of the PZPR.

It took Andrzej several weeks to convince him. He was checking in the statistical manual all that Andrzej was telling him about the epidemiology of mental diseases.

And Andrzej won. He received the green light to move the Department of Psychiatry from the premises of the big psychiatric hospital in the suburbs into the old building of the former military hospital in the very centre of the city. The moment of transfer was a great joy for Andrzej and Karolina, for their staff, and, above all, for the patients of the Psychiatric Department and their families. 'Our fight is not yet finished. We will fight to modernize this old building. But we are holding it strong and for ever,' said Andrzej, in the opening speech.

All the efforts of Andrzej and Karolina in the new place were now concentrated on creating the best conditions of treatment and resocialization for the patients, on obtaining the highest possible level of teaching for the young psychiatric residents, and on inspiring the interest in research in their co-workers. As chairman of the department, Andrzej was encouraging the existence and flourishing of various trends in research in psychiatry: social psychiatry, biochemistry, electroencephalography, psychopharmacology, and psychotherapy. This eclectic attitude, at the same time, expressed a relaxation from the bureaucratic slavery dictated in the Stalinist era. It also gave the possibility of finding among the various trends the most promising in establishing guidelines. There was a constant inflow of information from the collaboration with the Department of Psychiatry in France and in Switzerland, and with the Institute of Psychiatry in London. Very soon the department gained prestige internationally, and Andrzej and his co-workers were invited to many conventions and conferences abroad.

The progress made in teaching and research in psychiatry and electroencephalography was, of course, of great satisfaction. However, after a short thaw, a new freeze in the political situation was starting. The hopes bound with Gomułka's return to forge a new Polish way to socialism were gone. Did Gomułka's return to power show once again that power corrupts or was it just manoeuvring under Soviet pressure? Whatever the mechanism of change was, the winds of freedom were no longer blowing.

There was no free expression in the press, which had experienced a great revival immediately after Gomułka's return to power. Now the press became more and more dependent on the hardliners who apparently took the upper hand in the Central Committee. In the late 1960s, the atmosphere became dense with suspicion. People were afraid that any criticism would be evaluated as a treacherous action against the existing regime. Stalin was gone, but also Khrushchev was annihilated, and the new powers in the Kremlin were held by hardliners. It became clear that, although Stalin had masterminded evil things, the fault was not only in his personality, but also in the system.

The goals of the Communist system, contained in various writings, were defined as abolition of social injustices and national aggression, caused by political, nationalistic and religious demagoguery. History has shown that the system did not fulfil these goals. The system, corrupted already by Stalin and his followers and artificially kept alive by a dull and rigid bureaucracy, not only did not realize the theoretical goals, but, on the contrary, was an obstacle for the future. It was an enhancement of the worse features of human nature. It was a paradise for party leadership, 'nomenclatura,' and all cohorts of 'apparatchiki.' They lived in luxury and were completely cut off from the life of the nation. Their lives were similar to those of great landlords in the feudal system. And they had tremendous power. If they accused you, the burden of proof of your innocence was yours. There was no presumption of 'innocent, until proved guilty.' In the Russian language was a saying for this: 'Dokazi chto ty ne wierlblud' (Prove that you are not a camel).

After a full day's work, treating patients, teaching students and residents, looking at the results of research, and designing new methods, very often they could not sleep at night. In a whisper (for a long time they had known that again they were bugged), they asked themselves what they were going to do, what were they doing in a party that propagates such a vicious system in practice although it is full of righteous words in theory. The PPS, to which they had belonged, had been 'swallowed' by the PPR in 1948 and, at that time, they had just experienced the 'cauldron' episode. At that time, fear and hope that it might change kept them from overtly declaring that they didn't want to stay in such a party as the PZPR.

After the death of Stalin and after the return of Gomułka to power, hopes for improvement in the party line revived. They believed that all the evil things were caused by Stalin and his henchmen. The speech of Khrushchev confirmed their judgment. There were a couple of years of thaw. But what would happen now? Why was the hard line, so similar to the Stalinist style of governing, having the upper hand now? Why did the new system not have a 'human face'? Why did it become so dangerous to express critical opinions? Why did everybody feel insecure and why was there so much to fear? Why did they stay so long in the party?

The answer was complicated, although it might appear simple to people who do not know firsthand the reality of life in Poland in those years.

One of the factors was that their professional work for patients and their didactic work for students and for specializing doctors was very fruitful, and their research work was advancing in a most satisfactory way. If they would now step forward and say that they did not like the political situation, all that would be ruined. They would again be fired and go into enforced exile. The story of the 'cauldron' would be unravelled with unpredictable consequences. It was dangerous not only for both of them, but for Estelle, who two months after Ludwik's passing away in 1952 had had to leave his fresh grave and go into exile with Andrzej and Karolina. Since then she had been troubled with various health problems. In 1965, she was eighty. The three years of exile in Łódź, when she was obliged to climb three flights to their apartment, had taken their toll on her

health. She had always had problems walking because of rheuma-
tism. All her life had been dedicated to her family. When Andrzej
and Karolina returned from work, they were always telling her
stories of their day in which she was very interested. She was a
person of unusual personal charm, and all the co-workers of Andrzej
knew and adored her. Heroic protest against party line would, for
Andrzej and Karolina, certainly be the right thing to do. However,
the price would be paid not only by them, but above all by Estelle.
The price would also entail mismanagement of the newly reorganized and flourishing department. The co-workers would wear the
stigma of having been pupils of an enemy of the political system; all
possibilities of obtaining foreign aid in the form of new
psychopharmacological medications would be cut off.

Were Andrzej and Karolina satisfied with not taking an official
and openly critical position? They were not, although they knew that
it would not change even a bit the position of hardliners and could
only result in sacrifices.

How very frustrating and dangerous was the opposition against
the official party line? Andrzej and Karolina had had a memorable
lesson in 1953 when they were penalized with expulsion from their
work and directed to work in the worst hospital that existed in
Poland. Their scientific work was ruined, their personal life was
changed, and they had had to remain in exile for three years. Then
came Gomułka and the thaw. People felt happy and secure with
their freedom of speech, of openness. Now, within a couple of years
of Gomułka at the helm of party, things had changed. Was this
independently minded Gomułka forced into dependency by the
Soviet Union, where Khrushchev was ousted and the freeze was
coming from the East? Or was Gomułka simply corrupted by power.
In the words of Lord Acton 'Power tends to corrupt and absolute
power corrupts absolutely.'

Whatever was the reason for this freeze, Andrzej and Karolina
were unable to change it. If they could flee from such a country,
perhaps they would have done so. But they would never flee from
Poland because, even when they were allowed to travel together,
Estelle, 'the permanent hostage,' remained and they would never
leave her alone.

They were depressed, disillusioned, and tired. The chasm between
what they *wanted* to say and to do, what they felt, and what they
could say and do was deepening from day to day. This internal battle

was destroying them because, at the bottom of their hearts, the idea of social justice in a democratic society was still alive.

VII

IN THE LATE 1960's, A NEW CANCER STARTED TO GROW IN the PZPR: anti-Semitism. One after another, people of Jewish origin, whatever their religion was, were removed from the army, from the government, from more responsible positions in the party. The dismissals touched also people at the universities and in scientific institutes, people who never were involved in politics, as well as people who were. This was not a religious anti-Semitism; it was an anti-Semitism based on racial principles. And it was not a sporadic phenomenon, based on personal dislikes; it was an official party line.

After the 'six-day' war in 1967 between Israel and the Arab States, diplomatic relations between all the countries of the Soviet bloc and Israel were broken. In Poland, anti-Semitism was so strong that Jewish people who were personally not yet dismissed were forced by different tricks to ask for dismissal and to emigrate. The emigrating Jewish people were forced to resign their Polish citizenship and all the rights to the old-age pension or any other pension that was due after twenty-five years of work. They could take with them their furniture and personal belongings, but their possessions had to be specified in detail and verified by the emigration offices and they also needed emigration documents to Israel. Once out of Poland, if they decided to emigrate to other countries, for instance, to the United States, they could do so with the help of some international Jewish institutions.

The cruelty of the problem resided in the fact that many of them did not want to leave Poland at all. They identified themselves as Poles of Judaic or of no religion. They were attached to Poland, which they had considered for many generations their homeland. They were perfectly integrated into Polish society; their children had been brought up as Poles; they did not identify themselves with Israel, although many of them were happy that at last the Jews had a land they could claim for their rights. Some of them had a critical attitude towards some of the actions of the state of Israel, and they preferred any other country than Israel if they were forced into emigration.

With this mass Jewish emigration, Poland lost many excellent scientists, physicians, lawyers, artists, specialists in technology, and men of letters. The Jewish people who survived the war in Poland or in the Soviet Union had now, over twenty years after the end of the Second World War, to leave Poland.

On one of the days of this mass exodus of Polish Jews from Poland, two representatives of the Committee of PZPR in the Warsaw Academy of Medicine came to Andrzej's office in the Department of Psychiatry. They asked how many Jews he employed in his department. Andrzej answered that he could not give them such information because the criteria that he used in hiring his co-workers were based exclusively on professional, scientific, and didactic skills and moral integrity, and not on race. He was educating them to become good specialists in psychiatry and to have a good relationship with the patients. This answer did not satisfy the party representatives. One of them told Andrzej: 'We know that among your medical staff are too many Jews. We know very well who is who, and according to our account there are four Jews here. We have information on three of them, and we are asking you the identity of the fourth. You cannot hide such facts from our party. We know also that it is possible that, in addition to those four, you are hiding some other disguised Jews in your department.'

This was too much for Andrzej. He rose from his chair and told them to leave his office immediately. His nerves were completely shattered. He was unable to speak; he was unable to perform the work that he planned for the day. He told Karolina that he was tired and asked her to accompany him home.

When they returned home, he told Karolina the story. Karolina could hardly believe it. Now, twenty-five years after the biggest tragedy in the history of mankind, after the extermination of millions of people because of racist theories, the representatives of a Communist party spoke in such a way and officially expressed anti-Semitism. And these were representatives of a party whose ideological principles were based on equality of all people and against any religious, nationalist, or racist discrimination.

'They came to you because they know that in your department is no place for racial discrimination. They know, of course, about my roots, and I know – only by pure chance – who is the "fourth Jew" for whom they are looking. We never spoke between ourselves about who is Jewish or not Jewish in your department, so you don't know who is the "fourth Jew." This "fourth Jew" is the best proof that they apply no religious criteria but purely racist ideas. It is a girl whose father was born Jewish, and was baptized. Her mother had no Jewish ancestors at all. The girl was born in a Catholic family and baptized immediately after her birth. Even Hitler could not find her at war-time as being Jewish, according the Nuremberg criteria. Only those PZPR members found that here is somebody corresponding to these criteria, but they will never find her because I am the only person who knows that. According to the same criteria, I am for them a Jew, although I have always identified myself as a Pole. Poland is, for me, my homeland and whatever I do here is dedicated to Poland. For them I am a Jew who is taking the place that belongs to a "genuine" Pole.

'My dear Andrzej, you and your parents risked your life every day during the Nazi occupation to save my life. And now, in the new Poland, you are going to risk your work. You are risking being fired from your department because you are not "on the line" with the party. They did not do anything as yet, but wait a while, you will see they will invent some stories to hurt me, and thus hurt you through me. Anyway, you decided to keep, or as they say "hide," your Jews in your department and we are continuing our work.'

The anti-Semitic movement was ravaging Poland with great intensity under the leadership of the PZPR. It was clear for Andrzej and Karolina that such a country as Poland, with all its heroic past, with all its sufferings, was not any more the same, under the present rulers. These rulers had depreciated the ideas of enlightenment and democracy. They had betrayed all heroic, honest Poles who were fighting against the Holocaust and risking their lives to save Jews. These rulers had defamed the memory of millions of innocent Jews exterminated during the Holocaust.

One of the friends of Andrzej and Karolina who was working in Polish television was fired from his position. He was told that his place must be given to somebody who is more Polish. This friend, of whose Jewish origin even they had been unaware, was one of the pre-war members of the Polish Communist Party. Another friend, who was an officer of the Polish army created in the Soviet union, and had great military merits, was fired from the army with no explanation. In 1967, many of their friends who were of Jewish origin lost their jobs and had no means to survive for more than a couple of months. In this way, they were forced to emigrate from Poland. Some of their friends were not fired directly but such pressure was exerted on them that they were forced to emigrate.

The first violinist of the Warsaw Philharmonic Orchestra was told that, because of his Jewish origin, he would not be allowed to travel abroad with the orchestra for guest performances. Many scientists of Jewish origin, university professors, were not allowed to travel abroad to take part in scientific congresses. A policy of injustice, of racial discrimination, was inspired and led by the Polish government and by the PZPR.

Among the members of the PZPR, however, were some eminent people who were categorically opposed to this policy. The Polish minister of foreign affairs, a former PPS member, Adam Rapacki, received from the leadership of the PZPR a list of the names of Jewish employees in his ministry with a recommendation that he fire all of them. He wrote his own name on top of the list and resigned from his post. He was always against the Stalinist rules. Very soon after his resignation, he had a heart attack and passed away. The voice of Rapacki and of other Poles who were against this racial policy had no influence at all on the leadership of the PZPR. No discussion of this problem was possible within the party. To declare a disagreement with this policy was considered to be an act hostile to the PZPR.

It was extremely difficult for Andrzej and Karolina to continue their work in this situation. It had become dangerous for them after the last encounter of Andrzej with the PZPR representatives. They did not have to wait long for action against them.

A couple of weeks later, when Karolina expressed her opinion on the problem of organization of scientific institutes as members of the educational committee of the Senate of the Academy of Medicine in Warsaw, it was said that her conceptions were not coincident with the party line. The problem discussed had nothing to do with the party line or any political question. Nevertheless, two days afterwards, Karolina was called to the PZPR Committee of the Warsaw Academy of Medicine, where they told her that her opinions were wrong because they were not 'in the party line.' After a very short discussion, the general conclusion was expressed that such a difference of opinion was significant. It indicated, they told her, that her brain was functioning in a different way from those of other 'genuine Poles.' In their opinion, Karolina did not have a 'Polish brain.' Karolina was so shocked by this nonsense that, for a moment, she did not reply. But, after a while, she said: 'I don't understand your point of view. I happen to be a specialist in brain physiology and pathology. A human brain is simply the brain of a human being. Nobody as yet has found a difference between a Polish brain and a German or Italian brain. This is pure nonsense, good as an argument for ethnic demagogy but not for members of a party based on international principles. I don't agree with you.' There was a long silence, and eventually one of them said: 'Comrades, here we have another proof of what a non-Polish brain is thinking.'

When Karolina returned home from this 'grilling,' her profound grief exploded. Her family and she herself had identified themselves all their lives as Poles. For twenty-five years she had been a Catholic. The PZPR were making no religious objections; their remarks were purely racist, very similar to the Nuremberg criteria.

One week afterwards, she received from the principal (rector) of the Academy of Medicine a letter, dismissing her from her position as member of the Senate's educational committee.

From this time an emotional change was building up in Andrzej's and Karolina's minds and hearts. They became emotionally less and less involved in Polish problems. Such a Poland was not their country. The nation had been betrayed by the racist PZPR leadership. They wanted to live in a country in which such bitter feelings of injustice would not be possible, in a country with which they would have no emotional ties with the past. They wanted to be somewhere where they could stay indifferent, in a country with no heritage of patriotic involvement. The PZPR had given them a great lesson in false patriotism. It did not mean, of course, that they became less attached to their profession, to their work, to their department, to their staff, to their patients, to all the help they could offer. These things remained their only connection with Poland. Painful, but real.

All of Karolina's and Andrzej's friends who were of Jewish origin were leaving Poland with feelings of exasperation and injustice. Many of them always had a Polish identity and were attached to the Poland that they considered their homeland. Now Poland was rejecting them, was expelling them in a brutal way, with no consideration for their emotional ties.

Each evening, from a small railway station in Warsaw, called Warszawa–Gdańsk, a train was leaving for Vienna, the connecting station for further emigration. This train, which carried as a majority of its passengers Polish people of Jewish descent forced to emigrate from Poland, was called in the years 1968–9 the 'Jewish' train. Each evening, the station was filled with the 'non-Jewish' Poles who were friends of those who were leaving for ever their homeland. The farewells were extremely sad – for those who were leaving and those who remained. It was unbelievable and shameful.

In 1969, Andrzej has decided to resign from the honour of being the president of the Polish Psychiatric Association. He could no longer stand the atmosphere of political intrigue and racial gossip. Before the convention, during which the election of a new president was scheduled to take place, a high official from the Ministry of Health told him who had been designated by the Ministry of Health to be elected. When Andrzej stated that such designations were against the charter of the Psychiatric Association, because the president was always elected by members and not nominated by the Minister of Health, the official declared: 'Our party, the PZPR, wants to have such-and-such person as president and the minister received such an instruction, we will act accordingly.' Indeed the designated psychiatrist was 'elected' according to the party's wish.

Andrzej's department was also subject to pressures from outside. Andrzej was still the chairman with great prestige as a specialist, a teacher, and a scientist, but some party members, probably instructed from outside, started to spoil the calm atmosphere necessary for serious work. These mean party members believed that the party's organization had special rights and prerogatives to control the chairman in selecting and promoting staff members. The only way to reduce their influence was to fire them. It was not an easy task to fire influential party members, but given their poor value from a professional, didactic, and scientific point of view, Andrzej had enough strength to proceed with finding for them other places of work and allowing them to ask for dismissal. A certain calm returned again to his department.

Andrzej and Karolina had still the retreat of their home, where Estelle, with her warmth and charm, was a most loving mother to both of them. Since Ludwik's passing, Estelle had lived with them. Seeing her warm, smiling, and charming attitude when they returned from work made them feel relaxed. It was like a soothing dressing on the wounds of every-day life.

During all this turmoil with the 'Jewish' question, Karolina could not detach herself from thoughts of how her father would feel if he had survived to see what was going on in Poland at present.

Then something unbelievable happened. Karolina received an anonymous letter in which it was written that she should leave Poland because she was a Jew and has no right to work in Poland and occupy a place that belonged to a 'genuine' Pole. Andrzej tried to console her, saying that such hate mail belonged in the waste basket, but he himself was deeply hurt. He thought that Karolina was right when she said that they would hurt him, hurting her. She felt more and more insecure and was thinking all the time: 'What will they invent to hurt us profoundly? My dearest love, who risked every day of his life to save my life, is he going to suffer because of me all his life? The fascist nightmare will never end. The criterion of race will always decide who is a first-class and who is a second-class citizen.'

The life of Andrzej and Karolina was exclusively concentrated on their work in the department. It was now their only link with Poland. All their efforts were concentrated on giving the best possible care to the patients, the best education to the students, the best ideas to their research work. They worked long hours in the department during the day, and very often they spent all night there because they were working on sleep disorders in the Laboratory of Electroencephalography. Their social life was very limited, and their only joy was to see Estelle in good shape when they returned home.

In 1969 Andrzej had to spend a couple of weeks in Geneva to participate in the work of the panel of experts on mental health in the World Health Organization. He was invited to participate in congresses in London, Mexico City, and New York. During his journeys, he missed very much Karolina and Estelle; he missed his co-workers and his department, but at least he could relax a little outside the tense atmosphere in Poland. The leaders of the PZPR were becoming more and more rigid and dogmatic. The anti-Semitic policy was putting on him such a burden that his life became more and more difficult. His links with his country, with Poland, were becoming less and less emotional, more and more distant.

VIII

IN APRIL 1970, ESTELLE HAD A SERIOUS ACCIDENT. SHE slipped on the floor of their apartment and broke her hip. Such a fracture at her age was dangerous. It was a tragic blow for Andrzej and Karolina. Estelle was the most important person in their lives. She was beloved by both of them, and she loved them both as a mother. They knew from photographs and her friends that, in her prime, she had been an extremely beautiful woman. She had aged gracefully, and had always been unusually charming. This charm captivated Karolina since she first saw Estelle. She was very kind to everybody, honest, open-minded, and always extending her hand to help anybody before being asked. To her, 'What could I do for you?' was not an empty phrase. She always wanted to do something for somebody. She was admired by all the friends of Andrzej and Karolina. Intellectually, she was always very active, reading books, writing her reflections on them, reading the news and watching TV to be 'au courant' on all events. She had always a very optimistic attitude towards life. After a day of hard work, Andrzej and Karolina always looked forward to being with Estelle and feeling her love.

Immediately after the accident, she was hospitalized and operated on in the Orthopaedic department of the Academy of Medicine. She did not feel well after the operation, and she had many serious complications. Everything was done to save her life, but her condition was debilitating. After four months of grave suffering, Estelle passed away in June 1970. She was buried in the same grave as her beloved Ludwik.

The last tie of Andrzej and Karolina with their past was gone. They had a feeling of very deep and painful emptiness. Estelle had always told them: 'the only thing that has a value in life is love. Without love life has no value.' Now they were without her love, her tenderness, her care, her musical voice, her attention. The emptiness was difficult to endure.

For a certain time, Karolina and Andrzej had had an invitation to come to McGill University in Montreal as visiting professors. Now, after Estelle's passing away, and feeling very unhappy with all that was going on in the new Poland, they decided to change for a certain time their life-style and accept the invitation.

They never spoke between themselves about leaving Poland for good. They always saw themselves returning. Now the idea of leaving Poland existed in them; probably for the first time in their lives this idea was not something that was absolutely excluded. It was something that was not yet verbalized. It was something drowsing in their hearts, something existing in their subconscious. But, in reality, they thought that, after a change of atmosphere for a certain time, after relaxing in a foreign country, they would return to the country for which they had worked all their lives.

Before their departure, they went once more to Orelec, the village of the tragic death of Juliusz, Dorota, and Zosia. They had this need to see once more the place of martyrs, of Juliusz and his family and many other people who were killed only because they were Jewish. They wanted to return once more to this place of tragic wartime and look from the forest on the hills near Orelec, to the road that Poland had travelled during the last twenty-five years. They wanted also to reflect on the ideas of such people as Janka and many other Polish heroes who died in their fight against the Nazis, how those ideas had been realized in Poland during the twenty-five years since the end of the war.

The village was silent, as always. The head of hamlet was a young man, born during the war. He knew that, during the war, Jewish people from Orelec and neighbouring villages had been murdered by the Nazis in the forest and that a mass grave had been erected after the war by the Polish government. Andrzej and Karolina told him the aim of their visit. He accompanied them to the house where Juliusz lived in exile with Dorota and Zosia. The house was now occupied by a Polish-peasant family, transferred from the pre-war eastern part of Poland, taken after the war by the Soviet Union. The furniture was changed, rooms and kitchen rearranged. In the backyard, there was still the old fence and the same tree.

The Polish family did not know that, during the war, the house had been inhabited by a Jewish family. They knew nothing about the tragic events in Orelec and about the mass grave on the hill. This Polish family consisted of parents and two daughters who were studying and, now, during vacation time, were staying with their parents.

Andrzej and Karolina went to see the school. It was closed during vacation, and the teacher absent. The windows were covered with curtains, and Andrzej could not see into the room where Janka had worked during the war.

They went to the square before the church. All was like in 1942, during the last visit of Andrzej to Orelec. The same church, the same houses around the square. The same sun in the sky.

But the people were not the same. The majority of the population came here after the war and knew nothing about the tragic events in 1942. The head of the hamlet had given Andrzej the addresses of five families, who were living in the village in 1942. They visited these houses. Only in one house was the memory of the tragic events still vivid. An old man told them in a very emotional way, with tears in his eyes, of the tragic events of April 1942. There was only a slight trace of the memory of those events in the other four families. They said that it was so long ago, it was difficult to remember. They knew only that the Gestapo had come to the village and taken all the Jewish families. They never saw those Jewish families again.

Andrzej and Karolina returned to the square before the church and from there they started the journey Juliusz and his family had made twenty-eight years ago. They were alone because the head of the hamlet was too busy with his administrative tasks to accompany them. They went to the road with the Christ in Sorrow. The chapel was still there, as was Jesus, in sorrow.

They continued slowly, the same way the Jewish martyrs had travelled so many years ago. From the crossroads to a narrow road up to the forest on the hill. They found the mass grave. They did not find the remnants of the ditches. Probably they were overgrown by dense bushes. They knelt before the mass grave. They could not talk, and in silence were thinking about the life of Juliusz, Dorota, and Zosia and their tragic death. They were thinking about Juliusz's belief that the sacrifices of the war would teach humanity to build a better future for humankind, and expel Evil from human hearts. And now they knew that his hope was never fulfilled. Evil was still present in human hearts; God had still no kingdom in all human hearts. In this country, in Poland, which was Juliusz's homeland, anti-Semitism was present again, inflicting pain and suffering on many people whose lives were dedicated to Poland.

They returned to the village, looked once more on Juliusz's house and on the roadside chapel, and returned to Warsaw.

One week later, they were in Switzerland, staying overnight in Zürich to take the morning plane to Montreal. They began their lives as visiting professors at McGill University.

PART FOUR

—

BEFORE THE NEW DAWN

Behold, the dwelling of God is with men.
He will dwell with them,
and they shall be his people,
and God himself will be with them;
he will wipe away every tear from their eyes,
and death shall be no more,
neither shall there be mourning
nor crying nor pain any more,
for the former things have passed away.

The Revelation to John
21:3–4

I

ANDRZEJ AND KAROLINA WERE RECEIVED AT McGILL University in Montreal with great respect and interest in the work they had been doing in Poland, especially in psychopharmacology and in electroencephalographic research on sleep. They also gave lectures to psychiatric residents. Other universities in Canada also invited them to deliver lectures, and everywhere they were met very warmly and with great scientific interest. At the same time, they were collecting from those universities new scientific data and administrative information, which could be useful for Polish psychiatry after their return to Poland.

In the years of thaw, when travelling abroad was easier, they had already made friends abroad, and they knew many psychiatrists in Canada and in the United States. Since their long stay in France in 1947, they had also had many scientific contacts in Western Europe. Those contacts enabled them to send their co-workers from Poland for fellowships and scholarships abroad. Now, in Canada, they were also looking for new scientific and training contacts. Although their visiting professorship to McGill University was for one year, the Polish Ministry of Health had given them permission to stay in Canada for only three months.

They had constant mail contact with their Department of Psychiatry in Warsaw through Dr Halina, the lady docent, an extremely dedicated psychiatrist. When Andrzej was absent during vacations or conventions abroad, Dr Halina always replaced him. Very well-trained professionally, she had a warm relationship with patients. An excellent teacher of students and young residents in psychiatry, she had also a great interest in the scientific problems. A devout Catholic, she was respected for her courage and integrity by all members of the department.

During the long and serious illness of the former chairman of the Department, Dr Halina, although the youngest of his co-workers, had taken on her shoulders all the responsibilities for the department. After the former chairman retired and Andrzej became chairman, she was his closest co-worker. Andrzej had full confidence in her honesty and knowledge of psychiatry.

She married a very charming and intelligent lawyer, who was the son of a highly respected professor of Roman law at Warsaw

University. Dr Halina and her husband were very close and reliable friends of Andrzej and Karolina, always ready to help them in difficult times, especially during the long illness of Andrzej's mother.

In addition to their mail contact with Dr Halina and with some other co-workers and friends in Warsaw, they had contact with the publisher of their recently finished book on present, more urgent, and controversial problems in psychiatry. They had already received galley-proofs for correction.

Although life was quite interesting in Canada, and they met some very nice people, they missed their department in Warsaw, and their co-workers. From a great distance, over the ocean, memory of displeasure was diminishing and nostalgia was prevailing. The work in their department was the essence of their lives, and they were eager to return to all the challenges of this work. It compensated for all their disappointments and worries of the life in Poland.

One month after their arrival in Canada, Karolina received from Warsaw a new anonymous letter. The unknown author wrote that she should stay abroad and that her return to the Department of Psychiatry would be very badly accepted by the 'genuine' Poles, Polish 'since their grandfather and great-grandfather.' She should understand at last that she was not and never would be a 'genuine' Pole because she was born a Jew, and she would die as a Jew. In Poland, there was no place for her. She was occupying a place belonging to a 'genuine' Pole. The nightmare of anti-Semitism reappeared and took its toll on both of them.

Karolina became depressed. She could not sleep at night. She lost weight, and had an intense exacerbation of her gastro-intestinal problems. She had to be treated in the out-patient department of gastroenterology of the teaching Hospital at McGill. Andrzej's health was also impaired, and he had a constant increase of blood pressure and had also to be treated in the cardio-vascular department of the same hospital.

During sleepless nights and long weekends, they were now discussing the problem of their future. Would they be able to return to a Poland, with its racist ideology? Would they be able to remain in the PZPR, the party showing now a fascist, racist face, hostile to them? When, after the war, they had joined the Polish Socialist Party, the charter of this party had nothing common with the PPR, which, under the forced 'unification,' 'swallowed' the PPS and became the PZPR. Their hopes of change in the PZPR were nourished by the thaw, when Gomułka returned to power. Gomułka was still in power, but it was not the same Gomułka, the independent spirit. It was a racist Gomułka in a racist party.

If they returned to Poland, first of all, they should withdraw from membership in the PZPR and be prepared for the consequences of this decision. They knew that it meant that Andrzej would be fired from his position as chairman of the Department of Psychiatry in Warsaw. Both of them would probably lose their jobs in this department and be barred from any other university department in Poland. The only employer in this totalitarian state was the government. And the government would repeat its dull statement that it could not permit youths to be instructed by traitors to the PZPR ideology. They would have no possibility of teaching, nor of scientific research, of travelling abroad.

In the files, scrupulously held by the Ministry of the Public Security, was certainly the story of the 'cauldron' and the suspicions of spying for God-knows-whom in 1948. There was also the story of firing them in 1953 for non-conformism from the Institute of Psychoneurology. Anything could happen; in addition, Karolina was, in their opinion, a Jew, and a Jew had no place in Poland.

At the beginning of November 1970, Karolina received from Warsaw another anonymous letter with similar content, but much more aggressive, vulgar, and rude.

This was the last straw. The decision was already made in Andrzej's mind and in his heart. He had no doubts that he should not expose Karolina's and his own health and all their future life for a country in which the ruling party was officially propagating racist anti-Semitism. The anonymous letters were its symptoms; the conversation about the national identity of Karolina's brain in the PZPR Committee in the Academy of Medicine in Warsaw was another symptom. Inquiries in Andrzej's office about the percentage of his Jewish co-workers was yet another symptom. The situation, which had existed for over three years, with firing Jews from all jobs and enforcing their emigration from Poland was not a small personal story. It was the story of a nation that permitted to grow inside it the cancer of racial hatred, and of a Communist party running amok with racism. It was impossible to continue life in such a country. They had invested all their hopes, all their lives in the wrong place. They were already fifty-six years old. They had worked all their lives in Poland, and for Poland. They had a feeling that they had done a good work for Polish psychiatry, but they could not continue to live under such a system.

This was Andrzej's decision, and he made it with the same conviction with which he had decided to marry Karolina in the time of the Nazis. Karolina knew that the essence of Andrzej's life was his department in Warsaw. She did not want to influence his decision; she had a terrible feeling of guilt, because she felt that they wanted to hurt him by hurting her, and that they had achieved their goal. All their dreams about a change in the new Poland were gone with the wind.

Andrzej decided to write a letter to one of the secretaries of the Central Committee of the PZPR to tell the people of the PZPR, and of the government, why he had decided not to return to Poland. He wrote this letter, made photocopies of it, and sent them to the Minister of Health, to the secretaries of the PZPR, to the principal of the Academy of Medicine, and to Dr Halina in the Academy of Medicine in Warsaw. In this letter, he blamed the PZPR for the existing situation and the racial politics of discriminating, forcing Polish citizens – who, if one applied the Nuremberg criteria, were considered as Jews – to emigrate, depriving them of work. He gave concrete examples of what he had seen and heard from the official representatives of the PZPR in the Warsaw Academy of Medicine. This racial anti-Semitism was strictly bound, he said in his letter, with the same hard line as in the Stalin era, and rigidly enforced by a totalitarian system. People were afraid to say what they really thought; they were blindly obeying the directions of the PZPR. The PZPR was denying the right to independent unions. As an example, he cited the order of the Minister of Health who was dictating to the members of the Polish Psychiatric Association whom the PZPR wanted to be elected as president of this association. Such an order, which was enforced, made the elections a pure formality and changed the free elections into a PZPR nomination. The principal of the Academy of Medicine was forced by the PZPR to fire Karolina from the Senate's educational committee, because the PZPR Committee of the Medical Academy had determined that her brain was not 'genuinely' Polish. The totalitarian system of thinking and governing was perverting human relations, and the fear of repression was making automatons of human beings. Poland was becoming a country where freedom of thinking was abolished, and the rules of law were powerless.

As Andrzej's and his wife's ideas concerning the evolution of post-war Poland were in absolute dissent with such an ideology, which made of Poland a country of fear and injustice, they did not want to return. He could not tolerate such a situation in which his wife, a survivor of the Holocaust, was persecuted by the anti-Semites in the PZPR, and he, as the chairman of the Department of Psychiatry, was asked by the PZPR how many Jews he was 'hiding' in his department. For these reasons, neither he nor Karolina would return to Poland and would instead continue their work abroad.

They sent these letters by registered mail, to be sure that they were delivered to the addressees. It was mid-November 1970, just two weeks before the term allowed them by the PZPR to stay as visiting professors in Canada ended. They returned to their residence in Montreal in a very desperate mood, with a great sadness in their hearts, but with a deep conviction that their decision had been inevitable. After hours of rest, they recovered a certain calm and a certain relief that they had done something that should have been done a long time ago.

They never asked for asylum. After three months, they went to the immigration office to extend their visitor's visa from three months to one year, i.e., for the full term of the invitation. They were told by the immigration officers that it would be more convenient for them to take a landed-immigrant visa, because it does not need another renewal after a three-month period. With their credentials, they could easily obtain it. It would also give them the option of staying in Canada as long as they wished and obtaining, after five years, Canadian citizenship. It did not mean any commitment, although they would be most welcome by Canada as Canadian citizens.

All that did not alleviate their sadness. From now on, it was a curtain of mist over all their feelings, a nostalgia enveloping all their thoughts and deeds.

Two weeks after mailing the letters to Poland, Andrzej received a phone call from the Polish Consulate in Montreal; the Polish ambassador from Ottawa would be coming next day to Montreal and he wanted to speak with Andrzej and Karolina in the office of the Polish Consulate in Montreal. Andrzej declined the invitation and proposed as the place of meeting his own office at McGill. He knew that, under international law, consulates and embassies were extraterritorial places. After negotiations, it was concluded that the meeting would take place in the Ritz-Carlton hotel in Montreal.

It was a very painful encounter for both of them. The Polish ambassador was a nice, cultivated person – an intellectual. He had received from his superiors instructions to convince them to return to Poland. His superiors had found that many of Andrzej's claims were justified, and the PZPR wanted to repair many mistakes that it had made and had pledged to fight such abuses in future. The situation would certainly improve and, for the sake of Polish medical science and education, they should return to Poland to continue their work, which was very highly appreciated by his superiors.

Andrzej's answer was kind, but short and determined. He had spoken already in Poland about these problems with many high officials in the PZPR and, although they told him that in general he was right, they were unable to do anything more than give him vague promises. At the same time, many of his interlocutors told him that his outlook was wrong and that he had to study more Marxism-Leninism to avoid becoming an enemy of the Communist regime.

Andrzej concluded his answer, saying with great bitterness: 'If you really want to change the situation, do that without us. We are tired, discouraged, and seriously convinced that this "version of Communism" cannot work. The trials of socialism "with a human face" in Czechoslovakia were ruthlessly destroyed by armies of other countries, and I am ashamed that, among the "other countries" destroying Dubcek's efforts, was also Poland and the Polish army.

'I hope that a day will come when somebody will emerge and do something positive for a socialism "with a human face." The concept of the dictatorship of proletariat is, in reality, the dictatorship of a communist bureaucracy, of "apparatchiki," completely detached from the nation. Our best wishes are with you, and we hope that a day will come when party bureaucracy will be abolished and a democratic system will be built. But, for the time being, we will stay apart. We waited for it in vain for a quarter of century.'

Karolina, listening to Andrzej, could not contain her tears. She told the ambassador the tragic story of how her parents and her only sister were murdered by the Nazis in Orelec, how Andrzej and his parents had saved her, risking their own lives, and how many heroic Polish saviours were helping Polish Jews. And now, in the new Poland, the Communist party, which has in its charter ideals of freedom, equality, and fraternity, is officially propagating racist ideas.

'This is not a pogrom with a bunch of criminals attacking and looting Jewish shops and houses; this is an official program of the PZPR, which is ruling Poland. How can I stay in Poland if, after all my work for this country that I love, the party organization tells me that I am not a "genuine" Pole, basing its opinion on racist criteria. The party has deprived me of my country, of Poland of my dreams.'

At the end the ambassador told them that they did not have to make a decision right away, that the Ministry of Health would wait one year for their final decision and keep for Andrzej his chair, so that he could return to his position any time during the coming year. If they chose to stay abroad, the Polish government would provide them the so-called consular passports, so that, retaining Polish citizenship, they would have the privilege of travelling to and from Poland with no special permission.

Andrzej accepted the last proposal and promised to send the necessary applications to the Polish Consulate in Montreal, together with the fees for such passports. However, he told him also that it would be a disservice to the Department of Psychiatry to keep it without a chairman for one year, because his decision was final and irreversible. He asked the ambassador to give him the assurance that the PZPR would not enforce firing from his department any of his co-workers of Jewish origin, and to take into consideration that, in his opinion, the best-qualified person to be his successor was Docent Halina. She was professionally, scientifically, and morally prepared for such a responsible work and position.

They exited the Ritz-Carlton together with the ambassador. It was a cold and windy evening. The ambassador very kindly invited them to his embassy car, waiting for him. Karolina, extremely tired and touched by the conversation, automatically approached the car. Andrzej stopped her at the last minute, explaining to the ambassador that, after such an exhausting conversation, a walk in the cold air would do them good. He knew that the cars of embassies and consulates were also extraterritorial.

They saw the ambassador to the car and then walked alone through the cold and windy streets towards their Montreal apartment. They could not talk. They were full of anguish and sorrow. In the cold Canadian weather, the Poland of their dreams was always in their hearts.

II

THAT WAS THEIR LAST OFFICIAL CONTACT WITH POLAND. They never received the consular passports, although they sent the required forms and fees to the Polish Consulate in Montreal.

They received from the Ministry of Health in Warsaw a letter, saying that their book on contemporary problems of psychiatry would not be published. The principal (rector) of the Academy of Medicine in Warsaw sent them dismissal letters from their positions in the Academy of Medicine. Although they anticipated the dismissals, it was a very painful experience.

There was also some good news. After a couple of months, Dr Halina was appointed as acting chairman and professor of the Department of Psychiatry in Warsaw. None of Andrzej's co-workers who were of Jewish origin were fired from the department. They met a delegation of Polish psychiatrists at a convention in Rome, and they brought to Andrzej this positive news.

At the beginning of January 1971, they received the status of landed immigrants and Canadian travel documents, allowing them to travel abroad. Canada, the new country of their choice, was from the first moment of their arrival very helpful. The Canadian government wanted people who were arriving here to work and give all their experience and services to the Canadian citizens. Nobody ever asked them about their political opinions, if they were Liberal or Conservative.

When they were travelling on lecture tours through Canada as visiting professors, they had offers of tenure from various universities. They decided to accept the invitation from Laval University in Quebec City for several reasons. The first reason was emotional. Quebec was closer to Europe than any other province. Another reason was that this university offered them the best opportunities for research work, with a fully equipped laboratory for electroencephalography and sleep research for Karolina, and development of a special unit for scientific research for Andrzej. Both of them were appointed full professors at Laval University in Quebec City. They could continue and expand their scientific research in electroencephalography and psychopharmacology. They had also some didactic duties for residents in psychiatry. They always liked to teach and considered it a refreshing duty. Andrzej often referred to it as to their 'gardening nursery' duties. As full professors at Laval University, they were given the rights to practise medicine in the Province of Quebec and also the right to practise as psychiatrists within the framework of Medicare.

Their relationship with the members of the Department of Psychiatry was very good. Many psychiatrists were attracted to collaborate with them. They trained good and responsible EEG technicians and held special lectures to introduce the methodology of scientific research in this department. Laval University, founded in 1820, was the oldest in Canada. It was a French university in the province of Quebec, and the French language was for Andrzej and Karolina like their mother tongue because they had spoken and learned it from their childhood.

In their personal life, they had to begin from scratch. They arrived in Montreal with two pieces of luggage each, just enough for the three months permitted to them by the PZPR. They had to buy clothes for the harsh Canadian winter, snow-boots and other things to be well equipped for this difficult climate. They rented an unfurnished apartment, the furnished accommodation being beyond their means. Housing was extremely cheap in Poland, and they could not believe that, in Canada, rent consumed about one-third of their wages. Furniture was expensive. They bought only one piece of new furniture, a mattress; the other pieces were second-hand or pieces borrowed from their friends. On the naked walls, Karolina glued with Scotch tape some twigs with evergreen leaves to make their living quarters more attractive. They ate in the cafeteria of the teaching hospital. Even with all the financial precautions, it was difficult to make ends meet because there was an unexpected expenditure, the car. Canada is an enormous country, and the distances are so huge that a car is not a luxury, but a necessity. As they did not have enough money to buy a car, they asked for a loan at the bank. No bank would lend them money because they had no bank account. They could, of course, ask any of their friends to act as guarantor for them, but Andrzej was too proud to do that. So, they accepted a loan from the car dealer, for which they had to pay high interest. The loan was for one year, but they had never had a loan in their lives, and rushed to pay it off in three months. And they were penalized for it, which was a normal thing in capitalistic countries but mystifying to the naive, non-capitalist newcomers. Many other things surprised them, but slowly they learned how to manage their personal affairs.

The essential problem was the sadness and nostalgia. It was not easy to detach themselves emotionally from the country of their childhood and adolescence, from the country in which they had invested all their hopes and enthusiasm. Although it was not the Poland of their dreams, rather a Poland of their deceptions and lost illusions, there was still a strong emotional tie, which probably would always remain in their hearts.

They were used to travelling abroad as invited lecturers or as guests of their friends, but they were always travelling with the certitude that they would be returning home. They always returned with joy, even though life was much easier for people in their position in foreign countries. With all the difficulties of daily life in Poland, with all the restrictions, there was always a hope that things would get better at home, that Poland would be again a country of free spirit. The happiness of being back home, of being again in the department so cherished by them both, was so great that, without any rest, they engaged in all their professional activities, and enjoyed personal friendships.

Now it was a quite different situation: they had decided to stay away for good. Andrzej once told Karolina in great anger and pain: 'For me, it would not be sufficient to tell them what I think of racism. I have to do something, even losing everything that I have created with such love for Poland, to show them how much in contempt I hold all that is going on now. I still hope that this will change.'

Adaptation to a foreign country at their age and with their system of values was extremely difficult. Therefore, Andrzej and Karolina had always at the bottom of their hearts pain and sadness, and the feeling that they would never be entirely happy with this new life. Their only happiness was that they were together, always with their love, and that they were free, free to think, free to say what they wanted to say, free to travel where and when they wanted. They were at last masters of their own lives, within, of course, the limits of their financial resources.

After so many years of fear, insecurity, lack or limitation of sincerity, certain disparity between thoughts and words, they were now not obliged to lock their true thoughts in the heads and express them in words that would not damage their lives. The process of 'limited sincerity,' was damaging to the thoughts themselves. Now, they saw how difficult it was for them to 'decondition' the fear of contact with other people. The totalitarian system was having a devastating effect on the characters of people, making them insincere under the pressure of constant fear.

In the political system of such countries as Canada, before an election each party announced its program via the mass media. They offered the possibility to discuss some or all problems of their programs. They publicized their views, praising their own programs and indicating the imperfections and errors of those of the other party or parties. Not all propaganda tools were honest but the citizens had the free choice of voting according to their preference. No enforcement was used to ensure a vote for this or another party, or to force participation in elections if a citizen was not interested in politics. On election day, the citizens voted as they wanted or did not vote at all. No pressure was put on any person by the existing parties. If the Conservative party was, for instance, the winner, a citizen could still keep his liberal opinions, and it had no influence on his personal or professional life or position. If the personal political opinions were inconsistent with the winning party, the citizen was not suspected to be an enemy of the state. There were no 'dissidents.' A citizen with opinions different from those of the ruling party was not labelled treacherous. He continued to work, to win respect and confidence. His personality was not distorted by the obligation to show the hatred for his political adversaries and by the obligation to follow verbally the political bible of the totalitarian regime.

They learned also in Canada the freedom of travelling abroad. In Poland, each journey abroad was bound with anxiety about whether they would receive their passports on time, or at all. Until the last moment, they did not know if they would participate in a professional convention, even if they were invited as lecturers and all their expenses were paid by the organizing committee abroad. The time during which they were allowed to stay abroad was limited by the bureaucrats from the Ministry of Health, and they were not permitted to accept an extension of the invitation, even for one day. After returning to Poland, they had to return their passports within twenty-four hours to the Ministry of Health, under the threat that they might never again receive permission to travel abroad if they were late returning them. As a rule, Polish citizens were not allowed to keep their passports at their homes.

In Canada, every Canadian citizen could receive within two to three days a passport, after paying a small fee; this passport was kept at home. The validity of passport was for three years. The time spent abroad depended only on the professional leave given by the employer and on financial capabilities.

All these positive factors, highly appreciated and cherished by Andrzej and Karolina, could not make them happy. They had suffered too much during the Nazi occupation. The tragedy of Orelec left a profound wound in their lives that time could not heal. And after the war, after hard, dedicated work in Poland for twenty-five years, after hopes and expectation that their always progressive views would be realized in the new Poland, they felt like bankrupts. Although, towards the last years of their lives, they could live in a free country, they always yearned after the non-existent Poland of their dreams. They missed their department, their collaborators, their friends, the nostalgic beauty of the Polish landscape, and the melody of the Polish language in the streets.

Being free citizens in a free country, they were always prisoners of their past. They always remained sensitive to any injustice. Living for a certain time in a free country, they saw that 'freedom' was not always well divided among the population of many so-called free countries. National health insurance did not exist in the leading country of the free world, equal education possibilities did not exist in many free countries, the old-age pension was not sufficient for old people to live decently.

This free world was, in reality, a world of hard competition, of hard work. There was no equal start for everybody. The ideal freedom in such countries was sometimes ridiculed, because what was freedom for one person or one class of people was slavery for another person or another class of people. There was an enormous difference between the unbelievable luxury of life and unnecessary waste of money on one side and the difficult life of unemployed, often homeless people. They had to witness that rhetoric was quite often in a great contrast with social achievements for the well-being of the majority.

Some politicians of the free world were, in their decisions, far from the human criteria of justice and respected only the reason of their state (*raison d'état*).

The reason of the state was measured by other moral parameters than the behaviour of individuals. However, there was a growing understanding that the reason of the state might imply, sometimes, perpetrating a crime. In such a way were judged the rulings of many imposed dictators in small countries.

These critical observations, important for personal integrity, could be made outside the iron curtain. Inside, the people were slaves of the dogmatic philosophy and of indoctrinated and indoctrinating ways of thinking of party bureaucrats. Outside, there was true freedom of thinking and freedom of speech.

During their stay in Canada, Andrzej and Karolina had the opportunity to make their scientific activity stronger and more effective. They had many scientific contacts not only within Canada, but also in the United States and Western Europe. The scientific collaboration was much easier than from Poland, where they were always under the supervision of the Ministry of Health and the party's bureaucracy. Now, they needed no permission to participate in scientific conventions or to organize scientific symposia. Their professional life, their scientific research work, was giving them much satisfaction.

During different scientific conventions, they had sometimes the opportunity to meet psychiatrists from Poland. This was, for them, always a very emotional experience. They were so eager to know what was going on in the Psychiatric department of the Academy of Medicine in Warsaw, what achievements their former co-workers had made. In their long talks at night after such encounters, they discussed each and every detail concerning life in Poland.

After five years of residence, they were granted Canadian citizenship without losing their former citizenship. The ceremony of granting citizenship was a happy event in their lives. They were formally adopted by a free country. This adopting country, Canada, was always a caring mother for them. From the beginning of their stay in Canada, they were given very good conditions of work and the rights to all benefits, such as medicare and the national and provincial pension plans. The greatest benefit of all was a total freedom of their political, social, and religious beliefs, freedom of thinking, speaking out, of travelling, and, above all, freedom from fear.

They missed Europe and, whenever possible, visited Western Europe, especially their beloved countries, France and Italy. As strong as their nostalgia for Poland was, they never visited Poland because they were simply afraid that, after entering it for a short visit, they might not be allowed to return to Canada. Each time they were in a country close to the Polish frontier, Andrzej said: 'Let us hope that one day everything will change and we will have the Poland of our dreams. Then we will be happy to see it again. But not now, not yet.'

During their travel abroad they had also the opportunity to visit some of the so-called Third World countries. Millions of people were in despair, miserably poor, starving and dying of hunger; children, undernourished, infected with tropical diseases, dying for lack of or insufficient medical help. Did the leaders of wealthy countries understand well enough that the same humane feeling should extend beyond any political frontiers? Patriotism encapsulated in the love and well-being of your own country seemed to be selfish.

Much of this selfishness was caused by the 'cold war.' It was impossible to realize the 'all-human' patriotism because of the still-simmering antagonism between the great powers that were primarily interested in competition to find better and more efficient 'deterrents' to another world war.

The cold war between the two superpowers was a major obstacle in uniting the large, strong countries in the fight against the misery and despair of the majority of people on earth. Tremendous efforts and enormous resources were accumulated to build an arsenal of nuclear bombs and other military equipment, sufficient to kill the population of all the earth. And yet the majority of the population of the earth was still starving and dying of hunger and diseases.

Andrzej very often at night, in his dreams, returned to the tragedy of Orelec during the Nazi times. He saw in his dreams the village, the forest on the hill, the woods under which were buried Juliusz, Dorota, and Zosia. And if, in his dreams, he met the shadow of Juliusz, he would tell him: 'Juliusz, my dear Juliusz, do not return to this earth. It is not yet the proper time for people like you to live here. Here, God is always represented in the wayside chapel in Orelec, in many other chapels and churches, in synagogues, mosques, and temples of various religions. But God is not always present in the hearts of the people. Juliusz, my dear Juliusz, return to the God in Heaven.'

III

IN MARCH 1974, ANDRZEJ AND KAROLINA HAD TO GIVE A lecture and participate in an international convention in Jerusalem, and later were invited to participate in another convention in Europe.

It was their first visit to Israel, the state of a nation that suffered the greatest racist crime in the history of mankind. During the Second World War were lost in the Holocaust six million innocent Jewish people, killed only because they were Jewish according to racist criteria. Karolina was one of the survivors of the Holocaust, and she was saved by the Catholic Poles. Andrzej was also a survivor of the Holocaust because, in marrying Karolina during Hitler's occupation of Poland, he was exposing himself to the same mortal danger as the Jewish people. There was only one penalty for the so-called gentiles who hid or protected Jews: death.

When the state of Israel was created in 1948, Andrzej and Karolina were still living in Poland. The creation of a state that could give citizenship to each Jew immigrating in it was accepted with great joy and pride by the Jewish survivors. Their lives were terribly shattered by fear of racist hatred and by the loss of their families. The creation of Israel was also an expression of international duty by other states, including the two superpowers. The Jewish people had now a state that could not only give them citizenship, but also represent their cause in an international forum. The two superpowers were the first to recognize Israel's right to exist and to establish diplomatic relations with it.

For the future story of Israel and Palestine, it was unfortunate that none of the Arab states recognized Israel's right to exist. The Palestinians, who had the right to form their own state within another part of the former British mandate over Palestine, did not want to accept only a part and they did not form on it their home-land. Therefore, the Gaza Strip went under the rule of Egypt and the West Bank of Palestine under the rule of Jordan. The people in Israel were waiting for many years for peace. In the meantime, they were exposed to numerous attacks from the Arabs, who did not recognize its right to exist.

The war of 1967 between the state of Israel and the Arab states of Egypt, Syria, and Jordan became a controversial issue in the international forum because of circumstances that led to its outbreak and because it was followed by Israel's occupation of Arab territories. The USSR, many countries of Eastern Europe, and also some other countries broke their diplomatic relations with Israel. The other superpower, the United States, all the countries of Western Europe, and many other countries maintained their diplomatic relations with Israel.

The tragedy of Israel and of its Arab neighbours, which started with the lack of recognition of the right of Israel to exist, became more complicated with the Israeli occupation of the territories.

Jerusalem was a unique city in the world, where one could see and cherish the history of three religions: there was the Wailing Wall, the only remnant from the temple of Solomon. It was a sacred place for Jewish people. There was the road of martyrdom through which Jesus went to Golgotha, a place sacred for Christians. They spent moments full of emotions on the Mount of Olives. There was the Dome of the Rock, from which the Prophet Muhammad ascended to heaven, a place sacred for the Moslems.

Andrzej and Karolina walked and walked through the streets of the Old City, under the spell of its past history, full of emotions and feelings that its streets and stones were witnesses of events that shaped so much the contemporary image of the world.

They went to Yad Vashem, and they were deeply moved by the pietism dedicated to the memory of the Holocaust. Karolina prayed for her parents and her sister and all her family who were victims of the Holocaust. Before leaving Yad Vashem, she presented herself to its officials as a survivor of the Holocaust and introduced Andrzej, who married her under Hitler's occupation and saved her life, risking his own and his parents' lives. When the officials heard this story, they rose to shake Andrzej's hand and tell him that they felt honoured to meet such a heroic person. One of them told Andrzej: 'Not only your wife is a survivor of the Holocaust. We consider you also as a Holocaust survivor because your life was at the same risk as the life of any Jew when you married your wife, although you are a gentile. We honour especially such heroic people in Yad Vashem. The trees planted here are in memory of victims of the Holocaust and for the glory of the heroic saviours of Jewish people. We call them "the righteous Gentiles." You should have such a tree here. Please fill out together with your wife forms with necessary data to enter in our files. It is our duty to leave for history traces of heroic deeds. It is a great privilege and honour for us to meet such a person as you.'

After leaving Jerusalem, Andrzej and Karolina went by a rented car to visit the sacred places in Nazareth and Bethlehem. Bethlehem, with its beautiful panorama, had such irresistible charm they returned there twice to keep for ever in their memories its unusual beauty.

They went to visit one of the most tragic monuments in the Jewish history, Massada, whose defenders preferred to perish rather than surrender under the Roman siege. Andrzej and Karolina were then thinking of a similar fate chosen by the hero of the Jewish uprising in the Warsaw ghetto, Anielewicz and his soldiers.

They saw the Dead Sea and its surroundings. Then, they visited a kibbutz and were full of respect for people working in an atmosphere of mutual understanding and friendship.

They went to the Gaza Strip and were horrified by the situation in which Arab people lived there. They knew that misery was there before the Israeli occupation, but nothing had been done until now to relieve their poor lives. There was no future under occupation for the unhappy Palestinians. They listened to their grievances, with greatest compassion and understanding. The occupation lasted already seven years and there was no end to it. How long would it continue? It was not a free life in a homeland of which they were dreaming. Andrzej and Karolina were so emotionally touched by all their stories that, wandering through the streets of the Gaza Strip, they lost their way out towards Tel Aviv. One of the Palestinians took care of them and accompanied them out. It was a heart-breaking visit.

In Tel Aviv, they visited Karolina's aunt. This charming old lady, who was the widow of Józef, Juliusz's only brother, was in 1941 deported by the Soviets with her husband and small children in terrible conditions to a place in Siberia named 'Zimnyj Gorodok.' She lost there her husband, and she survived in hard conditions with her children the period of the Holocaust, far away in Siberia. They returned to Poland, and their dream was to get away as far as possible from the Soviet Union. Therefore, in 1948, they emigrated to Israel. She received Andrzej and Karolina with great joy and respect. They also visited her son and her daughter and their families.

Before leaving Israel, they visited also their friends, Polish Jews who emigrated from Poland in 1948 and in the late 1960s after the outbreak of anti-Semitism and became Israel's citizens. Some of them were considering the 1967 war as a kind of pre-emptive strike; some called it a preventive measure. All of them were hoping that it would be followed by negotiations with mutual concessions to reach understanding and peace. Instead, there was an outbreak of another war in 1973. They evaluated it as a defensive war. All of them were for ending the occupation as soon as possible. They emphasized that any treaty with the Arab states must give Israel total security, and that such security could be obtained not only through negotiations with the Palestinians, but also by recognition by other Arab states the right of Israel to exist.

After this visit with friends, they tried to have a more optimistic attitude and to hope that the occupation was only an episode and would finish with negotiations with Palestinians and establishing peace and diplomatic relations with Palestinians and other Arab states. Nevertheless, the mere fact that Israel was a state occupying other territories was difficult for them to accept.

They boarded an El-Al plane to fly to Europe for another professional convention. After the plane took off, Andrzej saw that the passenger in the seat in front of him had stood up and was attaching a band to his arm. As it was very soon after take-off, Andrzej thought that this man might not feel well and intended to monitor his blood pressure. He loosened his seat belt and wanted to get up, but Karolina, who had not noticed anything because she was looking through the window, stopped him, afraid that he did not feel well. 'No,' Andrzej replied, 'I feel well, but the poor man in front of me seems to feel bad because he is preparing to take his blood pressure. I am going to help him.'

Karolina looked at the man in the row in front and just in time stopped Andrzej from offering his help. 'My dear,' she said, 'he is all right. It is something that has nothing to do with blood pressure. It might be interesting for you to know that the religious Jews are preparing for a special prayer, putting on their arm a sacred device and you will see in a couple of seconds . . . another sacred device on their forehead.' Indeed, the man in the row before them was now putting another device on his forehead. Karolina did not have an exact knowledge of all the Jewish rites, because she had been educated in a non-religious family, but she had heard about it. 'You see, my dear, now he is praying,' said Karolina. 'I am also going to pray for a safe journey. Just relax and try to sleep for a while. We are so tired.'

Andrzej closed his eyes and began to doze. After a while, he was awakened by a voice near to his ear. The old man from the row before him had finished his prayers and was talking aloud to him in great anger in Polish: 'Wake up, you Pole, wake up. You have to understand that you are no longer in Poland where you can kill the Jews or inform on them to the Nazis. I am speaking to you in Polish, in this dirty language which I promised myself not to use any more because I want to tell you what I think of Poles.

'Poles are a nation of anti-Semites, a nation that did business during the war denouncing Jews to the Gestapo. I hate you. I hate all the Poles. I hate your language. I hate your lover who is sitting here with you. This is a plane of my country. I and my family are protected by my country, and you will be unable to act against us here or in Europe. We are safe here and well protected against fascists. Your talk with your lover when I was preparing myself for prayer was disturbing me. This hated Polish talk. You are rich, you can travel, because you have stolen Jewish fortunes during the war, and she is well dressed because she has also stolen Jewish money.'

He stopped for a while because Karolina rose from her seat, and the old man had to let her pass. She did not go away. She stood close behind him, when he continued: 'I have spent during the war two years in the Jewish ghetto and three years in a concentration camp. I have the worst opinion from my experience with the Poles. This plane is a plane of Israel, and I don't want to hear any more Polish language. After all my sufferings, I have the right to it. Our leaders told us that Poles are born anti-Semites. Go back with your lover to your dirty country.' He finished shouting and wanted to return to his seat. It was impossible because Karolina was standing behind him. Andrzej knew from looking at her face and her wide-open eyes that she was very angry and was going to fight not only for him, but against all unjustified generalizations. He knew also that she was not going to hurt the old man who suffered so much in his life.

She started to speak in a low voice, in her beautiful Polish: 'Listen to me sir, I am speaking to you in Polish whether you like it or not because this is my mother tongue and you understand it well. We are now in the plane of a free country, and I know what are my rights. You are a poor Polish Jew who survived the Holocaust, who suffered terribly from the Nazis' crimes during the war. You suffered already before the war Polish anti-Semitism. But, at the same time, you are a dangerous fanatic because you are making unjustified generalizations. I want also to tell you that we are not lovers, but with God's blessing we are husband and wife, duly married. I hope you understand me, sir.'

The old man nodded his head, hypnotized by the shining eyes of Karolina. She continued: 'I want you to know, that we are both survivors of the Holocaust and therefore we understand your sufferings. When Hitler invaded Poland, I was a Jewish girl studying medicine in Cracow. At the same time, my husband finished his medical studies in Lwów. He is a Catholic Pole, or as you call it, a gentile. He and his parents not only were not anti-Semitic but they fought against anti-Semitism, which indeed existed among many Poles, but many Poles does not mean "all the nation."

'At the beginning of September 1939 I fled with my parents and my only sister to Lwów. This city, as you know, belonged before the war to Poland and at the end of September 1939 was occupied by the Soviet Union.

'In autumn 1940, I met this Pole and very soon we were both in love. Pay attention, sir, we were in love, we were not lovers. I became his fiancée with the permission of my parents and his parents, and we planned to be married at the end of academic year, in July 1941. He was working at the university where I was studying.'

Karolina paused. She could hardly speak, thinking of the past, of the tragedy of Orelec, of the heroism of Andrzej and his parents, of the offer of the bishop, of the hopes of Juliusz, of all the days and nights when she and Andrzej were shivering with fear that her origin might be discovered, which meant death for both. And now this man was condemning all the Polish nation. No, she could not start crying now, she had to fight for the honour of all decent Poles who risked their lives, hiding Jews or helping them in any possible way.

She continued: 'The German occupation of Lwów did not change the opinion of this Pole. He married me in July 1941, a couple of weeks after Hitler invaded the Soviet Union. You, sir, know very well how terrible is the fear of perishing, you understand very well how strong is the will to survive. These feelings were imposed on all Jews by the criminal regime of the Nazis. But you have also to understand that the same fear and the same will to survive existed in my husband, in his parents, and in other Poles, among them many Catholic priests who knew my origin and saved my life during the war. They consciously imposed on themselves this terrible fear to save me, to save *one* human being. Therefore, these Poles are for me heroes, and I cannot stand to hear somebody offending all the Polish nation. Without my husband and many other Poles, I would be today a particle of gas from the smokestacks of the crematoria in Auschwitz.

'May I ask you to understand one thing: it is extremely dangerous to make unjustified generalizations. If, according to your emotional declaration, all Poles are bad, thieves, dirty killers, you have to punish all of them. Recent history has shown us to what crimes such reasoning leads. My parents and my only sister perished during the Holocaust. All my family was killed by the Nazis.'

Karolina was now very tired and her voice was trembling. But she had to finish her mission.

'We know very well the anti-Semitism of many Poles before, during, and after the war. We left Poland four years ago, because my husband wanted to manifest in such a way his abhorrence and contempt for anti-Semitism. When you will pray again, ask God to give you more strength to fight this badly addressed nationalist hatred. Hatred is the dominant feeling among many people. But "many" people, does not mean "all" people. In our hearts God has to prevail over Evil.

'We do not ask you for an apology because we suffered enough in our lives and understand well your sufferings.'

Karolina returned to her seat close to Andrzej, but the old man was still standing near Andrzej's seat. When Andrzej looked at him, he saw tears in his eyes. Andrzej immediately stood up and said: 'Please don't cry, sir. As you see we are all survivors of the Holocaust and nothing should divide us after those terrible times. I want only to ask you to remember that each human being has the same rights in God's judgment. The sufferings of each human being are equally deplorable. The blood of each human being has the same value; each nation has the same rights, and we should have contempt for any unjustified generalizations.

'I cannot apologize in the name of Polish anti-Semites for all the sufferings imposed on you by them because I am myself fighting all my life against any kind of racism. In all nations, you can find decent people who fight against racism not only with words, but with deeds. All I want from you is not to forget our conversation when you return to your country, to Israel.'

Andrzej returned to his seat, with no resentment towards the old man. Karolina, however, was still unhappy and angry: it was not the first time that she had heard such an outbreak of hatred against the Polish nation from the Jewish people. Some of the Polish Jews abroad told her that they promised never to speak Polish because they hated even the Polish language. She did not tell Andrzej all these stories because she did not want to upset him by speaking of the Jewish hatred. Now he witnessed it, full blown.

He stood against it, like she, but he was so full of compassion for all the victims of the Nazis that he forgave the old man his outbreak. She would not forgive herself that she did not ask the old man if he would have behaved in the same way as Andrzej's father did in the matter of their marriage. Would he also, having only one son, put his son's and his own life at risk to save another human being's? She was also sorry that such outbreaks of hatred might become frequent in Israel, and Israel might damage its integrity and its pride in being a democratic nation.

A young stewardess pushing the cart with tea and coffee, who heard some fragments of the long conversation with the old man, asked Andrzej if she could help him with something. 'My dear,' Andrzej said, 'we were talking about the past. There is nothing that you could help in this respect. We hope that the new generation in all nations will do everything to prevent the recurrence of the terrible errors of the past. Thank you for the coffee.'

When they were waiting for luggage claim with the other passengers, the old man from the plane approached them and said in Polish: 'I wish both of you a happy time in Europe. Thank you both for what you told me. I will think about it and I hope that I will understand what you meant. I am an old Jew, and I don't want to be unjust. I was always an honest man. God bless you. I am sorry to have hurt you.'

They went to the exit.

The weather was beautiful, the temperature mild, the sky without clouds. They were happy to be together and to see Europe again.

IV

MANY PEOPLE IN POLAND, AMONG THEM ANDRZEJ AND Karolina saw the administrative and economic disasters caused by the totalitarian system where all the power was concentrated in the Communist party and in the Communist government. The slogan 'all power to the Soviets' at the beginning of the Soviet revolution was probably intended to give power to the councils (Soviets), conceived as a large representation of the population. In the course of years, it degenerated into giving all the power to the Communist bureaucracy.

In Communist Poland, like in other Communist states, all the power was assigned to two so-called verticals: ideological (PZPR) and administrative (government). The division of power existed on every level of the 'verticals.' On the highest, it was divided between the First Secretary of the PZPR together with Secretariat, Politburo, and all departments of the Central Committee of the PZPR and between the prime minister and his council of ministers. On the lower levels, it was divided between the provincial (Voivodenship) secretary and his bureaucrats and the president of the Provincial National Council and his bureaucrats. On still lower levels, it was divided, respectively, between the district (powiat) PZPR secretary with his bureaucrats and the president of the District National Council and his bureaucrats. The same division of power existed on municipal and regional levels.

The power sharing was based on the idea that the PZPR officials were analyzing if all the administrative decisions are in conformity with the principles of Marxism and they decide in more important matters presented by the administration. The administration had the task of elaborating professional problems of its competence. No decision could be made without PZPR approval.

In such a way an enormous number of bureaucrats were sitting simultaneously at their desks in the party and in the administration. The bureaucrats from the administration, although, in the majority, party members, were waiting for 'ideological' approval of PZPR bureaucrats, and therefore hampered in their work. The PZPR bureaucrats were slow in their decisions because they were afraid that their decisions might be not conform to Marxism, and some PZPR members on the higher level might accuse them of 'revisionism.'

Looking at it from Canada, in retrospect, Andrzej recalled some examples from his work where the decision-making process was destroyed by lack of competence and was dying not only from the lack of 'ideological' inspiration, but mostly from ideological consumption caused by the rhetoric bacillus. There were also cases where decisions were killed by the struggle at the crossroads of the corridors of power, where the persons fighting for more power were annihilating one another to show who is more powerful ('Kto kavo' means in Russian 'Who whom' will dominate).

A couple of months before they left Poland, Andrzej was asked by a high official in the Central Committee of the PZPR to visit him regarding some problems of psychiatry. This official, who before the Second World War was a member of the Polish Communist Party, was a modest and humble man made responsible for health affairs in the Department of Social Affairs in the Central Committee of the PZPR, although he was not a health professional.

Andrzej was informed by him that, in two weeks, the Department of Social Affairs of the Central Committee would convene a meeting of all eminent psychiatrists to discuss problems of psychiatry. He showed Andrzej a summation to be presented after the discussions. This summation contained only slogans and generalities. Andrzej, stunned by this, told him that it was impossible to make any summation before the discussions and that the important professional problems of psychiatry could not be dealt with in generalities. The official stated that it made no difference what would be discussed because, for him, the most important thing was to present the summation at the end of the discussion and send it immediately afterwards to the Secretariat. In the Secretariat, they would register it and put it into the files and wait for the decision of the party. He ended by stating that 'we know here in the Central Committee what is the party's line, and I have in my office people who worked on this problem.'

The meeting, indeed, took place in the Central Committee two weeks later, and the psychiatrists discussed very important professional problems and indicated their needs and priorities. The official from the Central Committee was present during all the discussions. At the end, he stepped up to the lectern and read the summation from a couple of sheets of paper. His statement made no mention of concrete proposals put forward at the meeting. It contained only generalities and promises that health, and especially mental heath, is of great concern to the party, and everything would be done to safeguard and protect the interests of the working class.

The participants of the meeting were greatly disappointed, but not surprised. They had heard several times such speeches, which were called 'speech-grass' (in Polish 'mowa-trawa') or 'dumb speech.'

After a couple of weeks, Andrzej called the same official and asked if the concrete proposals of the meeting had been sent to the Secretariat. He heard in answer: 'You heard my summation. I have given it to the Secretariat. It is registered in their files. The Secretariat knows perfectly well what is needed. Otherwise they would not be in the Secretariat. You just have to wait and see what happens.'

Nothing happened, and when Andrzej called him again after another two months with the same question, the answer this time was: 'We have some much more important political problems now in Poland than psychiatry. When the right time comes, we will deal with psychiatric problems.'

Unfortunately, such an approach to concrete problems was very common among the party's officials. Still, this type of official was not the most dangerous one. In the opinion of professionals, they were called 'innocuous' because, although they blocked progress, they were not vicious and, indeed, had no power to do any serious personal harm.

Other officials in the common opinion were 'dangerous' because they had enough power to harm, and even destroy people. Such were the officials who nearly destroyed Andrzej and Karolina in 1953. At that time, they were making preparations for great 'purge trials' in the Ministry of Public Security. The threatening atmosphere lasted a couple of years after Stalin's death. Many of the persecutors, feeling some time later that they might be put on real trial for their cruelties, fled abroad, profiting from the privilege of being able to grant themselves passports. Many of them asked for asylum in foreign countries, presenting themselves as victims of the same ministry where they were perpetrating their crimes. They were selling abroad false accusations of anybody whom they had once persecuted. This transformation from persecutor to persecuted did not surprise decent people in Poland.

An amazing social phenomenon appeared within a few years after the Communist party came to power in Poland. A new class of 'red bourgeoisie' emerged. Before the war, the members of the Polish Communist Party were persecuted and condemned for many years in prison. Now, after the war, they had not only freedom, but some of them, the 'apparatchiki,' immense power. They had forgotten the ideas for which they had fought and savoured all the privileges of power. They had the best apartments, special shops behind the 'yellow curtains,' stuffed with goods unavailable to the general population.

As the policy of the PZPR was to attract many people, it was to a certain degree invaded by people who wanted to make a career through the party and who were interested only in good positions in the bureaucracy and in being eligible for the perks of the 'apparatchiki.' Some of them had criminal records and were accepted into the PZPR anyway, since the PZPR, knowing their records, could manipulate them, using them as tools of cruelty and hiding behind them. This was the same sort of dirty trick used and inspired by Stalin.

Within the jungle of their own bureaucrats, the PZPR 'apparatchiki' fought one another for more power. Often a just cause could be lost in this struggle.

As an example, Andrzej recalled that, when he was fighting for the transfer of his department from suburbs to Warsaw, he wanted – to make his cause stronger – to ask for help the Minister of Defence and the PZPR Secretary of Warsaw. One of his friends, with whom he consulted, warned him not to. In her opinion, it was naïve, and Andrzej could lose everything not knowing where the balance of power rested and how to negotiate a path through the corridors of power. The PZPR Secretary of Warsaw was in a power struggle with the Minister of Defence. They were personal enemies. If Andrzej asked both of them for help Andrzej's cause would be lost. The promotion of his cause by both of them would provoke a negative reaction from both sides, jealous one of another. Her advice was to choose one of them, or none of them, and go to somebody who has a greater power than both of them. Although the powerful man was not a professional, Andrzej, convincing him, could be sure that nobody would oppose his decision.

Andrzej followed this advice, and although he convinced the powerful man, he himself did not feel well emotionally. It meant for him that using this kind of knowledge, he himself was, to a certain degree, manipulating the powers that be.

Still, there were in the PZPR, in the Central Committee, some very decent people, not corrupted by power. Not yet.

V

TIME RUNS RELENTLESSLY FORWARD, AND ANDRZEJ AND Karolina inevitably aged. They felt much more the burden of years. The difficulties and pains of their journey through the valley of tears were taking their toll on their health, and both are ailing.

In the valley of tears are some islands on the sea of tears. A small minority of its population lives comfortably and enjoys life on those islands. Some wealthy-enough people inhabit them. Nearly all the 'leaders' of various nations and social systems live there with their faithful bureaucrats. Some of these leaders are aware that the sea of tears surrounds their islands and are trying to diminish the number of people navigating through the sea. Some other 'leaders' increase the number of unhappy people, toppling their dependants into the sea.

The majority of the contemporary population is left to navigate through the sea of tears. Most of them, if not all, end their miserable lives by sinking in the sea.

This is the short story of the last decades of the twentieth century. If general civilization does not break down, future historians and scientists will have the opportunity to analyse all the social and ecological factors leading to this situation, and especially the aggressive destructive instincts of many human beings. If a general catastrophe ensues, only God will make the evaluation and judgment of this era.

No human being can avoid the end of the journey through the valley, at least physically. What will happen after the physical end is open to conjecture. Karolina has no doubts that, at the end, she and Andrzej will meet God and that their love will last for ever. Andrzej, the former agnostic, is now closer to Karolina's belief, simply because he will not admit that the end of their love is possible.

Andrzej and Karolina retired at the compulsory age of sixty-five from Laval University in Quebec City. Four years later, they closed their medical practice in Montreal and moved to Toronto. They have no patients any more, because they themselves are ailing and have to be treated. With all their physical illnesses, their intellectual and emotional life remains as vivid as it was at the beginning of their love.

They continue to work on professional problems. They often return in their thoughts to the past, and they carefully watch present events. Now they are writing this book.

Future historians and scientists will easily discover that life in the second part of the twentieth century was characterized by an enormous discrepancy between the conceptual and imaginative power of human thought and the weakness of human social instincts. There was a rapid development of all branches of science, in medicine, physics, chemistry, astronomy, communications, etc. Around the earth is turning a space station; new ones will follow with most sophisticated laboratories.

Andrzej and Karolina are full of enthusiasm for the rapid progress of science. At the same time, however, they are afraid that personal interhuman relations are not progressing at the same pace as the intellectual powers of the brain. Not all scientists have high moral standards, similar to those of Albert Einstein, Robert Oppenheimer, Frederic Joliot-Curie, Andrei Sakharov, and Jonas Edward Salk. Not all political or religious readers reach the moral level of Pope John XXIII or of Pope John Paul II. Let us not forget that people are living in the atomic age, and that enormous destructive forces are in the hands of many political leaders.

One evening, when Andrzej and Karolina were talking about the very beginning of mankind, Andrzej said jokingly: 'At the very beginning, when God created Adam and Eve, the progenitors of mankind, He was already very tired after days of hard creative labour. He had also some doubts about whether his work was perfect, because, at the end of each of the former days, He used to say that the work was good. He did not say this after the last day of creation. He wanted to look at Adam and Eve for a certain time and, if necessary, make some corrections. He located Adam and Eve in a very pleasant place called Paradise, and told them: 'Enjoy your lives, but do not procreate without my permission. I have to be quite sure that my creative work concerning you both was good and that you are indeed made in *my* image, after *my* likeness. The quality of your soul is my greatest concern. If it does not reflect my image, although you are physically beautiful and able to enjoy life on this remote planet, you might procreate mankind under the influence of Evil. Therefore, my dear Adam and Eve, I am asking you to wait with the act of procreation. If you procreate without my permission, it could be a calamity for all future humanity. It would be an original sin, and you will be punished and expelled from Paradise. I have to rest after my work and you have to wait.'

'As you know, Karolina, the rest is history. Evil disguised as the serpent seduced them to procreate. They were expelled from Paradise. Eve gave birth to two sons, Cain and Abel. Abel was slain by Cain, and the atrocities mar the history of mankind.'

Karolina, amused by Andrzej's interpretation of the beginning of mankind, said: 'I have to make a short remark. I believe that God acted perfectly well and, in His way, gave human beings free will. They could choose between good and bad, between Good and Evil. The history of mankind is the history of the fight between God and Evil.

'The sea of tears in our valley is the best evidence of the choice human beings made. We will soon know through the space telescope invented by Hubble, the secrets of the galaxies. However, we still do not know the dark sides of human consciousness. Perhaps, one day somebody will build another telescope through which we will see the essence of Goodness and how to avoid Evil. This could not only enrich astronomy, but improve our knowledge of human consciousness, of the mechanisms of human instincts.'

When Andrzej and Karolina were talking of the analysis of the second half of the twentieth century by future historians and scientists, it seemed to them clear that they would come to the conclusion that the Holocaust was the greatest crime in the history of mankind.

The Second World War finally ended when the United States dropped the first atomic bomb on Hiroshima and the second on Nagasaki. They killed and wounded over 200,000 of the civilian population.

As a result of the Second World War, two great superpowers emerged: the United States and the Soviet Union. The United States created the European Recovery program, called the 'Marshall Plan.' This plan helped to rebuild the economy of Western European countries and secure for their populations a comfortable level of life. At the same time, the Soviet Union, dominating the Eastern European countries, brought to them, and also to itself, economic disaster and a fanatical, utopian ideology with tremendous sufferings.

Very soon after peace was reached, another war began between the two superpowers: the 'cold war.' Hatred and aggression were present now between them, between the leaders of the United States, representing the free world, and the leaders of Soviet Union, representing the Communist world. After all the crimes committed by Stalin that ruined twenty million lives, in the era of Brezhnev, although there were no more such crimes, the policy of 'exporting' the Soviet revolution continued. In many countries, especially those of the Third World, the Soviet Union directly or indirectly organized Communist guerrillas. The greatest tragedy of the guerrillas was that, seeing no help from rich countries, they believed that they were fighting for a better future for their own poor countries. The actions of the guerrillas provoked a cruel answer from the leadership of the 'Free World' in order to defend freedom and capitalism, or capitalism and freedom. The means of defence were very often far from democratic principles. The poor countries were crushed by the power of the U.S.-backed dictators such as Somoza, Marcos, Battista, the Shah of Iran, Noriega, and others. On both sides were growing aggressive and destructive instincts, leading to dehumanization. The sea of tears in the valley of the remote planet was larger and still growing.

The stories of gulags and the bloody tragedies of Soviet peasants and intellectuals during Stalin's time are known not only from the writings of Soviet dissidents like Alexander Solzhenitsyn or Joseph Brodsky, but from official data published now in the Soviet Union, at the time of leadership of Mikhail Gorbachev.

During the 'cold war,' both superpowers accumulated such an enormous number of nuclear weapons that the population of the remote planet – Earth – could be destroyed within one hour. Enormous sums were spent for this goal, with neglect not only of the safety of the environment, but, above all, of the economic and social needs of many nations, belonging to one or another power's sphere of influence. The Soviet Union garnered the biggest cache of conventional and nuclear weapons. At the same time, the standard of life of its citizens dropped to new lows and the economy was in shambles. The old Communist slogan 'be watchful' survived Stalin's era, and poisoned the joy of life. The people were looking everywhere for enemies and were themselves either persecuted or persecutors.

The situation of the Third World was tragic: millions of men, women, and children were dying of starvation in Ethiopia, Bangladesh, India, and many other countries. The help given by the rich countries was very small. Many countries remained indifferent to those sufferings. Mother Teresa in Calcutta dedicated all her life to the cause of the poor and sick. The dimensions of this disaster are so great that legions of such saints as Mother Teresa would be needed to relieve the fate of the poorest.

This era of 'cold war' between the two superpowers was characterized by so-called regional conflicts. They were, as a matter of fact, real wars, with arms, and 'regional' only because they did not directly involve the two superpowers in a world cataclysm. There was a war in Korea, in Vietnam; there were wars between the Arab states and Israel, between Iran and Iraq, between the Soviet Union and Afghanistan, to name just a few. The roots of these regional acts of bloodshed were always buried in racial, national, political, or religious fanatical concepts. In some countries religious leaders became political dictators, and the religious dogmas became incorporated in political concepts, which led to dictatorial regimes. This sounds very much like a repetition of the Inquisition. Yet, it happened in the twentieth century.

The situation in the Middle East is especially complicated. In Lebanon, Moslem factions are fighting with Christians, Christians are fighting among themselves, terrorists of different orientations are kidnapping innocent people from Western countries. In the North of Lebanon are based Syrian military forces, and in the south is a small zone occupied by Israeli military forces since the Israeli invasion and consequent retreat from Lebanon after an unpopular war in 1982.

The occupation by Israel of the West Bank and the Gaza Strip since the 1967 war eventually provoked, in 1988, the Palestinian Intifada. This is an example of the classical painful response of natives to occupation, and its cost is human life. Up until the first months of 1990, about seven hundred Palestinians had been killed and thousands wounded by Israeli soldiers, among them many children and women. About forty Israelis have died in the violence.

Israel could prove itself as a democratic country if it began as soon as possible peaceful negotiations with the Palestinians and brought a fast end to the occupation of the West Bank and Gaza Strip. Israelis and Palestinians will for ever be neighbours, and the only way for both nations to survive and flourish is not only peace, but friendship, mutual help, and understanding.

The anti-apartheid action against racial discrimination in the Republic of South Africa has caused for a long time atrocious repercussions from the South African regime. The legendary leader of anti-apartheid movement, Nelson Mandela, spent twenty-seven years in prison, jailed by the white rulers of South Africa.

Andrzej and Karolina presume that the task of future historians and scientists should be finding a means of strengthening the positive social instincts of human beings in all nations. It is extremely difficult to acquire the knowledge of how to improve interpersonal relationships. Without such an improvement, the human future looks very dim, even in democratic countries.

The value of democracy depends on the people creating it. If democracy loses its innocence; if the conception of freedom is hurt by greed; if the controversial relationship between patriotism, liberty, and human consciousness is misunderstood, then democracy is no longer democracy. It is heart-breaking to see how often her pristine beauty is raped by people who let her then drift towards meretricious manners. True democracy has to be guarded like the apple of the human eye.

Vaclav Havel, Czechoslovakian president, said recently in his speech before the U.S. Congress (1990): 'Without a global revolution in the sphere of human consciousness, nothing will change for the better in the sphere of our beings as humans and the catastrophe towards which the world is headed – be it ecological, social, demographic or a general breakdown of civilization – will be unavoidable.'

Andrzej was thrilled to find in these words the same ideas he presented in his article published in 1973 in the *American Journal of Psychiatry*: 'A united world is the only hope of contemporary mankind. If such a world is not realized, then we may be faced with another solution. A day will come when a man with a club in hand will emerge from the cave to begin once more the history of a perhaps more happy humanity. This would mean that we are not the right edition of the species "homo" that is labelled "sapiens."'

However, Andrzej and Karolina, reading these conclusions, felt that the present situation (1990) of the world does not allow one to make such an apocalyptic prediction. Why? Because the 'cold war' came to an end. Whether this end would be interpreted as the failure of Communism and a victory for democracy in the free world, or as a sign that the two superpowers and other countries understood that the 'cold war' was tragic for billions of human beings, the fact remains that the end of the 'cold war' means that a new era for mankind is beginning.

The end of the 'cold war' is the most important and most optimistic event of the last decades of the twentieth century. It is seen by many as the dawn of a new era for humanity, as a hope that a new sunrise is coming that will follow a night that lasted too long.

The changes in the Soviet Union are remarkable. After seventy years of the utopian, fanatical ideology of Communism, new conceptions of Mikhail Gorbachev, namely 'perestroika' and 'glasnost,' are bringing an end to the era of Stalin and Brezhnev. The unveiling of Stalin's crimes is the final gravestone under which this era of misery will be buried. Under Mikhail Gorbachev's program, the Soviet Union should become a confederation of free states with human democratic socialism and with no imperialistic ideas for export. He and his collaborators know that a turbulent period lies ahead: the switch from a state with an economy controlled by the state and the party to a market-oriented economy, the teaching of 'glasnost' to people indoctrinated by fearsome watchfulness is not easy.

The heart of 'perestroika' and 'glasnost' should be given an adequate pacemaker, to prevent its collapsing from a too slow or a too rapid beat. He and his collaborators, like Shevernadze, probably understand that the human conscience of the Soviet people has been distorted after seventy years of life under imperialistic, 'watchful' Communism. The general atmosphere of lack of confidence, the paranoiac 'watchfulness' labelling millions of people as 'enemies,' led to their persecution and death.

Already in the first years of 'perestroika' and 'glasnost,' the realization of those ideas provokes an outbreak of national and religious fanaticism in some of the republics of the Soviet Union. The main thing is to keep the reforms on the path of legal processes without violence and force, using only peaceful means and negotiations.

The hopes of Andrzej and Karolina for a better and happier future are nourished by the news of peaceful revolutions in countries of Eastern Europe that have found their freedom and liberated themselves in a peaceful way from Soviet domination. They feel especially enthusiastic about Poland, their homeland. A simple Polish worker, an electrician from the Gdańsk shipyard, Lech Wałesa was the precursor of the Eastern European revolution against imperialistic Communism. He organized an *independent* Polish trade union, Solidarity. He was awarded the Nobel Prize for Peace when still fighting for the very existence of Solidarity. And eventually, after years of peaceful fight with Communist-imposed way of 'nominating' the leaders of a trade union, he prevailed with his adherents and led Poland into the free world. One of the most distinguished members of Solidarity, Tadeusz Mazowiecki, became Poland's prime minister, winning a great respect for his moral standard, even among his former adversaries.

The democratic changes in Central and South America, the fact that Nelson Mandela, finally released after twenty-seven years in prison, can now sit at the negotiating table with the white representatives of the South Africa government to negotiate a ban on apartheid, the negotiations concerning disarmament, the approach of the integration of European Unity in 1992 – all these and similar events are optimistic signs for the future in the minds of Andrzej and Karolina. With all this wishful thinking and political naïveté, they understand that it takes time to grow roots that are solid enough to resist the winds of still existing conservative opposition and to allow the flowers of freedom to bear fruit.

The tragedy of Tiananmen Square is one of the examples when progressive, peaceful movements were choked by adverse forces. One hopes that the great Chinese nation will eventually find its own way towards democracy. The way forward demands not only an enormous human effort, but also wisdom in strategy and knowledge of old forces that will not easily give up their power.

The obituary of Communist imperialism can already be written. However, its failure does not mean automatically that everything about the Western alternative is perfect. The United States, the leader of the Western Free World, has many problems of its own: decline of its educational system; increased incidence of crime and drug addiction, of homelessness; lack of any kind of medical insurance for over 10 per cent of its population (30 million); serious environmental problems; crumbling of the infrastructure of roads, bridges, and other constructions.

However, the end of the 'cold war' gave to the United States and other countries more financial opportunities to appease human needs and solve internal difficulties.

Many people, think, as do Andrzej and Karolina, that the coming decades of the twenty-first century will make people much closer to a united mankind with collaboration and no confrontation. Perhaps such believers are wrong, and their dreams will never come true.

Perhaps they are right, and mankind will navigate towards a society that, in the words of Julian Huxley, is 'world united *de iure*, submitting itself to a unitary system of self-government.'

In his article, cited above in this book, Andrzej wrote in 1973: 'Interdisciplinary efforts by biologists, physicians, psychologists, sociologists and pedagogues are needed to prepare a scientific program in order to diminish the discrepancy between the conceptual power of human thought and the weakness of social instincts. This is an agenda for many generations of scientists. Most, if not all, systems of education should be changed; we are already faced with such demands from the younger generations. It is not only a question of the program of studies but of their ethical framework. There should be much more studies of mechanisms through which there can be proper channelling of aggressive and other destructive instincts, as well as study of negative reinforcement of such instincts starting in early childhood, the reduction of aggression by genetic selection based on chromosomal investigations, the sublimation of instincts, the means of discharging some of them onto substitute objects and the responsible channelling of the militant enthusiasm of the youth. Principles of human relations between individuals and nations must be subject to imprinting from childhood.'

Andrzej and Karolina believe that now, after the end of the 'cold war,' advanced efforts should and can be made towards revolution in the sphere of human consciousness. This will give much more happiness to mankind than an accumulation of nuclear weapons and other means of destruction of human beings in confrontation.

EPILOGUE

—

TOWARDS THE END OF THE JOURNEY IN THE VALLEY OF TEARS

'If I speak in the tongues of men and of angels,
but have not love,
I am a noisy gong or a clanging cymbal.
And if I have prophetic powers, and
understand all mysteries and all knowledge, and
if I have all faith, so as to remove mountains,
but have not love, I am nothing.
If I give away all I have, and if I deliver my body to be burned,
but have not love, I gain nothing.

Love is patient and kind; love is not jealous or boastful;
it is not arrogant or rude.
Love does not insist on its own way; it is not irritable or resentful;
it does not rejoice at wrong, but rejoices in the right.
Love bears all things, believes all things,
hopes all things, endures all things.
Love never ends . . .'

First Letter of Paul to the Corinthians
13:1–8

IT WAS A BEAUTIFUL LATE AFTERNOON AT THE BEGINNING of March. Andrzej and Karolina were resting on the balcony of their hotel room after a convention in California. The air was calm, and balmy with the perfume of flowers. The palms were standing still, their leaves untouched by any wind. The sun was already approaching the peaks of the mountains, bathed in splendid golden-rosy colour.

'It is such a gorgeous evening that you could feel you are in paradise,' said Karolina. Andrzej took her hands and said: 'Perhaps one day the people will wake up at sunrise, live throughout a sunny day, and there will be quiet nights with no nightmares. But I don't think that this will happen during our life on this earth. We had sunny days always in our hearts since the day we met. But outside were terrible storms, threatening darkness at night time, fear and despair. We survived because of our love. Our love was and is the essence of our lives. Our love is very simple and at the same time complicated, clear and transparent and at the same time full of mysticism. It is unifying not only our bodies. Our souls are inseparable in this love. And with such love, there is no place for hatred of any human being. You have to extend this love to others. However, this love cannot embrace people who have lost human face, who are destroying the moral values of humanity and endangering the very existence of human beings. And, therefore, my love, you have to fight against them.'

'You are, my dear, a strong believer, and all that I said you could briefly define: we cannot negotiate with Evil, we have to fight with it.'

Karolina smiled and put her head on Andrzej's shoulder. For a while they did not talk. They looked at the sunset.

After a while Karolina said: 'Yes, I am a believer. I think that God is with me since the day of my birth. I changed my religion but I did not change my God. I believe in a God who represents for me all that is good, noble, and honest in the world, in the universe. I have to follow Him in those values. The religious rites are beautiful, have a historical value, but they are not, by themselves, with all the due respect, the essence of my religion. You can sometimes be close to God without religious rites, and you can be far away from God, observing scrupulously all the rites. I have also to recognize that being in a church or in any place of worship helps you to concentrate on values given by God. The mass prayers, followed by handshakes and feelings of brotherhood with others, seem to me of great importance.

'And what about you, my dear? What about your hesitations between faith and disbelief? For me, you are always close to God, whether you admit it or not. God is in your soul, because you are honest and full of goodness. Do not be afraid to meet God "in person." Finally, we will know what is to be really good. And we will always be together with our love.'

'And maybe we will understand all the mystery of human existence. We will understand that in creating the human being God has given him the free will to act with good or with bad intent. In such a way a potential evil was born. It is in human beings, inside each of us, and it can be defeated only by the good intent of each of us. To be good, you have to fight with yourself and listen carefully to the voice of God, who is in your soul. Any political, economical, or social program, although theoretically excellent will fail if the souls of human beings will be overpowered by dark forces.'

Karolina kissed Andrzej and said: 'I think that you had just that in mind when you were speaking of a fight against Evil. When the day will come for us to see our God, we will ask Him: "God, give people more strength to fight against dark forces. Evil has the seducing face of power. Give the human beings the strength to take off the mask of power and see the real, monstrous face of Evil. They were suffering so long and so much, seduced by different faces masking Evil. Help people to make some fundamental changes in their consciousness, give them the courage to reject the false shrine of doctrines, and they will be able to change their fate."'

They were very close one to another when Andrzej said: 'We are approaching the end of our journey in the valley of tears. You promised me that we would find a better place beyond. Would it be difficult for you to tell me if the valley we will be leaving soon will stay for a long time with tears? I believe, like you, that this depends only on the human beings in this valley, on their consciousness and courage to change their fate in overcoming the dark forces.'

Andrzej was holding tight to Karolina's hand. His existential anxiety was gone. The past was known, and it was full of atrocities. The future could only be better. God seemed to Andrzej to be very close and listening to them. They closed their eyes, holding each other close. When they opened their eyes, it was already dark. The peaks of the mountains were scarcely visible. A mild, very mild wind was blowing from the east. Sometimes such mild winds bring long-lasting, beautiful weather.

The writing was concluded on March 16, 1990.

AN AFTERWORD

VARIOUS THREATENING ELEMENTS EXIST OUTSIDE AND inside us. Around us we face natural disasters to which – knowingly or unknowingly – we contribute in the form of damage to air, land, and water. Inside us are elements that threaten our physical or mental health and our social instincts.

In the presence of such extrinsic and intrinsic threats, there is no room, no rationale for conflict between persons, nations, races, religions, and classes. A unified humanity could face natural and human dangers successfully through means, sooner or later emerging from advancements of science. All our efforts should be concentrated on the quelling of those threats. Fighting between ourselves will only augment existing dangers, which might ultimately destroy us. Awareness of this is growing. Changes in human consciousness do not come fast or easily. It is our responsibility to imprint in generations to come, from earliest childhood, the principles of humane social relations.

During our lifetime, we have seen that understanding and compassion are deeply implanted in human beings. Their name is legion. An example: the poem "Là-bas" (see page 68). It was written by a poet and painter from Montreal. Pierre Mathieu was a child at the outbreak of the Second World War. He was never in Poland, has never seen war or concentration and extermination camps. He has only heard and read about them. Yet his emotions plummet to a state of ultimate despair over vain efforts to escape the trap of 'fours crématoires.' He feels kith and kin with the victims: 'mes frères, mes soeurs, mes élus du martyre sans pareil!' Many people feel like he does; some are close to the experience; some have still an existential bitterness or indifference; some are full of hatred. We hope that a day will come when all mankind, nurtured by mutual understanding, love and compassion, will look with joy, and no fear, at a clear starlit sky from any place on clean land and sea. With no changes in human consciousness, the earth, the remote planet, might one day become a gas chamber for the unhappy human kind.